# Welcome!

## English for the travel and tourism industry

**Second Edition**

## Teacher's Book

Leo Jones

CAMBRIDGE
UNIVERSITY PRESS

CAMBRIDGE UNIVERSITY PRESS
Cambridge, New York, Melbourne, Madrid, Cape Town,
Singapore, São Paulo, Delhi, Mexico City

Cambridge University Press
The Edinburgh Building, Cambridge CB2 8RU, UK

Published in the United States of America by Cambridge University Press, New York

www.cambridge.org
Information on this title: www.cambridge.org/9780521606608

© Cambridge University Press 2005

First published 1998
Second edition 2005
7th printing 2012

*A catalogue record for this publication is available from the British Library*

ISBN 978-0-521-60660-8 Teacher's Book
ISBN 978-0-521-60659-2 Student's Book
ISBN 978-0-521-60662-2 Audio Cassettes (2)
ISBN 978-0-521-60661-5 Audio CDs (2)

ISBN 978-0-521-60660-8 Paperback

# Contents

# Thanks

I'd like to thank everyone whose hard work, fresh ideas, helpful comments and criticisms have enhanced this book immensely.

The following teachers tried out the pilot lessons and reported on their experiences using them with their students:

Núria Cáceres in Sabadell, Spain; Jennyfer Chai-Chang in Valencia, Spain; Rose Cheung in Hong Kong; Suzanna Harwood in Athens, Greece; Patrick Lawlor in London; Mary Mumford de De Santiago in Guadalajara, Mexico; Bill Pellowe and Jayne Feldart in Fukuoka, Japan; Robin Walker in Oviedo, Spain; Nursel Yalçin in Aydin, Turkey

The following teachers reported on the pilot lessons:

Maud Dunkeld in the UK; Josette Hober-Ondersuhu in Grenoble, France; Antoinette Meehan in Tokyo, Japan; Inge Spaughton in Stuttgart, Germany; Gabriella Tavella in San Martin de los Andes, Argentina

Will Capel inititated the project and guided it through its many stages

Tony Garside edited the book and guided the project efficiently and sympathetically through to publication

Tim Douglass produced and edited the recordings

Stephanie White designed the Second Edition at Kamae design

And thanks to the people who took part in the interviews:

Sally Garside; Jane Sparkes; Janine Cording at AOSSA Travel in Brighton; Fiona Bowers and Sam Wilkinson at Dig in the Ribs in Brighton; Rob Allan, Emma Bray, Mark Fancy, Lisa Thomas and Emma Whiting at the Grand Hotel, Brighton.

Tony Robinson and Annemarie Young edited the Second Edition. Thanks to them both!

# Acknowledgement

TourismConcern, London, for the 'The Himalayan Tourist Code', page 101.

# Introduction

## What is *Welcome!*?

This is the Second Edition of *Welcome!*

Apart from its new design, this new edition includes:

- several new reading texts
- practice in writing emails
- many new photos and cartoons

The CDs and cassettes are exactly the same as the First Edition.

*Welcome! – English for the travel and tourism industry* is an intermediate level course in communication skills for people who deal with visitors and tourists as guests, clients, passengers or customers.

The course is divided into 10 Modules consisting of 4 or 5 sixty-minute Lessons each, covering:

- situations students might find themselves in during their work (but only where English would be used), focusing in particular on
  - carrying out their job efficiently with people who don't speak their language
  - helping guests or clients
  - solving problems
- vocabulary development
- functional language — developing a polite and friendly tone of voice, with exercises and tasks, including role play and pronunciation work
- improving students' listening skills
- improving students' reading skills
- discussion activities to encourage students to improve their communication skills generally and develop confidence and fluency
- grammar revision to help students to use English more accurately.

*Welcome!* is not intended to be a course in 'survival English' for people who aspire to go no further in their careers than taking orders or cleaning rooms — though, of course, most people in travel, hospitality and tourism do have to 'start at the bottom'. *Welcome!* prepares students to deal with many different situations in which they may find themselves in their work, not just the most predictable ones: to be an effective English speaker, you have to be able to cope with unexpected occurrences, not just the predictable. You have to be able to engage in conversations with clients, offer them advice and reassurance, speak to others on their behalf, and so on. *Anyone* who deals with visitors or tourists needs to be able to give directions, recommend excursions and visits, talk about local places and customs, explain local habits and rules — if necessary in English, and often using English as a lingua franca with foreign people whose own English may not be very good.

## Who is *Welcome!* for?

*Welcome!* is for people training for a career or already working in the following travel and tourism industries:

- hotels (hospitality)
- restaurants (catering)
- cafés and bars
- camp sites and self-catering accommodation
- transport: airlines, ferries, road, rail
- travel agencies
- car hire
- working for tour operators or as local reps
- public sector tourism: tourist information offices, tourist boards
- leisure activities and tourist attractions (pools, theme parks, castles, galleries, museums, etc.).

They are likely to be people who realise that they can't make do with 'survival English' and who probably aspire to more senior, responsible jobs in their industry, where meeting the public and a confident command of English are essential.

The professional training involved in each of the above areas is clearly different. Nevertheless, apart from the job-specific terminology, the English-learning needs are very similar. When it comes to using English, the communication skills that the people in all these industries require have a great deal in common — and all of them need to deal with visitors and tourists.

The course is primarily aimed at students who are still in training or doing an in-service language course. Although no previous work experience is assumed, many of these students will have gained some experience during placements and holiday work. Some may also have experience as clients themselves. The discussion questions will encourage students to draw on their (perhaps limited) work experience and to use their common sense. As time goes on during their course, the students may well acquire more experience through holiday work and work placements.

The material works best at intermediate level, but it is designed to be flexible and can be used with mixed-ability classes.

The students may have studied English for some years at school, with varying degrees of success, and there is likely to be a wide range of English ability within each class. What they may well have in common is an unfamiliarity with pair and group work and a fear of making mistakes when they speak. What they need is to build up their confidence and fluency, expand their vocabulary, be able to understand spoken English easily, and improve their accuracy. Also, they need to develop a polite, friendly, confident tone of voice and way of behaving in English.

# How is *Welcome!* organised?

Each Module focuses on a different theme. Within each Module there are four or five Lessons. The Modules are colour-coded in the Student's Book for ease of use.

Modules covering GENERAL themes alternate with Modules that cover more specific themes (*in italics below*). The more specific themes, such as *Food and drink*, are relevant for ALL students, even if they don't expect to have anything to do with food and beverage preparation or service in their work. This is because everyone who deals with visitors and tourists needs to be able to describe local cuisine and drinks. Moreover, as people change jobs and find themselves having to do unexpected things as their careers develop, they may have to wait tables, explain food and beverage items on a room-service menu, work in reception or advise guests on travel arrangements. They will need to know about all the aspects of their organisation and the situations their clients and employees may find themselves in.

| LESSONS | MODULE | THEME |
| --- | --- | --- |
| 1–4 | Different kinds of people | Dealing with clients in face-to-face situations |
| 5–10 | *International travel* | *Transportation by air, sea and rail* |
| 11–14 | Phone calls | Using the telephone with clients |
| 15–20 | *Food and drink* | *Food and beverage service in bars, cafés and restaurants* |
| 21–24 | Correspondence | Correspondence with clients |
| 25–30 | *Accommodation* | *Dealing with guests in hotels and booking accommodation* |
| 31–34 | Money | Dealing with payments and foreign exchange |
| 35–40 | *Travelling around* | *Public transportation, car rental, motoring and giving directions* |
| 41–44 | Problems | Helping clients to solve their problems, dealing with complaints and advising clients about safety |
| 45–50 | *Attractions and activities* | *Recommending activities to clients and describing your region; discussing the effects of tourism* |

Each Lesson is a double-page spread and contains material for a 60-minute classroom session. Each Lesson is divided into two to four sections (A, B, C, and so on), each of which is usually divided into a series of steps (1, 2, 3, and so on). One of the Lessons in each Module focuses on a topic which the students discuss, usually provoked by a reading passage.

*Welcome!* is designed to be flexible. Feel free to select the sections or steps that are most relevant for your class. You might, for example, decide to place less emphasis on writing skills and skip some of the Writing tasks — or spend a long time on them if your students need to improve their writing skills greatly.

If you find that there's more material in the book than you can cover in the time you have available, you'll need to *select* the exercises or sections within a Lesson that will be of most benefit to your students. Indeed, it's recommended that you *do* select among the activities, since not everything in the book is likely to be equally relevant to every group of students. Many of the Modules are 'free-standing' and don't depend on having done the work in a previous Module. You may decide to deal with the Modules in a different sequence from the way they are presented in the Student's Book and this won't affect the way that the course works. However the Modules do become progressively more difficult.

If your classroom sessions are shorter than 60 minutes, you may have to skip some sections. Alternatively, you may prefer to continue a Lesson in the next classroom session. This is easily done because each Lesson in Welcome! is split into separate sections.

If your classroom sessions last 90 minutes, you may find that most Lessons provide enough material, especially if your students are rather weak in English and need to take their time with the role plays. However, the 'extra' 30 minutes in your classroom sessions can be devoted to work on specialised professional terminology (see page 8), extra work on grammar (see page 12) or topical or locally-relevant reading texts (see pages 11–12).

# Pair work and Group work

Many of the activities in Welcome! work best with learners working together in pairs or small groups of 3 to 5 students. The larger the class, the more these student-centred activities make sense, because:

- they give everyone a chance to speak
- they allow real conversations to develop, as opposed to isolated language practice
- they free learners from the fear of making mistakes, or losing face in front of the whole class and the teacher.

Of course, it's true that learners are more likely to make mistakes in this situation, but it's far better for a whole class to be talking, with mistakes, than for them all to be listening to the teacher and answering questions one at a time in turn.

While the students are working in pairs or groups, spend this time going around the class, eavesdropping on the students. If you think it's helpful, join in sometimes and offer encouragement, advice or suggestions. Make notes on any important mistakes you hear while you're going around — but don't spend time actually correcting the students' mistakes while they're trying to express themselves.

The teacher has three main things to do while the students are involved in working in pairs or groups:

1 Getting things started: make sure everyone knows what to do and possesses the necessary vocabulary to do it

2 Monitoring the groups at work and deciding when to stop the activity

3 Leading a short follow-up discussion after each activity — answer any questions, point out any significant mistakes, and perhaps do some remedial work if necessary.

**Introduction**

Although accuracy is an important aspect of language learning and should never be ignored, it is far more important for learners to be able to communicate effectively. Most grammatical mistakes don't seriously affect communication. No learner should be (or even can be) corrected every time he or she makes a mistake. Indeed, if that happened, many students would become so inhibited that they'd be afraid to speak at all! No one can learn a foreign language without making mistakes and mistakes are actually an essential indicator of what learners still need to learn. On the basis of mistakes you overhear, together with the questions you're asked, you can plan any remedial teaching your class may require. It's only when students actually make mistakes that you can find out what their difficulties are — and then you should take action. There's no point in trying to anticipate mistakes.

If your class doesn't contain an even number of students, there will be an odd person out for pair work. Rather than becoming his or her partner yourself, it's best in such cases to make one 'pair' a group of three, with two members of the group sharing one of the roles. Make sure it's not always the same three who have to do this every time though!

It's a good idea to rearrange groups and pairs frequently: this will help to keep the class feeling fresh and receptive to different people's ideas. It may, however, sometimes be necessary to make sure that the more outgoing learners are kept together in the same group, so that they don't intimidate the less confident ones. Similarly, the shyest learners may gain more confidence if they talk only with each other, at least for a while. You may have to constantly compromise between offering variety and playing safe when arranging pairs and groups.

While using *Welcome!* your learners will be participating in enjoyable speaking activities. Their enjoyment may tempt them to lapse into their mother tongue from time to time. When this happens, you might find it helpful to remind them that every member of the class has a common aim: to improve their English. Indeed, one of the guiding principles of the material offered here is to foster a spirit of co-operation and friendship in the class — you are a team with a common purpose, and each member of the team has a part to play in the success of the course. Agree together on a rule that only English may be spoken in your class — that may sound like a tall order, but it may be necessary.

### How to discourage students from using their mother tongue

- Remind them that your class may be their only opportunity to use English during the week.
- Go round monitoring and whenever you overhear a pair or group speaking their mother tongue, remind them firmly of the English-only rule.
- Introduce a system of 'fines' (rather like a swear box) for students who don't use English.
- Demonstrate what to do before the students are split into pairs or groups, using one of your more confident students as your own partner while the others listen. This will help everyone to get into the discussion or role play more quickly.
- Separate students who persistently use their mother tongue and put them with students who do use English in class — but not if they have a bad influence on anyone they sit with.

- Make sure everyone knows simple transactional phrases they can use to manage their interaction. Make a list of phrases like these on the board (or as a poster for the classroom):

  Who's going to begin?
  You begin.
  Which role are you going to take?
  Whose turn is it?
  What are we supposed to do?
  What do you think?
  I didn't hear what you said.
  I don't agree.
  What does this word mean?
  Let's ask the teacher about this.
  How much longer have we got?
  I think we've finished. What should we do now?

  — and add further similar phrases to the list or poster as the need arises.

Students may need reminding of these phrases from time to time if they continually seem to be using their own language to manage their interactions.

# Mistakes and correction

As stated above, though accuracy should never be ignored, it's far more important for learners to be able to communicate effectively. To speak English fluently it's important to develop confidence and this is impossible if you're afraid of making mistakes. Students shouldn't be corrected too often as this may have an inhibiting effect and make them 'mistake-conscious'. You can't learn a language without making mistakes, and mistakes are a useful indicator of what students still need to learn. In real life, after all, people have to communicate with each other *in spite of* the mistakes they may be making and the limited amount of English they know.

Students should certainly be corrected when they make serious errors, but it's usually best to point out any mistakes that were made after the class have completed an activity, rather than interrupting *during* the activity. While students are working in pairs or groups, and you're going from group to group listening in, you *might* be able to make the occasional discreet correction without interrupting the flow of the conversation, but normally it's better to make a note of some of the errors you overhear and point them out later.

While your students are speaking, you may overhear them making mistakes in pronunciation, intonation, grammar, vocabulary or style, but rather than mentioning every single mistake you've noticed, it's more helpful to be selective and to draw attention to certain points that you think your students can improve. It's less confusing to focus on just one type of error at a time by, for example, drawing attention to pronunciation errors after one activity and then to vocabulary errors after another and to grammar errors after another. Accuracy is something that takes a long time to develop and it can't be achieved overnight!

In writing, where errors are more noticeable, accuracy is much more important. When marking students' written work, you can't really overlook some of their mistakes as you might do if they were talking. However, it's helpful to show students which of their mistakes are more or less serious and to distinguish between different kinds of mistakes.

Give students a chance to correct their own mistakes by <u>underlining</u> the relevant parts or showing in the margin whether there's a mistake in grammar (*G*), word order (*WO*), vocabulary (*V*), punctuation (*P*) or spelling (*Sp*) or, of course, using your own method.

A tick (✓) is a nice way of showing that an idea has been well expressed.

# Vocabulary

As they work through *Welcome!*, the students will be learning more and more vocabulary. Some of this is presented in special Vocabulary exercises (such as Section A on page 24 in the Student's Book), some occurs in context in the reading texts (such as the article on page 12) and in the recordings — and some is encountered within the instructions and questions in the Student's Book.

It's impossible to predict which vocabulary items are 'new words' for your students — you are the only person who can judge what vocabulary your students may need to learn. The final choice about which 'new words' to highlight should be made by the students themselves, guided by you, their teacher.

There's a vocabulary list for each Lesson in the Teacher's Book. These are the important words that the students need to know or learn in order to deal with the material in the Lesson. All the difficult vocabulary items are listed and defined, but for the recordings only the important words are given. You may need to consult a dictionary for definitions and further examples of the words used in different contexts. Where different terms are used in British and American English, both items are included in the Vocabulary lists (GB = British English, US = American English).

From these vocabulary items you should select the ones which your students need to remember: encourage them to highlight these items in their own books (see Highlighting vocabulary below). In some cases, if any of the words are likely to confuse or disconcert your students, you might decide to write up some of them on the board and discuss their meanings before everyone starts work on a particular section.

It's important to limit definition of vocabulary to those words that are essential to the task. Students can often understand a conversation or a reading text and then successfully complete the activity without understanding every word. In fact, learners should be encouraged to develop a tolerance for ambiguity, so that they don't panic or give up hope when they see an unfamiliar word. In addition, by dealing only with essential vocabulary you can prevent vocabulary work from taking up the entire classroom session. Where possible, urge students to guess the meaning of the word from its context.

Guessing meaning from context is a very important reading and listening skill. At first students may need your guidance, but as their skill develops they will be able to do this on their own. Explain to the students that guessing words from context involves:

- looking in the text or among the words in the same list for clues about the word
- thinking about what you know of similar words
- using your knowledge of the world.

For instance, look at the advertisement on page 9 in the Student's Book. Students may not know the word *escorting*. You can lead them to guess the definition by asking them to look at each occurrence of the word in the ad (there are three) and asking them to suggest another word that would fit in each context (e.g. *taking*, *accompanying*). If the students do work out meanings for themselves, they're more likely to remember the new words than if you define the word for them ('going with someone as a guide') or if you tell them the equivalent word in their own language.

There may be other words in each Lesson (particularly in the recordings and reading passages) which aren't in the Vocabulary lists and which students may ask about. You should be prepared to answer questions about these words or have students look them up in their dictionaries.

## *Highlighting vocabulary*

Highlighting vocabulary in their Student's Book turns each person's book into an 'instant revision aid'. Every time they look back at sections they have already done, the vocabulary they want to remember 'jumps out from the page', reminding them of the vocabulary items and showing the words in contexts. Just leafing back through previous units in a free moment (on the train, tram or bus, for example) will help them to revise vocabulary really easily.

What students should *not* do is highlight whole paragraphs of text (as if they were memorising passages from a text book for an exam). The selective approach of highlighting just a few chosen words on each page is much more effective.

In the recordings the students should listen for information and not try to spot unfamiliar vocabulary. Indeed, students should be discouraged from worrying about vocabulary when their main task is to understand the information that the speakers are communicating — which is what happens when we really listen to people in the flesh or on the phone. The Vocabulary lists in the Teacher's Book only include the most important 'new words' used in the recordings. You may find it helpful to go through the Transcript of the recording before the classroom session, highlighting in your Teacher's Book any more vocabulary which you think your students need to know before they hear the recording — these might be key words they don't know, or unfamiliar words that might distract them from concentrating on understanding the gist or from performing the task.

## *Vocabulary notes*

Apart from highlighting new words students should be encouraged to store vocabulary in other ways: a loose-leaf personal organiser or Filofax is particularly useful for this. This is best done by topic, with each new topic starting on a new page. Fresh pages can be inserted whenever necessary and the pages and topics can be rearranged easily.

## Specialised terminology

*Welcome!* does not cover specialised terminology. If all the members of your class are training to enter a particular profession, such as Catering, Hospitality or Leisure management, they will need extra work on the specialist vocabulary of that profession. The vocabulary that is in *Welcome!*, even in the Modules that cover specific themes, such as *Food and drink*, is 'general travel and tourism vocabulary', which people in every branch of the industry need to know.

Technical vocabulary or jargon that is special to a particular trade, industry or firm isn't covered in *Welcome!* You may need to devote special classroom sessions to this with your class, using supplementary exercises or reading texts covering your students' specialised area.

# Types of activities and exercises

Don't worry if the occasional activity fails to take off or seems to fizzle out with a particular class. Open-ended exercises in particular are inherently unpredictable. An activity that falls flat in one class might be very popular with a different class. Bear in mind the attitudes and prejudices of your class when you are selecting the activities you're going to do, and be prepared to 'sell' the idea of an activity to them if you believe it to be a particularly worthwhile one. Some activities are 'easier' than others, but this may not depend so much on the nature of the activity or the level of English required as on the imaginations, opinions, experience, versatility and knowledge of the participants themselves. Above all, though, the activities are designed to be enjoyable — because students who are enjoying their course are still eager to continue improving their English and are receptive to new ideas.

## Role play

Many of the activities in *Welcome!* involve students taking on specified roles in pairs.

Students are asked to play a role in order to simulate the kind of situations in which they may find themselves when dealing with clients or guests. This is an ideal way of preparing for real-life situations in which students may find themselves in their work.

One problem with such role plays is that only one person can play the role of 'member of staff' and the other person has to be the 'guest' or 'client' — which they won't have to do in real life. Unfortunately, the only way round this it to do each role play twice, changing roles. Usually, in *Welcome!* this is built into the structure of the role play or recommended in the instructions in the Student's Book.

However, students can actually learn quite a lot from playing the guest's role. It gives them insights into how members of staff ought to behave and speak, and enables them to give useful feedback afterwards to the 'member of staff' about the way he or she has dealt with them. Make sure there's time for everyone to give feedback before they change roles, or move on to the next step.

Some of the role plays involve telephone conversations. Students should sit back-to-back for telephone role plays, to simulate the essential fact that we aren't able to see the person we're talking to on the phone, and have to communicate only with our voices, not gestures and eye contact.

During a role play, you should go round the class monitoring, listening in to what is going on and offering individual advice and vocabulary suggestions. Make a note of the errors you overhear so that you can draw everyone's attention to them in the feedback / follow-up stage at the very end of the activity or section.

If you have a video camera and recorder available, many of these role plays can be recorded for playback, analysis and discussion later. This will enable students to 'see themselves as others see them', which may be slightly traumatic at first, but very beneficial in the long run. If you are going to do this, keep a copy of one of the recordings you make at the beginning of the course — then you'll be able to play it again later in the course to show your students how much progress they have made. An audio cassette recorder (with a good directional microphone) can be used in the same way.

Some Lessons contain an extended role play / simulation. These are integrated activities, including role play, processing written information (such as a timetable, reservation chart or itinerary) and writing, as well as problem-solving and decision making.

Here's a list of the extended role play / simulations:

| LESSON | TITLE |
|--------|-------|
| 10 | Organising a trip |
| 20 | Welcome to our restaurant! |
| 30 | The perfect hotel . . . (includes a hotel description) |
| 49 | A nice day out |

## Speech balloons

Useful phrases are presented in speech balloons. Students should decide which of the phrases are going to be most useful to them and highlight them. The phrases they already know and use should not be highlighted. They have opportunities to use the phrases in a role play that follows in the same Lesson — but should try to remember them to use in later Lessons too.

## Communication Activities

Some of the activities in *Welcome!* are called Communication Activities. These are shown in the Student's Book with this symbol: ⊙ . Their purpose is to simulate real situations as closely as possible. When we're talking to another person, we don't usually know what information the other person has or what the other person is going to say. In other words, there is usually an 'information gap'.

The Communication Activities are on pages 108–126 of the Student's Book. As you'll see, they are jumbled up in random order, so that it's not possible to find your way through them easily. This means that students will find it difficult to 'cheat' by looking at each other's information. The object is for the students to find out what their partners know and to tell their partners what they know. In this way an 'information gap' is created and bridged — and communication takes place.

In these information gap activities two or three students are each given different information, such as different role descriptions, and then have to bridge the gap in a conversation or phone call: the Communication Activities work in the same sort of way as role cards.

As students perform the Communication Activities, you can go around the room and make yourself available for help with vocabulary and instructions, as needed.

Here is a brief description of each Communication Activity, for quick reference:

| LESSON | DESCRIPTION | CA NUMBERS | | |
|---|---|---|---|---|
| 4 | Six short role plays | 1 | 17 | 33 |
| 6 | Customer satisfaction questionnaire | 3 | 19 | |
| 7 | Taking a reservation | 5 | 20 | |
| 8 | Explaining itineraries | 2 | 18 | |
| 9 | Airport codes | 6 | 21 | |
| 13 | Answering enquiries | 8 | 23 | |
| 14 | (Model notes) | 37 | | |
| 14 | Taking phone messages | 9 | 24 | |
| 24 | (Model letters) | 38 | | |
| 25 | Phone calls | 7 | 22 | |
| 26 | Checking in | 4 | 30 | |
| 28 | Giving information | 11 | 26 | |
| 29 | (Extra information for the travel agent) | 36 | | |
| 31 | Changing money | 14 | 32 | |
| 33 | Explaining a bill | 10 | 25 | |
| 38 | Car hire | 13 | 28 | |
| 40 | Giving directions | 15 | 31 | |
| 41 | Helping with problems and difficulties | 27 | 34 | |
| 42 | Dealing with complaints | 12 | 35 | |
| 46 | Giving advice | 16 | 29 | |

## Discussion

Some discussions are provoked or introduced by short recorded texts or interviews, photographs, or reading passages. The discussions are designed to work best in small groups — though if your whole class is very small, a whole-class discussion may sometimes be preferable. Some examples of this are in Lesson 2: Section A is a warm-up discussion to set the scene and encourage the students to share their experiences, and D2 is a follow-up discussion as the outcome of reading the text in D1.

Students should be encouraged to discuss the issues and activities they have been dealing with. Even though this has no direct relevance to dealing with guests or clients, discussion is an ideal way of helping the students to develop their confidence and fluency in conversation. Moreover, particularly in small groups, discussion also gives everyone a chance to use and consolidate the vocabulary that they have encountered in the Lesson. You'll find that discussion arises naturally after many of the activities throughout this course, such as reading a text, and particularly after students have taken part in a role play.

Discussions are by their very nature open-ended. This means that they may go on for a long time if everyone gets interested and wants to have their say. But it also means that sometimes nobody will have much to say. In this case there's no point in forcing the students to have opinions — instead, move on to the next Step in the Lesson. Many of the discussions are provoked by questions in the Student's Book. It's to be expected that some of the questions will be less provocative than others — and some sets of questions may fall flat with one class, and be a great success with another.

If you anticipate silence or apathy when a discussion is proposed, it's possible to get things going by beginning the discussion as a whole class, asking everyone to suggest some ideas and then dividing the class into groups to continue their discussion.

Once the discussion is under way, you should go round the class monitoring, listening in to what is going on and offering individual advice and vocabulary suggestions. Make a note of the errors you overhear so that you can draw everyone's attention to them in the feedback / follow-up stage at the very end of the activity or section.

At the end of each Lesson in *Welcome!* students should be given a chance to raise any queries or doubts they have. Sometimes it may be a good idea to ask them to explain how they benefited from doing a particular section. This may sound like asking for trouble, and in some classes you might really be opening a can of worms by asking this kind of question! But it's very reassuring for students to find out that the other members of the class have had similar difficulties and that others have found the activity useful.

You should also provide the students with feedback, pointing out errors you have noted down and congratulating them on the activities they have performed well.

## Pronunciation

The Pronunciation exercises in *Welcome!* are all fairly straightforward. They begin with a closely-controlled repetition exercise with a recorded model, followed by practice in pairs. They are different from the other role plays in that the students are focusing solely on pronunciation, and don't have to worry about deciding what to say or how to react.

The emphasis in these exercises is more on a friendly, helpful tone of voice than on pronouncing individual words correctly. This is a recurring theme in *Welcome!* — the need to adopt a tone of voice that guests and clients will perceive as welcoming, efficient and helpful, together with a demeanour that shows that you are sincere, willing to listen and help, and friendly. A smile is worth a hundred words!

The first Pronunciation exercise is on page 10 in the Student's Book.

## Dialogues

Before embarking on a role play that requires everyone to 'think on their feet' and decide what to say and how to react, students sometimes have to complete a dialogue with alternate lines missing, sometimes choosing suitable phrases from speech balloons.

These dialogues are best done in pairs so that the students can discuss different alternatives. There are usually several possible ways of completing each line. This kind of exercise helps the students to realise that life isn't a phrase book — there are many different ways of saying the same thing and many different ways of reacting to what other people say.

There's a recorded model dialogue to play to the class when they've finished the exercise — but this isn't intended to be 'the perfect dialogue'.

The first dialogue is on page 15 in the Student's Book.

## Listening

The purpose of the Listening exercises is to give students practice listening to authentic spoken English and to develop skills to make them better listeners. There are tasks for the students to do which are designed to help them to understand the main points that are made — and discourage them from listening to every single word or worrying about what they don't understand.

Listening is a skill that requires the students to concentrate on what they *do* understand and not to worry about all the things they don't understand. If, for example, a speaker says something unclearly, there's no point in worrying about this if it means that you stop listening to what speakers say next — just as in real life we have to ignore the words we don't understand and concentrate on the main points that are being made. It would be impossible for the students to acquire this skill if the only English that they were exposed to was always slow and simple. Using the recordings in *Welcome!* will help the students to do this better.

The reason why we haven't printed the Transcripts in the Student's Book is because if the students had a transcript to refer to, they might use it all the time when they're listening to the recordings — and this wouldn't help them to acquire the skill of understanding real life conversations (where the speakers don't hand out transcripts of what they're going to say!).

However, from time to time, you may decide to photocopy the occasional transcript from the Teacher's Book — but you shouldn't do this too often.

Some of the recordings are totally natural, and some are improvised so that they resemble English as it is actually spoken in a variety of realistic situations. The voices represent a variety of authentic regional and non-British accents, and the speech contains the normal hesitations, pauses and interruptions that occur in authentic spoken language.

Here's a recommended procedure for the Listening exercises:

1   Do the warm-up or pre-listening exercise, if there is one.

2   Explain what the recording is about, how many speakers there are, who they are and where they are.

3   Set the counter to zero.

4   Play the recording all the way through so that students can imagine the situations, get used to the voices and get the gist of what is being said. (If the recording is too long for this, just play the first 15–20 seconds, then rewind to zero.)

5   Play the recording again and this time ask everyone to decide on their answers to the questions in the Student's Book.

6   Get everyone to compare their answers. If they haven't managed to answer all the questions, they may need to hear the recording again.

7   If necessary, play the recording again so that everyone has another attempt at getting the answers they missed before.

8   Finally, play the recording for a third time and ask them to just sit back and listen. Maybe they could note down any questions they want to ask you at the end, or note down vocabulary or expressions that were used — or just relax and enjoy the conversations while soaking up ideas and vocabulary.

The first Listening exercise is on page 8 in the Student's Book.

# Writing

*Welcome!* is mostly about improving speaking and listening skills, but there is at least one Writing task in each Module and Lessons 21–24 focus on letters and emails to clients.

Depending on the needs of each class, you may decide to vary the emphasis on the Writing tasks. Writing is an important way for the students to consolidate what they've learnt — writing

things down helps with remembering vocabulary, for example. So, even if your students are mostly interested in improving their speaking and listening skills, they should do most of the Writing tasks in *Welcome!*

The Teacher's Book contains model versions for some of the Writing tasks, which you can photocopy as handouts for your students when they've made their own attempts.

Here's a recommended procedure for the Writing tasks:

1   Discuss with the class some of the ideas or information they might include in their writing.

2   Brainstorm ideas from members of the class and write the most interesting ones on the board, perhaps including a few of your own.
    OR
    Arrange the class into groups to discuss what they're going to write and make notes.

3   Ask everyone to do the task as homework, so that they can do it at their own speed without any time pressure or distractions — and so as to reserve class time for speaking and listening activities, which can only be done in class.

4   Everyone does the Writing task at home. Ask them to leave enough room in the margin for you to add corrections and comments later.

5   Back in class, before they hand it to you for marking, arrange the class into pairs or groups and get them to read each other's work. Any piece of writing should be an attempt to communicate ideas to a reader. If students know that their peers are going to read their work, they're more likely to try to make it interesting, informative and entertaining! If you, their teacher and 'critic', are the only reader, the process of writing is much less motivating. Students can learn a lot from reading each other's ideas — and from each other's comments on their own work. A piece of written work should be regarded as a piece of communication, not simply an opportunity to spot the grammatical errors that students make.

6   Collect the work and take it away for marking.

7   When marking their work, give students a chance to correct their own mistakes, as discussed on page 7, perhaps by underlining the relevant parts or showing in the margin whether there's a mistake in grammar (G), word order (WO), vocabulary (V), punctuation (P) or spelling (Sp).
    A tick (✓ ) is a nice way of showing that an idea has been well expressed.

8   Return the work to the class and allow everyone enough time to write their corrections. Go around the class answering questions and checking the corrections whilst they're doing this.

9   (In Lessons 21–25 only) Finally, perhaps, give out a photocopy of the model version. Give everyone time to read it through and compare it with theirs.

Here's a list of the Writing tasks in *Welcome!*

| LESSON | WRITING TASK |
|--------|--------------|
| 1 | Describing your job |
| 10 | A letter explaining an itinerary |
| 14 | Taking messages (+ Model version in Communication Activity 37) |

*Model version in the Teacher's Book

Besides the above, there's plenty of practice in taking notes and filling out forms.

If your students are taking an examination where they'll have to write compositions, letters, brochure descriptions, menus, etc., they may need to do more writing practice than is included in *Welcome!* The best source of such material may be their exam syllabus and past papers.

# Reading

There are several Reading texts in the book, of different lengths. Most of these are authentic texts and hence contain vocabulary which the students may not know. Just like listening, reading requires students to concentrate on what they *do* understand, rather than panic when there are some words or phrases they don't understand — see Vocabulary on pages 7–8. The tasks and questions that accompany each Reading text are designed to help the students to understand the main points, not catch them out. Most Reading texts are followed by a discussion or role play activity.

There's an important difference between an authentic (unsimplified) text and the specially-written instructions and role play material in *Welcome!* Authentic texts do contain vocabulary that the students should learn to use themselves, but they also include more 'advanced' vocabulary that students at this level just need to understand (or even ignore). Students may need some help in deciding which category new words fit into. You can help them by reading each authentic text before the Lesson and highlighting the vocabulary items that you think your students should try to remember — these will only be words that are going to be useful in their work, and words they may encounter again.

A substantial amount of time can be saved in class if the longer reading texts are prepared as homework before the Lesson. This gives everyone time to look up unfamiliar words and get to grips with the content at their own pace. Then the answers to the questions can be discussed in class and more time will be available for other exercises and activities, such as role play or discussion.

If you can't rely on your students to prepare the Reading texts, and they have to read them in class, make sure they don't get obsessed with insisting on having every unfamiliar word in a text explained to them. This would be a waste of time because every text can be understood without knowing the meaning of every word. Correspondingly, it may not be a good idea to 'exploit' each

text too thoroughly by drawing the students' attention to every item of vocabulary it contains — just the items that are most relevant to their needs.

The texts are accompanied by questions for the students to answer, or a task. These questions and tasks direct the students' attention to the main points of the text and encourage them to react to the ideas or information in the text and talk about their own experiences.

Most of the texts that the students have to read are letters or faxes from clients, timetables or itineraries, booking forms, advertisements, brochure extracts and short informative passages. But some Lessons include a longer reading passage, focusing on an interesting or controversial topic, together with a discussion activity.

Here's a list of these 'Read and discuss' texts:

| LESSON | TEXT TITLE |
|---|---|
| 3 | Your first visit to a ryokan |
| 5 | What to do if . . . you're afraid of flying |
| 19 | Mediterranean diet and the Atkins diet |
| 29 | Hotel descriptions |
| (34 | Is service included? — this is a 'Listen and discuss' Lesson) |
| 39 | Welcome to Florida |
| 43 | Traveler safety tips |
| 47 | Advertisements for Spain and Thailand |
| 48 | A brief history of Mexico |
| 50 | How to be a responsible tourist |

You may wish to supplement the reading passages in *Welcome!* with your own choice of topical or more specialised texts photocopied from magazines or newspapers, according to your students' needs and interests. In particular, English-language texts which have local relevance, such as texts about an aspect of tourism in your students' country or region are particularly suitable.

# Functional language

Each of the Modules which have a general theme include useful phrases (in the speech balloons) and practice in using functional language in various situations. Each of the more specific Modules contains one Lesson that has more general relevance (beyond the theme of the Module), covering functional language that the students need in all kinds of situations. Here is a list of those Lessons:

| 6 | Asking questions |
|---|---|
| 13 | Answering enquiries |
| 28 | Giving information |
| 37 | Offering and requesting |
| 46 | Making suggestions and giving advice |

# Grammar

*Welcome!* doesn't revise grammar systematically, but it does include some Grammar revision exercises, where relevant. If your students require more practice in English grammar, they should use exercises from a grammar practice book, such as *Essential Grammar in Use* by Raymond Murphy (CUP).

Grammatical errors should be corrected when they affect communication, but otherwise correction is best reserved as feedback after the students have completed a discussion or role play. (See Mistakes and correction on page 7.)

Here's a list of the Grammar revision exercises:

**LESSON**

| | |
|---|---|
| 5 | *can/can't*, *have to* and *should/shouldn't* |
| 6 | Questions |
| 8 | *If . . . sentences (first conditional)* |
| 9 | *If . . . sentences (second conditional)* |
| 20 | *Did you do it? / Have you done it?* |
| 25 | *If . . . sentences (first conditional)* |
| 27 | Prepositions |
| 37 | *to . . . / -ing* |
| 39 | *have to, mustn't, should, shouldn't, can, can't* |

## Advice boxes

Throughout the book there are Advice boxes styled as post-it notes. These suggest ways of behaving and dealing with clients or guests. The advice given in these boxes should be discussed, rather than taken at face value.

These helpful tips are a regular feature of this book, giving everyone some advice on how to deal with clients. Make it clear to everyone that they should feel free to disagree with some of the advice. Some students with experience of dealing with clients may feel some of the advice slightly patronising. Some of the tips may be controversial or may not accord with the customs or habits of people in your students' country.

# THE TEACHER'S BOOK

Before each Lesson, it's advisable to read the teaching notes for each section and prepare ahead what you'll be covering in class. This is particularly important in the role plays and the Communication Activities where you'll need to know who's doing what and when.

Here's a summary of what is in the Teacher's Book:

## Aims

The aims of each Lesson are clearly stated in the Teacher's Book. These should be explained to the class so that they know what they're supposed to be doing. At the end of the Lesson you and they can evaluate to what extent those aims have been achieved.

## Vocabulary

There's a Vocabulary list for each Lesson in the Teacher's Book. These are the important words that the students need to know or learn in order to deal with the material in the lessson. All the difficult vocabulary items are listed and defined, but for the recordings only the important words are given. You may need to consult a dictionary for definitions and further examples of the words used in different contexts.

From these Vocabulary items you should select the ones which your students need to remember: encourage them to highlight these items in their books (see Vocabulary on pages 7–8). In some cases, if any of the words are likely to confuse or disconcert your students, you might decide to write up some of them on the board and discuss their meanings before everyone starts work on a particular section.

## First of all . . .

If there isn't a warm-up activity in the Student's Book, a warm-up is suggested in the Teacher's Book as an easy way in to each Lesson.

## Procedure

A recommended procedure is given for each Lesson. The procedures are more detailed in earlier Lessons than in later ones, as you and the class get used to the way the different kinds of activities normally work.

Suggested timings are *not* given for individual sections because there's no knowing how long they'll take — it all depends how difficult, or how interesting, your students find a section, and how long it takes to answer the questions they ask.

## Answers, suggested answers and sample answers

Answers are given for exercises where only one answer is acceptable for each question.

Suggested answers are given for more open-ended exercises, and for some of the questions that the students are asked to discuss.

Sample answers are given for questions that have many possible answers — just to give you an idea of what to expect or to give as prompts to students who have no ideas.

## Transcripts

A complete transcript of each of the recordings is provided. Occasionally, you may wish to photocopy one of these to help your students with a Listening exercise — but only occasionally. The transcripts include all the features of spontaneous spoken English, including hesitations, false starts and ungrammatical utterances.

## Model letters, emails and faxes

In some Lessons a model version of a Writing task that the students have to do is included in the Teacher's Book. This can be photocopied and handed out to the class, if you wish.

## If there's time . . .

Most Lessons in the Teacher's Book contain ideas for extra activities. If time allows, you can do these with your students if they would benefit from or enjoy more work on a particular topic. Some of these are questions for further discussion or longer discussion activities.

## Vocabulary puzzles

Pages 103–107 of the Teacher's Book contain a Vocabulary puzzle for each Module, which you can photocopy and give to your students. These puzzles revise some of the vocabulary the students have encountered in the Module. The puzzles can be done in pairs in class, or for homework.

At the end of each Module in the Teacher's Book you can find the solution to the relevant Vocabulary puzzle.

Thank you for reading this introduction. Good luck with using *Welcome!*

*Leo Jones*

# 1 Working in travel and tourism

The first Module (Lessons 1–4) covers various aspects of dealing with clients in face-to-face situations. The basic skills introduced and revised here are required in the whole of the book.

## Aims

Begin by explaining to the class the aims of Lesson 1, which are to improve their ability to:

- engage in pair work (which may be a new experience for some students)
- understand the main information in authentic recordings (and not to worry about words and phrases they can't understand)
- compare different kinds of work in the travel, tourism and leisure industries
- talk about their own preferences.

(It may be necessary to reassure them that 'improving their ability' doesn't mean 'becoming perfectly proficient' — it means making some progress so that they are *better* at each skill than they were before!)

## Vocabulary

In the Teacher's Book you'll find a list of important Vocabulary items for each Lesson. These lexical items are words and phrases that are introduced in the Lesson, some of which students may not have come across before.

Your students may be unfamiliar with the following words and expressions in Lesson 1. You may need to explain some of them — or you may prefer to ask the members of the class who do understand them to explain them to the others. Or you may prefer to wait until your students ask you to explain them.

| | | |
|---|---|---|
| **aspects** | **general public** | **rewarding** |
| **coach excursion** | **hourly rate** | **routine** |
| **decisions** | **nightmare** | **seasonal** |
| **dream** | **package tour** | **shift** |
| **duty** | **paperwork** | **supplement** |
| **duty manager** | **pressure** | **team** |
| **emergencies** | **rep (representative)** | **tips** |
| **escort** | **repeat customers** | **uniform** |
| **feedback** | **responsibilities** | **varied** |
| **flight** | | |

Students should highlight the items they want to remember in their own books — this means vocabulary which is new to them as well as words and phrases they already understand but which they (or you) feel they should try to use more often in their own speech.

Among the items in the list will be some which are less relevant to your students, or which they don't really need to remember and use, as well as many that some or all of them already do know and

use. The list doesn't include all the words in the interviews which students are unlikely to know, because the task can and should be completed without understanding every word that's spoken.

## First of all …

If everyone already knows everyone else, start straight in with Section A, but if some or all of the members of the class are together for the first time, get everyone to introduce themselves by answering some of these questions:

> What's your name?
> Where are you from?
> Where do you work/study?
> What do you do?
> What are you studying
> Why are you doing this course?

> My name's …
> I was born in … but now I live in …
> I work/study in …
> I'm a …
> I'm doing a course in …
> Because I want to …

Perhaps remind everyone that we usually answer the question:
**What do you do?**
by saying:
**I'm <u>a</u> student, or I'm <u>a</u> receptionist.**

Alternatively, put the students into pairs and ask them to interview each other and then report on their partner to the whole class. Introduce yourself in the same way too.

**A** This is a warm-up and preparation for the listening exercises in Section B. Seeing the quotes in writing will help everyone to understand what the speakers are saying when the recording is played later.

As some of your students may not have worked in pairs or in groups before, it may be necessary to demonstrate how some of these discussion activities might go. You can do this by acting out each conversation with one of your more confident students. Make it clear that these are 'fluency activities' where the emphasis is on communicating ideas and not worrying about making mistakes. They should try to keep talking — and ask for help with vocabulary when necessary.

Arrange the class into pairs. If you have an odd number of students in the class, there should be one group of three. Answer any questions that come up about the vocabulary in the quotes.

Ask everyone to discuss the questions, making it clear that this is an opportunity for them to practise their English. The actual answers to the questions are less important than discussing in English because at this point, before they hear the recording, the answers are a matter of opinion. Students can only improve their speaking skills by talking in English, so if some of your students are talking in their own language, stop the activity and try to convince them that they *can* manage the discussion in English.

True, their conversation may not be so wide-ranging or elaborate as it would be in their own language but this *is* an English lesson, after all! (See **How to discourage students from using their mother tongue** on Introduction page 7.)

Reassemble the class and ask one or two pairs to give their answers to the questions, but don't tell them if they're right or wrong at this stage.

# If there's time ...

Ask the class for their views on these questions:

- Which of the statements describe the *pleasant* parts of their work?
- Which describe the *unpleasant* parts?
- Which of the statements would you make about the work you do (or expect to do)?

**B1** The recording consists of four interviews with real people talking at their natural speed. If your students aren't used to hearing native speakers, this may cause some consternation at first because the speakers aren't speaking s l o w l y   a n d   c l e a r l y for the benefit of foreign learners.

So, before you play the recording, point out to everyone that the four speakers are 'real people' talking at their normal speed. They may need to hear the recording several times before they understand all the information. The purpose of this first listening is to give everyone a chance to get used to the voices. They don't need to be able to understand everything the speakers say.

Play the recording, pausing it for a few seconds between each speaker, so that everyone can reflect for a moment before the next speaker begins. (In the Transcript the relevant quotes are printed in **bold italic type**.)

## Answers

1  Jane — flight attendant
2  Lisa — hotel receptionist
3  Janine — travel agent
4  Fiona — waitress

**2** Before playing the recording again, ask everyone to read through statements 1–8, and answer any questions about vocabulary.

Play the recording, pausing it between each speaker to give everyone time to decide on their answers. These questions help them to focus on the main information. If they can answer these questions, they have understood the main points — even though they couldn't catch every word that was spoken.

Give everyone time to compare their answers in pairs. If there are questions that they disagree about, or if there are some they can't answer, play the recording again.

Ask the class to give their views on these questions:

- Which of the four jobs sounded most interesting?
- Why?

## Answers

1✓  2✗  3✗  4✓  5✓  6✗  7✓  8✓

# Transcript   5 minutes 29 seconds

**1**

JANE:  My name is Jane Sparkes, I fly cabin crew for British Airways long haul.
I enjoy the most about my job the fact that *I have no routine*. I do things…um…unexpectedly. I can be called out, so I don't know what I'm going to be doing maybe next week or the month after. I like the fact that all flights are different, *I meet different people*, and *I go to different places*. *I have lots of responsibilities in my work*. The prime one…er…the major one is safety. If anything ever happened to the aeroplane, I'm there to get people off as quickly and as safely as possible. But that's something that I've never had to do in a really bad emergency and I hope I never will have to do. In between, or rather instead of that kind of responsibility, *I look after people* during the flight — I suppose you could say I just give them food and drink — but flying is a…is a strange environment for a lot of people, it's a…a…it's a disconcerting environment and they need to be reassured, looked after. Food and drink I suppose really is the least important aspect of my job, it's safety first, keeping everything under control, making certain that everybody feels reasonably comfortable.

**2**

LISA:  *We do*…um… *different shifts*, we do lates and earlies. On an early …um…it's basically checking everybody out and dealing with guest accounts…um…checking arrivals for the next day, dealing with their requirements, allocating rooms. Um…on a late…um…generally checking people into the hotel, making dinner reservations for them …um…t here's…*there's also a lot of*…um… *paperwork* … *It's very varied*. I mean, *there's never a dull moment* …um… *you just meet so many different people*, specially in this hotel we have a lot of conferences, a lot of international guests. And the atmosphere is good in the hotel as well, you know, with your work colleagues, and it's a very enjoyable job. People complain. Um…you just have to not sort of take it personally and just apologise to them and, you know, pass on comments or get the duty manager to help them.

**3**

JANINE:  My name's Janine Cording and I'm a…I'm sales manager with a small travel agency.
We specialise in selling flight only, we don't sell package holidays here. Um…we can sell hotels and car hire, um…we can also sell…um…tours abroad, but as a general rule we don't sell a package at all. I love it. Yeah, it's…I'm very interested in travel and to be able to…um…deal with that field that I'm interested in, *it's very rewarding*, yeah. I enjoy talking about my own travel experiences …um…I enjoy…um…seeing other people going off on their travels, it's very…it's…*it's enjoyable seeing other people's dreams coming into reality*, that's what I enjoy I suppose. I try to encourage people to send me a postcard, so…um…er…I often hear from people in that way or I ask them to come back into the shop, particularly if I've spent a lot of time putting something together for them *it's always nice to have some feedback*. We do have a lot of people who come back to us just to let us know how things have gone. We have a lot of repeat customers.

**4**

FIONA: My name's Fiona Bowers, I'm a waitress.
Basically we work on a rolling two-week rota. I do about four shifts a week, which is *part-time…um…the weekends are obviously the busiest* and that's when we make our real money, and basically I come in at five, set the restaurant up ready for the evening and wait for the people to pour in. *We get paid an hourly rate and then we get tips on top of that* which vary incredibly. Like if you do a day shift, like now, you make no money. And if you do Saturday night, you make an awful lot of money, but you work for it really hard. Um…*I enjoy the people I work with*, really, mostly, I mean the job …anybody who's waited will tell you *it's really hard work* and *dealing with the general public can be a complete nightmare at times*, but the people I work with make it for me. They're all young, round my age, we all go out together and just enjoy…enjoy each other's company.

**C 1** Arrange the class into an even number of pairs — this may entail having two groups of three. Encourage everyone to use vocabulary related to jobs, e.g. *seasonal work, wear a uniform*, as well as using the phrases in the speech balloon.

While this is going on, go round the class answering any questions that may come up, particularly about the vocabulary in the advertisement.

Guessing meaning from context is a very important reading skill. At first students may need your guidance, but as their skill develops they will be able to do this on their own. Explain to the students that guessing words from context involves:

- looking in the text for clues about the word
- thinking about what you know of similar words
- using your knowledge of the world.

For instance, in the advertisement, students may not know the word *escorting*. You can lead them to guess the definition by asking them to look at each occurrence of the word in the ad (there are three) and asking them to suggest another word that would fit in each context (e.g. *taking, accompanying*). If the students work out meanings for themselves, they're more likely to remember the new words than if you define the word ('going with someone as a guide') or tell them the equivalent word in their own language.

### Suggested answers

The answers are all contained in the advertisement. What you'd enjoy or not enjoy is a matter of opinion.

**2** While the discussion in Step 1 is still in full swing, rearrange the pairs into groups of four (or five). Besides giving everyone a chance to find out about each other's views, this gives them a chance to restate their views with more confidence, and to a larger 'audience'.

### 3 Writing

This task should be set for homework. But it may be helpful for everyone to spend a little time working together in pairs or small groups making notes on what they are going to write.

Here's a suggested procedure for the Writing task:

**1** Discuss with the class some of the ideas or information they might include in their writing.

**2** Brainstorm ideas from members of the class and write the most interesting ones on the board, perhaps including a few of your own.
OR
Arrange the class into groups to discuss what they're going to write and make notes.

**3** Ask everyone to do the task as homework, so that they can do it at their own speed without any time pressure or distractions — and so as to reserve class time for speaking and listening activities, which can only be done in class.

**4** Everyone does the Writing task at home.

**5** Back in class in their next classroom session, before they hand it to you for marking, arrange the class into pairs or groups and get them to read each other's work. Any piece of writing should be an attempt to communicate ideas to a reader. If students know that their peers are going to read their work, they're more likely to try to make it interesting, informative and entertaining! If you, their teacher and 'critic', are the only reader, the process of writing is much less motivating. Students can learn a lot from reading each other's ideas — and from each other's comments on their own work. A piece of written work should be regarded as a piece of communication, not simply an opportunity to spot the grammatical errors that students make.

**6** Collect the work and take it away for marking.

**7** When marking their work, give students a chance to correct their own mistakes by underlining the relevant parts or showing in the margin whether there's a mistake in grammar (*G*), word order (*WO*), vocabulary (*V*), punctuation (*P*) or spelling (*Sp*) or using your own method. A tick ( ✓ ) is a nice way of showing that an idea has been well expressed.

**8** In the following classroom session, return the work to the class and allow everyone enough time to write their corrections. Go around the class answering questions and checking the corrections whilst they're doing this.

## If there's time …

Arrange the class into small groups and ask them to discuss these questions:

- What are the advantages of getting promotion in your line of work, apart from a higher salary?
- Why do people choose to work in the travel and tourism industries?

## Finally …

**1** Draw everyone's attention to the Advice box (styled as a post-it note). These helpful tips are a regular feature of this book, giving everyone some advice on how to deal with clients. Make it clear to everyone that they should feel free to disagree with some of the advice. Some students with experience of dealing with clients may feel some of the advice is slightly patronising.

**2** Remind everyone what the aims of this Lesson were. Do they feel that they have improved these abilities?

# 2 Being friendly and helpful

## Aims

Begin by explaining to everyone the aims of Lesson 2, which are to improve their ability to:

- recognise and produce a helpful and friendly tone of voice
- give clients the feeling that they are welcome.

## Vocabulary

| | |
|---|---|
| *appreciated* | *genuine* |
| *appreciative* | *impatient* |
| *book a table* | *member of staff* |
| *challenging* | *put someone at their ease* |
| *check-in desk (at an airport)* | *recommend* |
| *first impression* | *reservation* |
| *frown* | *staff* |

**A** Arrange the class into groups of three or four. The purpose of this warm-up discussion is to encourage everyone to think of times when they were themselves clients, guests or customers — and to consider how they were treated. If anyone has stayed in a hotel or travelled by plane recently, they should talk about those experiences too.

Reassemble the class and ask the students to tell the others about any *bad* experiences they had and any memorably good experiences. (Establishments get repeat business thanks to the courtesy, friendliness and helpfulness of the staff, not just the skills of the chef, the quality of the coffee and the range of goods they stock.)

**B 1**  Play the recording, pausing it for a few seconds between each conversation. One conversation demonstrates how not to behave. The students should concentrate on the way the people are speaking, not on what they're saying.

### Suggested answer

The receptionist (photo C) in the second conversation is the one who behaves in an unfriendly, unhelpful way. It's more the tone of his voice than the words he says that give this impression.

**2**  Play the recording again. This time the students should listen for what each client's problem is and the location of each recording. Both parts of the task should be reassuringly easy.

### Answers

| | | | |
|---|---|---|---|
| Conversation 1 | 1 | The client is nervous. | b at a check-in desk |
| Conversation 2 | 3 | The reservation hasn't been made. | a at a reception desk |
| Conversation 3 | 2 | The guest hasn't had her order taken. | c in a restaurant |

## If there's time ...

 Play the conversations again and ask the class to give their views on these questions:

- How do their voices show they're being polite, helpful and friendly?
- Which of the problems was the easiest to cope with — and which was the hardest?
- Which member of staff dealt with the problem most effectively?

## Transcript   2 minutes 47 seconds

**1**

| | |
|---|---|
| CHECK-IN CLERK: | Good morning, sir. |
| PASSENGER: | Oh, good morning. |
| CHECK-IN CLERK: | Could I see your ticket please? |
| PASSENGER: | What? Oh yes, er…sorry. Here you are. |
| CHECK-IN CLERK: | Thank you, Mr Robinson. |
| PASSENGER: | I was wondering, er…could I have a smoking seat, please? |
| CHECK-IN CLERK: | I'm afraid this is a non-smoking flight, sir. Would you prefer an aisle seat or a window seat? |
| PASSENGER: | Erm…well, I'm not sure. You see, it's the first time I've flown and I, well, I'm feeling a bit uneasy about it. Wh…What I really want is the safest seat! |
| CHECK-IN CLERK: | Oh I see! Well, there's really nothing to worry about. Let's see, I can give you an aisle seat right next to one of the exits. Then you'll have more leg room, too. |
| PASSENGER: | Oh good. Oh, well that sounds all right. |
| CHECK-IN CLERK: | And could I just see your passport, please? |
| PASSENGER: | Um…oh yes…um…here you are … |

**2**

| | |
|---|---|
| RECEPTIONIST: | Good evening, sir. |
| GUEST: | Good evening, my name's Smith. I have a room booked for tonight. |
| RECEPTIONIST: | Oh right, I'll just check … what was your name again? |
| GUEST: | Smith, John Smith. |
| RECEPTIONIST: | Smith? Er…well, there's no record of a reservation here. Did you make your reservation by phone? |
| GUEST: | No, by fax. I've got a copy of your reply here, look. |
| RECEPTIONIST: | I see. Well, there's nothing on the computer. |
| GUEST: | Well, do you have a room? |
| RECEPTIONIST: | I'll just check … Oh! Yes, we seem to be half-empty tonight. |
| GUEST: | Well, can I have a room then? |
| RECEPTIONIST: | Yes, I suppose so, I'll … |

**3**

| | |
|---|---|
| CUSTOMER: | Excuse me. |
| WAITER: | Yes, madam? |
| CUSTOMER: | I'm ready to order now. |
| WAITER: | Oh, I'm sorry, I thought you were waiting for someone to join you. |
| CUSTOMER: | Well, I was but she hasn't come and now I want to order. |
| WAITER: | Certainly, what would you like? |
| CUSTOMER: | I'll have a Caesar salad and a grilled fillet steak. |
| WAITER: | How would you like your steak cooked? |
| CUSTOMER: | Medium, please. |
| WAITER: | Would you like French fries with your steak? |
| CUSTOMER: | Yes, please. |
| WAITER: | And would you like the salad as a starter or with your main course? |
| CUSTOMER: | As a starter please … Oh, just a minute. Hello, Mary! |
| MARY: | Sorry I'm late. |
| CUSTOMER: | That's all right. I've just ordered. |
| MARY: | Oh, let me just look at the menu. |
| WAITER: | Please, take your time. Would you like me to come back in a couple of minutes? |
| MARY: | No, no, I know what I want. To start with I'll have … |

PHOTOCOPIABLE © Cambridge University Press 2005

**C 1** Arrange the students into pairs. Perhaps remind everyone that it's not just the words you use but the way you say them that makes something sound polite or impolite.

## Suggested answers

*Could you tell me your name, please?*
~~*What do you want?*~~
*It's a pleasure.* ✓
*Certainly.* ✓
~~*Do you want something?*~~
*May I help you?* ✓
*It's no trouble.* ✓
~~*Obviously.*~~
*Is there anything I can do for you?* ✓

## 2 Pronunciation

Play all three conversations on SB page 10 through once. Then play the first conversation and pause the recording. While it's still fresh in their minds ask the pairs to role play the conversation twice, switching roles the second time they do it. Then do the same with the second and third conversations. [37 seconds]

Reassemble the class and ask one or two pairs to perform each of the conversations. Correct anyone who doesn't sound helpful and friendly.

Finally, play all three conversations again to leave everyone with a 'good model' in their minds.

**D 1** Arrange the class into an even number of pairs. The prioritising task encourages the students to decide which points are the least relevant.

**2** Combine the pairs into groups of four (or five). First they compare their 'three most important pieces of advice' in the document. Then they talk about their own experiences. Students with no experience of dealing with clients should use their imaginations and discuss what they *will* enjoy and what they *will* find most difficult. They should try to come up with another answer to each question.

Reassemble the class and ask the groups to report on their extra answers.

## Suggested answers

I can learn about different countries.
Everyone is pleasant if you treat them right.
I like seeing new faces — it's never boring.
I don't have enough time to talk to clients and make them feel at ease.
It's frustrating not being able to speak English as well as I'd like.
People complain about things which I can't do anything about.

## If there's time …

Put the information below on the board and then arrange the class into groups of three or four. Ask them to discuss this topic:

* How do your behaviour and your appearance influence the impression you give to other people? Decide together what effect the following have on the impression you give to people:

YOUR EXPRESSION:
blinking   smiling
frowning   looking down
looking someone straight in the eye

THE NOISES YOU MAKE:
yawning   sniffing
humming   whistling

BODY LANGUAGE:
folding your arms
standing up straight
hands in pockets

CLOTHES AND ACCESSORIES:
uniform   casual clothes
fashionable clothes   tie
shorts   short skirt

## Finally …

**1** Draw everyone's attention to the Advice box. If anyone disagrees with the tips there, encourage them to say so.

**2** Remind everyone what the aims of this Lesson were. Have the aims been achieved?

**3** Ask everyone to read through the text *Your first visit to a ryokan* on SB page 12 before the next Lesson. This will save time in class.

# 3 When in Rome …

## Aims

Begin by explaining the aims of Lesson 3, which are to:

- increase the students' awareness of cross-cultural issues (different nationalities behave in different ways)

- stimulate discussion — each Module has one Lesson which focuses on an issue connected with travel and tourism, usually with a reading passage as its starting point. Discussion is a valuable way of developing fluency and confidence.

## Vocabulary

| | | |
|---|---|---|
| *beard* | *ignoring* | *over-familiar* |
| *formality* | *informality* | *rucksack* |

in the text:

| | | |
|---|---|---|
| *blanket* | *fellow-guest* | *slip* |
| *changing room* | *gown* | *slippers* |
| *communal* | *hot spring* | *soak* |
| *cover* | *mattress* | *stool* |
| *cushion* | *pan* | *towel* |
| *electrical heating unit* | *robe* | *undress* |
| *faucet (GB tap)* | *sheet* | |

## First of all …

Draw everyone's attention to the title of the Lesson and ask:

- How does the phrase continue? (See SB page 13.)

- Is there an equivalent expression in your own language?

- What does it mean? (If you're in a foreign country, behave like the locals.) Is this something visitors to another country should do? Do visitors to your country do this?

**A 1** The text comes from a publication for first-time visitors to Japan. The Japanese words printed in italics won't be found in an English dictionary (except perhaps *futon*), but they're all explained in the text.

If the students haven't already read the text for homework, ask them if they know anything about visiting Japan, and how life is different there. (They sleep on the floor, they eat raw fish, etc.)

If/When they have read the text, go through the answers to make sure there are no problems.

With an authentic text like this, it's a good idea to be prepared for the questions your students may ask about vocabulary — go through the text in your own copy of the Student's Book and highlight the words your students might find difficult (e.g. *slippers*, *faucets*, etc.). Be ready to explain these words if you're asked — but encourage the students to guess the meaning of such words for themselves if they can, using the clues within the text.

Many of the words that they might not know can be guessed from the context. For example, in paragraph 3, the words *mattress*, *sheets*, *cover* and *blankets* can all be guessed, and some of these are illustrated in the pictures. However, they don't need to understand all these words in order to complete the task successfully. (See **Vocabulary** on Introduction pages 7–8.)

## Answers

**1** B   **2** A   **3** C   **4** E   **5** F   **6** D   **7** G

**2** Highlighting with a fluorescent highlighter is recommended here — and also for highlighting new vocabulary items (see **Vocabulary** on Introduction pages 7–8). If you don't want your students to use highlighters, they could underline the points in pencil or note the points down in their notebooks.

**3** Arrange the students into pairs or groups of three for this discussion.

Reassemble the class and ask some pairs to report on their discussion and compare the lists of Dos and Don'ts they have come up with.

## Suggested answers

Do …

- Prepare for your visit by reading a good guidebook and making a list of places you want to go to.

- Stay in bed and breakfast places, not impersonal hotels.

- Try to meet local people and ask them to recommend places to go to.

- Travel long distances by public transport, not by car.

- Rent a bike to get around smaller places.

- Try local dishes when you eat out.

- Go on locally organised coach trips — they're a good way to meet people and learn about the country.

Don't …

- Spend all your time in the capital.

- Try to see all the sights.

- Forget to pack warm clothes — it can be cold, even in the summer!

**B 1** Arrange the class into an even number of pairs. This 'quiz' isn't a test, it's designed to stimulate discussion — some of the answers are debatable or a matter of opinion.

## Suggested answers

**1** d (He may be a guest, not an intruder.)

**2** a or b

**3** d (He should be addressed as 'Mr Fernandez'.)

**4** b ('Northern' and 'southern' people feel comfortable talking to each other at different distances. Northern people, such as

Germans, Canadians or British people, like to be further apart than southern people, such as Mexicans, Italians or Brazilians.)

**5** d (The other questions seem too personal.)

**2** Combine the pairs into groups of four or five. When everyone has had time to think of more examples of possible misunderstandings, reassemble the class and ask each group to report.

### Suggested answers

- Other examples of problems with family names:

  – a Chinese man called Mr Lo Win Hao should be addressed as Mr Lo

  – a Polish man who writes his name as Wajda Andrzej should be addressed as Mr Wajda.

- A smile can be used to cover embarrassment by the Japanese and some other nationalities.

- Direct eye contact with someone can be interpreted as an aggressive stare by some nationalities.

- If you blink too often, people might think you're insincere or lacking in confidence.

- Giving a present with the left hand is considered bad manners in some countries.

## Finally ...

**1** Draw everyone's attention to the Advice box.

**2** Find out if the students are now more aware of cross-cultural issues than they were before this Lesson. (It's impossible to generalise about the way people from a particular country behave — everyone is different, and well-travelled people tend to modify their behaviour to suit the country they're in.)

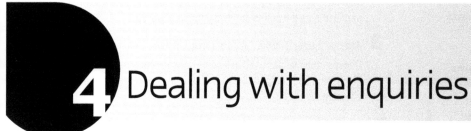

# 4. Dealing with enquiries

## Aims

Begin by explaining to the class the aims of Lesson 4, which are to improve their ability to:

- deal with enquiries in a helpful way
- respond to clients' enquiries appropriately, using suitable phrases.

## Vocabulary

| | |
|---|---|
| *available* | *kiosk* |
| *clues* | *luggage label* |
| *delayed* | *observer* |
| *dialling code* | *overlook* |
| *dialling tone* | *overnight bag* |
| *eye contact* | *porter (US bellboy)* |
| *flight* | *public transport (US transportation)* |
| *impersonally* | *two blocks from here* |
| *journey* | |

## First of all ...

Ask everyone to look at the photo on SB page 14. Ask them to suggest what kind of enquiries guests might make at the reception desk — what questions might they ask? If anyone has work experience, ask them to remember some (routine or more unusual) questions they've been asked by guests.

**A1** Play the recording, pausing between each conversation while everyone ticks the appropriate box. Then play it again while they fill in the blanks.

Go through the answers and answer any questions that come up.

### Answers

**1a** a room for someone else

**1b** 406

**2a** by bus

**2b** 60

**3a** breakfast service finishes

**3b** from 6.30 to 9.30 on weekdays and from 7.30 to 10.30 at weekends

**2** Play the recording again. The phrases the receptionist uses are printed *in bold italic type* in the Transcript.

Arrange the class into pairs. After comparing their answers, they should discuss the questions below the speech balloon.

### Suggested answers

The phrases that are used are:

*Good evening. How can I help you?*
*Is there anything else I can do for you?*
*Have an enjoyable day!*
*You're welcome.*
*You're very welcome.*
*It's a pleasure.*

The phrases in the balloon on the left in the Student's Book would be used when a guest is checking in. The middle four would only be used when welcoming a guest who had stayed with you before.

The phrases in the balloon on the right would be used when dealing with a guest who comes to the reception desk during the day, perhaps with an enquiry, like the guests in the recording.

## Transcript  2 minutes 21 seconds

### 1

| | |
|---|---|
| RECEPTIONIST: | **Good evening**, Mr Grey. **How can I help you?** |
| GUEST: | My colleague, Mr Black, is coming here next week. I think he's arriving on Tuesday. |
| RECEPTIONIST: | I'll just check the computer ... No, it's Wednesday for three nights. |
| GUEST: | I see. Well, could you make sure he gets a really nice room? 306 is my favourite. |
| RECEPTIONIST: | I'll just check if it's free ... No, I'm afraid it isn't. But 406 is just the same, a bit higher up and it has the same view. |
| GUEST: | Oh good, er…could you reserve that one for him then, please? |
| RECEPTIONIST: | Certainly. |
| GUEST: | Thank you very much. |
| RECEPTIONIST: | **You're very welcome**, Mr Grey. **Have an enjoyable day!** |
| GUEST: | Thank you! |

### 2

| | |
|---|---|
| RECEPTIONIST: | **Good evening**, Mrs Abbot. **How can I help you**? |
| GUEST: | Yes, can you tell me how long it takes to get to the airport? |
| RECEPTIONIST: | Would that be by taxi or public transport? |
| GUEST: | Oh, the flight's not till 6 o'clock, so I've probably got time to take the bus. |
| RECEPTIONIST: | Well, the buses leave every hour on the hour and the journey takes about 30 minutes. |
| GUEST: | Fine. So if I catch the 5 o'clock bus ... |
| RECEPTIONIST: | Well, no, you should check in no later than an hour before your flight, so you should take the 4 o'clock. You can buy your ticket on the bus. |
| GUEST: | Oh, right. Thanks very much for your help. |
| RECEPTIONIST: | **It's a pleasure**, Mrs Abbot. **Is there anything else I can do for you?** |
| GUEST: | Ah, yes, can you tell me ... |

### 3

| | |
|---|---|
| RECEPTIONIST: | **Good evening**, Mr Williams. **How can I help you?** |
| GUEST: | Good evening. I'd just like to know the latest time I can have breakfast in the morning. I'm really tired and I don't want to get up too early. |
| RECEPTIONIST: | I see, well tomorrow's Saturday and at weekends breakfast is from 7.30 till 10.30. If you get there by 10.15, that should be fine. |
| GUEST: | Good, OK. What about it in the week? |
| RECEPTIONIST: | On weekdays breakfast is from 6.30 till 9.30. |
| GUEST: | I see, fine thanks. Good night. |
| RECEPTIONIST: | **You're welcome**. Good night, Mr Williams. Sleep well. |
| GUEST: | Thanks. |

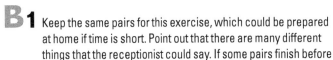

## B1

Keep the same pairs for this exercise, which could be prepared at home if time is short. Point out that there are many different things that the receptionist could say. If some pairs finish before the others, put them together with another speedy pair and ask them to compare answers.

When most of the pairs have finished, reassemble the class and ask the students for their ideas. Accept all reasonable suggestions and only correct the ones that are grammatically incorrect.

## Suggested answers

*(in bold italic type in the Transcript below)*

## 2 Pronunciation

Play the recording a couple of times, first for everyone to compare what they've written with the model version, and then to use as a model for the Pronunciation exercise.

## Transcript  50 seconds

| | |
|---|---|
| RECEPTIONIST: | Good afternoon, Mr Johnson. How nice to see you again! |
| GUEST: | Thank you, it's very nice to be here again. How are you? |
| RECEPTIONIST: | **Oh, I'm fine, thanks.** |
| GUEST: | Good. Now, I asked for my usual room when I made the booking. Is it available? |
| RECEPTIONIST: | **Er…well, no. I'm afraid not. I've had to put you in Room 101.** |
| GUEST: | Oh, well, never mind. Room 101 does overlook the garden too, doesn't it? |
| RECEPTIONIST: | **Oh, yes, it does. It's a very nice room. How long will you be staying with us?** |
| GUEST: | Oh, until Friday I expect. But is it all right if I let you know for sure tomorrow morning? |
| RECEPTIONIST: | **Oh, yes, that will be fine.** |
| GUEST: | Good. Thanks very much. Don't worry about a porter. I've only got this small overnight bag. |
| RECEPTIONIST: | **Well, if you're quite sure. Here's your key. Room 101 is on the first floor. Now you turn left at the top of the stairs ...** |

## C Role play

Before beginning this activity, please familiarise yourself with the information that the students will be seeing in **Activity 1** on page 108 of the Student's Book, **Activity 17** on page 116 and **Activity 33** on page 124. Allow plenty of time for this activity, bearing in mind that there are six short role plays to be done, some of which may have to be repeated.

Each conversation is 'observed' by a third student, who eavesdrops, or listens in, on the conversation and gives the others feedback after each role play, paying particular attention to the tone of voice used by the member of staff. The roles keep changing so that everyone gets *two* turns at being the member of staff. If the observer judges the member of staff to be unfriendly or impolite, the role play should be done again. Be ready to adjudicate if necessary!

As this is their first Communication activity, make sure everyone understands what the purpose of this kind of information gap activity is — see Introduction page 9). There's no need to look at each other's information because we're trying to simulate the unpredictability of real life situations.

Arrange the class mostly into groups of three — with some fours if necessary — sharing the roles, as if they're arriving together, or meeting a guest together.

Tell everyone to look at the appropriate Activity and read the instructions there. They shouldn't begin yet. Make sure everyone understands what they're supposed to do. Then tell them to start.

## If there's time …

Ask each group to 'perform' one of the interactions with the rest of the class 'observing' and offering feedback.

## Finally …

1  Draw everyone's attention to the Advice box.
2  Remind everyone what the aims of this Lesson were. Have they been achieved?
3  Ask everyone to read through the text *Afraid of Flying?* on SB page 17 before the next Lesson. This will save time in class.

# Different kinds of people: Vocabulary puzzle

Photocopy the Vocabulary puzzle on page 103 for everyone to do in pairs in class, or for homework. The answers are given here but they shouldn't be given out at the same time as the puzzle!

## *Answers*

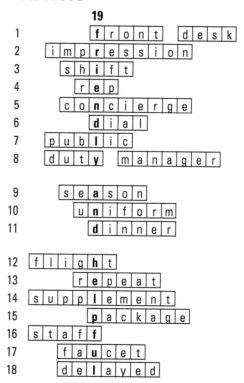

# 5 Different ways of travelling

This Module (Lessons 5–10) covers various aspects of transportation by air, sea and rail. Motoring and local transportation is covered in Travelling around (Lessons 35–40).

## Aims

Begin by explaining to the class the aims of Lesson 5, which are to improve their ability to:

- compare their experiences of different modes of transport
- cope with an unsimplified authentic text without needing to understand every word.

## Vocabulary

*annoying   coach   drunk   modes of transport*

in the text:

| | | |
|---|---|---|
| *anxiety* | *ignorance* | *strap yourself* |
| *bounce* | *loosely* | *thunderstorm* |
| *breath* | *pack* | *tighten* |
| *carry-on bag* | *retire* | *turbulence* |
| *dehydrate* | *roar* | *unfasten* |
| *excitement* | *specialize* | |
| *flight attendant* | *squashed* | |

 **A** This is a warm-up activity, introducing the topic of transport. The photos show a coach, a train, a plane and a ferry. After the groups have discussed the questions, reassemble the class and ask them to report on their findings.

**B 1** Throughout the book there will be short grammar review exercises. If your students need more extensive grammar revision, they should use supplementary material.

Note that there are many different possible answers in this exercise — see 2 below.

**2** Arrange the class into an even number of pairs. This Writing exercise could be set for homework if time is short. There are a large number of possible answers.

### Suggested answers

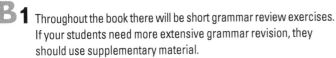

(The students are only expected to write six sentences, not this many.)

On a long-distance bus or coach you can't talk to the driver and you have to remain seated during the journey.

On a train you should show your ticket to the conductor but you shouldn't annoy the other passengers.

On a ship you can't open the window but you can sing songs.

On a plane you have to wear a seat belt and you can't open the window.

On a long-distance bus or coach you can't stand up during the journey and you shouldn't drink alcohol.

On a train you don't have to wear a seat belt and you can stand up and walk around during the journey.

On a ship you can't talk to the captain but you can smoke.

On a plane you can drink alcohol but you shouldn't get drunk or sing songs.

**3** Combine the pairs into groups of four. After the students have compared sentences, reassemble the class and ask each pair to read out one of their sentences.

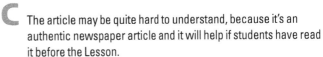 **C** The article may be quite hard to understand, because it's an authentic newspaper article and it will help if students have read it before the Lesson.

Read it through before the Lesson in your own copy of the Student's Book and highlight the words you think your students may not understand, so that you can be ready to explain them if asked. Most of the difficult words can be guessed from their context, and students should be encouraged to do this rather than expect their teacher to be a 'walking dictionary'!

## Answers

**1st column**

Now all you can do is ~~stand~~ sit for hours on end,

Flying is much safer than travelling by ~~air~~ road

**2nd column**

How can the ~~drivers~~ pilots see where they're going when it's cloudy?

Have a good night's sleep the night ~~after~~ before you have to check out in

Arrive at the airport a long time before you have to check ~~out~~ in.

**3rd column**

choose a seat near the ~~back~~ front

Don't drink alcohol – it ~~will~~ won't help you relax and it will dehydrate you

Sit down, ~~unfasten~~ fasten your seat belt,

Their success rate is very ~~low~~ high, apparently.

**D 1** Get the students into pairs. Encourage any students who have flown to lead and talk about their experiences of flying.

Try to reduce stress (see the answers for C above).

**2** Keep the same pairs for this activity. Halfway through the activity, ask pairs to swap roles.

## Finally …

Remind everyone what the aims of this lesson were. Have they been achieved?

# 6 Asking questions

## Aims

Begin by explaining to the class the aims of Lesson 6, which are to:

- improve their confidence and accuracy in using direct and indirect questions
- make them more aware of a polite tone of voice when asking questions.

These functions are not restricted to international travel situations.

## Vocabulary

| | |
|---|---|
| *APEX ticket* | *furnishings* |
| *balcony* | *laundry service* |
| *cancel a reservation* | *lobby* |
| *cashier* | *maid* |
| *change planes/trains* | *non-stop flight* |
| *check-in time* | *poolside* |
| *cleanliness* | *press a suit* |
| *concierge (GB hall porter)* | *quality* |
| *continuously* | *questionnaire* |
| *direct flight* | *round trip ticket* |
| *doorman* | *snack bar* |
| *en route* | *spell your name* |
| *equipment* | *stay over* |
| *food and beverage* | |

## First of all ...

Write up the answers to some questions on the board (as on the right below). Ask the students to suggest what question came before each one (given in brackets on the left below):

(Where do you come from?)   *I come from Madrid.*

(What time did you get up this morning?)   *I got up at 7am.*

(How did you get to college?)   *I came on the metro.*

(How long have you been learning English?)   *I've been learning English since 1992.*

*etc.*

**A1** Arrange the class into pairs. There's no need to go through the answers because they're all in the recording which you'll be playing later.

## Answers

**1** b (or c)  **2** g  **3** e  **4** f  **5** h  **6** c  **7** d  **8** a

**2** The recording gives the answers to the task in A1. As you play the recording, pause it for a few seconds between each conversation.

## Suggested answers

The impolite people were the travel agents in conversations 4 and 6 and the client in conversation 8.

## Transcript   1 minute 37 seconds

**1**

| CLIENT: | Do I have to change planes anywhere? |
|---|---|
| TRAVEL AGENT: | No, it's a direct flight. |

**2**

| CLIENT: | Can I get an APEX ticket? |
|---|---|
| TRAVEL AGENT: | Yes, but only if you stay over Saturday night. Is that all right? |

**3**

| CLIENT: | Is it best to fly from Paris to Lyon? |
|---|---|
| TRAVEL AGENT: | Not really, it's better to take a train. |

**4**

| CLIENT: | I'm...er...booked on a flight to New York tomorrow, but I can't travel then. What should I do? |
|---|---|
| TRAVEL AGENT: | Would you like me to cancel your reservation? |

**5**

| CLIENT: | What time do I have to be at the airport? |
|---|---|
| TRAVEL AGENT: | Your check-in time is 5.30 and your departure time is 6.30. Do you want me to book you a taxi? |

**6**

| CLIENT: | Does the flight stop anywhere en route? |
|---|---|
| TRAVEL AGENT: | No, it's a non-stop flight. |

**7**

| CLIENT: | Does the train go all the way to Venice? |
|---|---|
| TRAVEL AGENT: | No, you have to change trains in Bologna. Is that OK? |

**8**

| CLIENT: | How much is a round trip ticket to Tokyo? |
|---|---|
| TRAVEL AGENT: | Is that economy class or business class? |

## If there's time ...

Arrange the class into pairs and ask them to practise the exchanges, with the travel agents trying to sound as polite as they can.

# B1 Grammar

This exercise can be done in pairs, or working alone. See the Transcript for the correct questions and play the recording so that the students can check their answers. However, there are several possible variations which are grammatically correct, for example: *When are you supposed to check in? Could you tell me your full name? How would you like to pay?* etc.

## 2 Pronunciation

Play the recording a couple of times, then arrange the class into pairs for them to do the pronunciation practice.

### Transcript  57 seconds

1  What time does your flight leave?
2  What time do you have to check in?
3  How many people are there in your party?
4  What is your full name?
5  What kind of room would you like?
6  When will you be leaving?
7  How are you going to pay?
8  When would you like your wake-up call?

## 3 Role play

Before the students begin working in pairs, it may be helpful to have the whole class interview you in the role of a visitor from another country (the UK or the USA, for example). Perhaps point out that they don't have to use every one of the question words.

### Answers

How long have you been in this country?
How much time are you going to spend here?
What part of the country do you come from?
What kind of food is most popular in your country?
What time do people usually have dinner?
When do the stores close on a weekday?
Where do most tourists go to in your country?
Which is the most beautiful region?
Who is your country's president/prime minister?
Why do tourists enjoy visiting your country?
What did you come to this country for?

# C1

Make sure everyone notices the word order in the indirect questions. Ask the class to suggest some more questions they could ask beginning *Could you tell me … ?*

For example:

*Could you tell me where you live?*
*Could you tell me where you parked your car?*
*Could you tell me what your passport number is?*
*Could you tell me what time you'd like your wake-up call?*

## If there's time …

Ask the class to rephrase the questions in B2 as *Could you tell me … ?* questions.

## 2

This exercise can be done in pairs, or alone.

### Answers

3  Could you tell me when you arrived in this country/here?
4  Could you tell me who you gave the tickets to?
5  Could you tell me which day you're leaving?
6  Could you tell me when you'd like it returned/ready (by)?
7  Could you tell me why you'd like to see him/her?

# D1

Arrange the class into pairs (with one group of three if necessary) as they read the covering letter to guests and discuss the questions.

### Suggested answers

Because they help the hotel to improve its service.

Because, if they return to the hotel another time, the service may be better.

## 2 Role play

In this role play one student looks at **Activity 3** on SB page 109, the other at **Activity 19** on SB page 117. (If there is a group of three, two students should share the roles in Activity 3.) Allow plenty of time for this activity, so that everyone has a turn at asking the questions. Please familiarise yourself with the two questionnaires so that you can deal with any queries your students may have.

Before they begin the role play, allow everyone time to read through their information and make sure they understand what they have to do.

## Finally …

Remind everyone what the aims of this Lesson were. Have they been achieved?

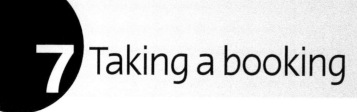

# 7 Taking a booking

## Aims

Begin by explaining to the class the aims of Lesson 7, which are to improve their ability to:

- deal with clients' ticketing and booking arrangements
- talk to clients about their requirements.

## Vocabulary

| | | |
|---|---|---|
| date of birth | method of payment | return flight |
| diet | outward flight | sea view/harbour view |
| honeymoon | preferred | supplement |
| initials | reservation form | tour operator |
| insurance | | |

## First of all ...

Ask the class about their national airline(s) and other foreign airlines they know — what kind of reputation and image does each one have? If they were going to fly somewhere, would they have a preferred airline? And is there one they'd prefer not to fly with? Why?

**A** You may need to play the recording two or three times for everyone to get all the information. If necessary, pause the recording after each piece of information has been given, so that the students have time to write their answers in the spaces. (One piece of information isn't asked for.)

### Answers

| | |
|---|---|
| return flight from | Athens to Zurich |
| date and time of outward flight | 7 July after 2pm (if possible) |
| date and time of return flight | 19 July after 6pm (if possible) |
| number of passengers | one |
| type or class of fare | economy |
| preferred airline | Swissair or Olympic |
| method of payment | Visa |
| name | this is what he forgot to ask! |
| address | 290 Amalias Avenue |
| telephone number | 323 7089 |

### Transcript   1 minute 27 seconds

CLIENT:  Good morning.

TRAVEL AGENT:  Good morning, how can I help you?

CLIENT:  I'd like to book one return ticket from Athens to Zurich, please.

TRAVEL AGENT:  Certainly, do sit down, please.

CLIENT:  Thank you.

TRAVEL AGENT:  Right. Could you tell me when you'd like to travel?

CLIENT:  On the 7th of July.

TRAVEL AGENT:  What time of day would you like to travel?

CLIENT:  Mm, I'd prefer a flight that leaves after 2 o'clock if possible.

TRAVEL AGENT:  And how about the return flight?

CLIENT:  Um…coming back on July 19th. After 6 o'clock if there's a flight that late.

TRAVEL AGENT:  Right. Is that economy class?

CLIENT:  Yes, economy class — I can get an APEX fare, can't I?

TRAVEL AGENT:  Yes, you can. Do you have a preferred airline?

CLIENT:  Um…Swissair*, or Olympic — it doesn't really matter.

TRAVEL AGENT:  And how will you be paying for the ticket?

CLIENT:  By Visa.

TRAVEL AGENT:  Fine, and could you tell me your address?

CLIENT:  Yes, it's 290 Amalias Avenue — that's AMALIAS.

TRAVEL AGENT:  And do you have a phone number where we can contact you?

CLIENT:  Yes, it's 323 7089.

TRAVEL AGENT:  Right, that's all I need to know. I'll just check the computer to find out about availability.

\* Swissair is now Swiss.

**B** Arrange the class into pairs to fill the blanks in this one-sided dialogue — it could be set as homework if time is short. If your students are likely to find it very difficult, play the recording first to give them an idea of what's going on — but they shouldn't try to memorise every word, of course!

Play the recording of the model version of the dialogue for the students to compare with, but note that there are various ways apart from the suggestions *in bold italic type* in the Transcript below that each blank can be filled.

The dialogue also demonstrates the kind of conversation they'll be having in the role play in Section C.

### Transcript   1 minute 1 second

TRAVEL AGENT:  Good morning, sir. How may I help you?

CLIENT:  Good morning. Can I make an airline reservation, please?

TRAVEL AGENT:  *Certainly. Where would you like to fly to and from?*

CLIENT:  From Athens to Istanbul.

TRAVEL AGENT:  *OK. And when would you like to travel?*

CLIENT:  I'd like to leave Athens on the 2nd of next month, returning on the 13th.

TRAVEL AGENT:  *Fine, all right. And what time of day would you like to fly?*

CLIENT:  I'd like to arrive in Istanbul by lunchtime, and be back in Athens by dinnertime.

TRAVEL AGENT:  *All right. And how many people will be travelling?*

CLIENT:  There'll be three of us — two adults and one child.

| TRAVEL AGENT: | *I see. Could you tell me how old the child is?* |
| CLIENT: | She's eight years old. |
| TRAVEL AGENT: | *All right. And is this economy class or business class?* |
| CLIENT: | Economy class — the cheapest fares you can get, if possible! |
| TRAVEL AGENT: | *All right. Do you have a preferred airline?* |
| CLIENT: | No, I don't mind which airline it is. |
| TRAVEL AGENT: | All right, I'll just check the computer to find out about availability … |

**PHOTOCOPIABLE** © Cambridge University Press 2005

## If there's time …

This Writing task can be done as homework:

Imagine that the tickets for the client in Section B have arrived at the travel agent's. Write a short letter to accompany the tickets being sent by mail.

## Role play

Arrange the class into pairs. One student looks at **Activity 5** on SB page 110, the other at **Activity 20** on SB page 118. Make sure everyone familiarises themselves with their information before they begin the role play.

By the end of the role play, which is in two parts, everyone should have filled out the booking form on SB page 21 on behalf of the client. Point out to everyone that they may have to spell out quite a number of the personal names and place names.

Finish by asking everyone to check their partner's form to make sure he or she has completed it accurately, with all the right dates, numbers and spellings.

## Finally …

Remind everyone what the aims of this Lesson were. Have they been achieved?

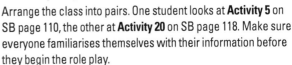

# 8 The best way to get there

## Aims

Begin by explaining to the class the aims of Lesson 8, which are to improve their ability to:

- advise clients on suitable routes
- explain routes and itineraries.

## Vocabulary

| | |
|---|---|
| *appointment* | *itinerary* |
| *booked into a hotel* | *misprint* |
| *confirmed reservation* | *reconfirm* |
| *connection* | *spot a mistake* |
| *freshen up* | *terminal* |

## First of all …

Ask the class when they use timetables in their daily lives. If they're planning a journey, what kinds of information do they look up before travelling (timetables, fares, routes, maps and street plans, guide books, etc.)?

## A1 Grammar

This quick exercise can be done in pairs or alone. The seven words in the list have to be used more than once because there are ten blanks to fill. (All the *if …* sentences are first conditionals.)

## *Suggested answers*

(Many variations are possible.)

| | | | |
|---|---|---|---|
| **2** | flies | 'll/will arrive | 8 o'clock |
| **3** | catch/take | 'll/will get | 9.40 |
| **4** | leave | 'll arrive | 14.25 |
| **5** | take | 'll arrive | 21.25 |
| **6** | reach | 'll have to fly | |

**2** Arrange the class into pairs. Point out that the extra information given with the timetables is important to solve the problems in the task. Note that there are no 'perfect answers' to these problems — the advice the students may decide to give is a matter of opinion. (Although the amount of irrelevant information in the timetables may seem excessive, in real life there's much more irrelevant information to wade through!)

## *Suggested answers*

**Mr A:** There are several possibilities: you could go by train, there's a Eurostar from Brussels at 7.25 which gets to Waterloo at 9.01. You can go by Underground from there to Canary Wharf very easily and quicky.

Alternatively you could go by plane and there's a Virgin Express flight at 7.25 to City Airport, arriving at 7.35.

If you don't mind being slightly late for your meeting, there's a later flight at 10.45, arriving at 10.50.

I don't recomend flying to Heathrow.

**Ms B:** The best way to go is to fly to Gatwick, which is only half an hour from Brighton. There's a SN Brussels Airlines flight at 7.45 which gets in at 7.45 British time to Gatwick. You'd probably get to Brighton by 9 o'clock with plenty of time to spare before lunch. There is a later flight, but it doesn't get to Gatwick until 16.50.

Alternatively you can get the bmi flight to Heathrow at 9.45, arriving at 10.05, it takes an hour to get to Central London and another hour to get to Brighton. You'll be there by 1 o'clock.

**Mr C:** There are various ways of getting to Cambridge. You can fly to London City at 14.00, then get the shuttle bus to Liverpool Street and then a train to Cambridge. You'd get there by 4 o'clock.

Or you can fly to Heathrow and take the Underground to King's Cross—if you get the bmi flight at 15.00 you'll get to Cambridge by about 6 o'clock.

Or you can take the Eurostar train at 14.56, getting to Waterloo at 16.25, the Underground to King's Cross and a train to Cambridge. You'll probably get there by 7 o'clock.

**Ms D:** If you're staying at Heathrow the last flight from Brussels is a bmi flight at 21.10 arriving at 21.25. You've just about got time for an early dinner in Brussels before you leave.

# If there's time …

Arrange the class into pairs. Ask them to play the roles of travel agent and client in the four situations in A1. They should change roles after each encounter.

**B1**

The deliberate mistakes encourage the students to read the document more carefully than they would if there were none. Don't discuss the mistakes at this stage before playing the recording.

## Answers

The two mistakes are towards the end of the itinerary:

In this line 21.30 should be 19.30 (2 hours before departure) — the client spotted this:

SUN 26 MAR CHECK IN AT OLYMPIC AIRWAYS DESK, TOKYO NARITA TERMINAL 2 BY (2130)

and in this line *Tuesday 28 March* should be *Monday 27 March* — the client didn't spot this:

(TUE 28 MAR) ARR BRUSSELS 1130

**2** Play the recording. Again, finding out whether or not the client spots the mistakes encourages the students to listen more carefully to the conversation.

**3** Explain to everyone that the recording is intended as a model for what they will have to do in the role play that follows — it shows one way that such a conversation might go and will help them to start their role play with more confidence. It helps them to get a feel for the kinds of things a travel agent might say in this situation. Then play the recording a second time, perhaps pausing it to answer any questions that may arise.

The phrases the travel agent uses are printed in **bold italic type** in the Transcript. The ones she doesn't use will also be useful in the role play.

*Transcript* 2 minutes 12 seconds

| | |
|---|---|
| CLIENT: | Good afternoon. |
| TRAVEL AGENT: | Oh, hello Mr Watson. I've got your tickets ready. |
| CLIENT: | Oh good. |
| TRAVEL AGENT: | If you'd just like to take a seat, *I'll just go through the itinerary with you* to make sure there are no mistakes. |
| CLIENT: | Fine, thank you. |
| TRAVEL AGENT: | Right. So, *first of all* you're leaving Brussels on Monday the 13th at 9.30 on *Sabena flight SN 600, arriving at Heathrow at 9.40. And we've booked you a room at this hotel for the night. |
| CLIENT: | OK. |
| TRAVEL AGENT: | Then the next day, that's the 14th, your flight from London to Sydney leaves at 12.15. It's Qantas flight QF 2 and you have to check in two hours before, so you should aim to leave your hotel at about 9 o'clock. |
| CLIENT: | Right. |
| TRAVEL AGENT: | And you get to Sydney the next day at 20.15 and you have a room booked at the Plaza Hotel till the 21st. |
| CLIENT: | Fine. |
| TRAVEL AGENT: | *After that* you go from Sydney to Tokyo on the 21st, leaving at 22.15 — *you have to check in* 90 minutes before. And in Tokyo you're booked into the Hilltop Hotel, as you requested, till the 26th. |
| CLIENT: | Right. |
| TRAVEL AGENT: | And then finally from Tokyo back to Brussels via Athens. |
| CLIENT: | Athens? |
| TRAVEL AGENT: | Yes, there aren't any direct flights on a Sunday, I'm afraid. |
| CLIENT: | Oh, well, never mind. |
| TRAVEL AGENT: | So you leave Tokyo on Sunday evening at 21.30. It's Olympic Airways OA 478. Check in at 21.30. |
| CLIENT: | Is that right? |
| TRAVEL AGENT: | Oh, no, sorry that should be 19.30 — two hours before. And you get to Athens at 8.05 the next day and your connection to Brussels is at 9.10 on OA 145, getting you back here at 11.30 on Tuesday morning. |
| CLIENT: | Oh, right. Well, that's fine. Well, thank you very much. |
| TRAVEL AGENT: | You're welcome Mr Watson, *I hope you enjoy your trip*! |
| CLIENT: | Thank you, goodbye. |
| TRAVEL AGENT: | Goodbye. |

*Sabena no longer exists. SN Brussels Airlines (airline code SN) still fly Brussels–London.

**International travel**

## 4 Role play

Arrange the class into pairs. One student looks at **Activity 2** on SB page 108, the other at **Activity 18** on SB page 116. The role play is in two parts so that both students have a chance to play the role of the travel agent. Before they begin the role play, make sure everyone reads their information through and understands what they have to do. Then answer any questions that arise before telling them to begin. Allow enough time for both parts of the role play.

The itinerary in **Activity 2** contains one mistake:

| 19 MARCH | SR109 | Los Angeles | 0850 | | | International Terminal 1950* |

*should read 0750

and the one in **Activity 18** contains a mistake too:

| 12 MAY | OS803 | Venice* | 1140 | Budapest | 1240 | |

*should read Vienna

## If there's time ...

Try to get hold of a couple of genuine itineraries produced by a local travel agent. Use these as the basis for another role play explaining the route.

## Finally ...

Remind everyone what the aims of this Lesson were. Have they been achieved?

# 9 Around the world

## Aims

Begin by explaining to the class the aims of Lesson 9, which are to improve their ability to:

- remember the names of countries and nationalities
- pronounce the letters of the alphabet easily and correctly.

## Vocabulary

**afford**  **flag**  **round-the-world trip**
**airport code**  **nationality**  **westwards**

## First of all ...

Ask everyone what nationalities most commonly visit their country:

- What languages do they speak and how many of them speak your language?
- How many of them expect to use English when they visit your country?

## A Vocabulary

Although not many people will recognise all of the flags, they should be able to work most of them out by process of elimination. Tell everyone not to linger over ones they don't know, but to do the ones they do know first. Again, with the nationalities everyone should do the ones they know first and come back to the more difficult ones later.

## Answers

| Australia | 3 — Australian |
| Austria | 9 — Austrian |
| Belgium | 21 — Belgian |
| Canada | 14 — Canadian |
| France | 7 — French |
| Germany | 11 — German |
| Greece | 10 — Greek |
| Hungary | 16 — Hungarian |
| Italy | 15 — Italian |
| Japan | 6 — Japanese |
| Malaysia | 17 — Malaysian |
| Mexico | 4 — Mexican |
| the Netherlands | 8 — Dutch |
| South Africa | 12 — South African |
| Spain | 5 — Spanish |
| Sweden | 13 — Swedish |
| Switzerland | 20 — Swiss |
| Thailand | 18 — Thai |
| Turkey | 19 — Turkish |

## If there's time ...

Ask the class what the five closest countries to their country are — and what is the nationality of a person from each?

## B1 Pronunciation

The pronunciation practice is 'disguised' in the puzzle. If your students aren't familiar with these airport codes, they may need some help. (Clue: all the places are listed from west to east). Make it clear this isn't a test — it's a game.

Don't discuss the right answers at this point, they're all in the Activities that follow.

**2** One student looks at **Activity 6** on SB page 110, the other at **Activity 21** on SB page 118. Explain that the pairs should continue their discussion, using the phrases in the speech balloon within their Activity.

## C1 Grammar

This open-ended grammar exercise refers to the countries listed in A. It should be done by students working alone. (All the *if ...* sentences are second conditionals.)

### Sample answers

If I could afford it, I'd go to Australia. I'd visit Brisbane and go diving at the Great Barrier Reef.

If I had enough money, I'd go to Austria. I'd go to the mountains and go skiing.

If I could afford it, I'd go to Belgium. I'd visit Brussels and eat mussels and chocolate.

If I had enough money, I'd go to Canada. I'd visit Toronto and then take a train ride to Vancouver.

If I could afford it, I'd go to France. I'd spend a week in Paris, enjoying the food and seeing the sights.

If I had enough money, I'd go to Germany. I'd go to Berlin and go to all the night clubs there.

If I could afford it, I'd go to Greece. I'd spend a week in Athens and then go island-hopping.

**2** Arrange the class into pairs or groups of three to compare their sentences. Go round correcting any grammatical mistakes you spot or overhear.

Reassemble the class and ask some students to tell you about the country they'd *most* like to visit and what they'd do there.

## D1

Arrange the class into an even number of pairs. Explain that it may be best for them to mark their east to west route on the map on SB page 25, using a pencil.

**2** Combine the pairs into groups of four or five for this activity. Draw everyone's attention to the useful phrases in the speech balloon.

# 10 Organising a trip

## Aims

Begin by explaining to the class that this Lesson consists of an extended role play / simulation. The aims of the Lesson are to improve their ability to:

- work together to solve problems, discussing them in English
- refer to times and dates easily and fluently.

## Vocabulary

| | |
|---|---|
| *accompany* | *routes* |
| *availability* | *sightseeing* |
| *city-centre (US downtown)* | *temples* |
| *places of interest* | |

## First of all ...

Ask everyone to look at the map on SB page 27 — can they identify the countries shown? Make it clear that this is a problem-solving discussion activity. As with most problems, there are going to be several correct ways of solving it.

## A1

Arrange the class into an even number of groups of three or four. As each group is 'competing' with the others to produce the itinerary that will be the most pleasing to the client, make sure that you have a good balance of students in each group. Ask the students to look at the email and decide what Ms Rivers wants — her itinerary to be arranged.

**2** Explain that the students are travel agents who have to plan the client's business trip. In case there is consternation at the unfamiliar surnames of the people Ms Rivers has to meet, just tell everyone to pronounce them as they're written.

Then let them get on with it and try not to intervene at all — answer questions about English but don't give advice about routes. The students should solve the problems together in their groups, without your help. It may, however, be necessary to refer them back to Ms Rivers' fax if they don't seem to be doing what she's asked them to do.

Allow everyone enough time to get to grips with the problem and attempt to solve it. There are many ways of solving the problem and the sample solution below (where the airports are flown to in alphabetical order) is not necessarily the best.

Each group writes an itinerary for their recommended route. If you're asked, tell the students that the recommended check-in time for international flights is 90 mins, and 30 mins for domestic flights.

**3** Combine the small groups into larger ones for them to compare itineraries.

### *Sample itinerary*

| | | | |
|---|---|---|---|
| Sun | 30 April | leave Madrid | 12.40 |
| Mon | 1 May | arrive Bangkok | 08.30 |
| Tue | 2 May | meet Ms Junsook | |
| Wed | 3 May | meet Mr Kasemeri | |
| Thu | 4 May | fly to Jakarta | 11.35 |
| Fri | 5 May | meet Ms Ramly + fly to Bali | 18.30 |
| Sat | 6 May | enjoy Bali | |
| Sun | 7 May | enjoy Bali + fly to Jakarta | 19.10 |
| Mon | 8 May | meet Mr Thayeb | |
| Tue | 9 May | fly to Kuala Lumpur | 11.30 |
| Wed | 10 May | meet Mr Al-Rahman | |
| Thu | 11 May | meet Mr Majid | |
| Fri | 12 May | fly to Osaka | 10.00 |
| Sat | 13 May | enjoy Kyoto | |
| Sun | 14 May | enjoy Kyoto | |
| Mon | 15 May | meet Mr Saito | |
| Tue | 16 May | meet Mr Kuriyama | |
| Wed | 17 May | fly to Singapore | 12.00 |
| Thu | 18 May | meet Mrs Tan | |
| Fri | 19 May | meet Mrs Chan | |
| Sat | 20 May | leave Singapore | 17.35 |
| Sun | 21 May | arrive in Madrid | 16.55 |

## If there's time …

Ask the students to vote for the best itinerary (votes for their own itinerary are not valid!).

## B Writing

Prepare this in class before everyone writes the letter for homework. Perhaps write up on the board some of the following suitable phrases that might be used in the letter:

*Dear Ms Rivers*
*I enclose a copy of the itinerary for your trip to the Far East.*
*Please let me know if you have any questions about it.*
*I have managed to fit in all of your appointments.*
*The only problem is that . . .*
*I'm afraid that on (date) it will be necessary for you to . . .*
*As you can see, everything fits together well.*
*You will be back in Madrid on (date) at (time).*
*I will go ahead and book the flights as soon as you give me your approval.*
*I have already provisionally booked the flights for you, so please let me know.*
*Yours sincerely,*

See Introduction page 11 for a recommended procedure for Writing tasks.

## Finally …

Remind everyone what the aims of this Lesson were. Have they been achieved?

## International travel: Vocabulary puzzle

Photocopy the Vocabulary puzzle on page 103 for everyone to do in pairs in class, or for homework.

## Answers

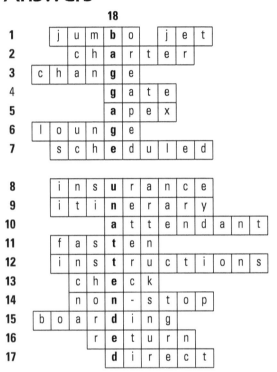

**18**

1. j u m **b** o | j e t
2. c h **a** r t e r
3. c h a n **g** e
4. **g** a t e
5. **a** p e x
6. l o u n **g** e
7. s c h **e** d u l e d

8. i n s **u** r a n c e
9. i t i **n** e r a r y
10. **a** t t e n d a n t
11. f a s **t** e n
12. i n s **t** r u c t i o n s
13. c h **e** c k
14. n o **n** - s t o p
15. b o a r **d** i n g
16. **r** e t u r n
17. **d** i r e c t

# 11 Using the phone

This Module (Lessons 11–14) deals with using the telephone with clients.

## Aims

Begin by explaining to the class the aims of Lesson 11, which are to improve their ability to:

- use the phone effectively and be aware of good and bad telephone behaviour

- answer questions from clients over the phone.

## Vocabulary

| | |
|---|---|
| confirm | payphone |
| cordless phone | sarcastic |
| efficient | tourist information office |
| interrupt | a written record |
| mobile phone (US cellphone) | |

**A** Arrange the class into pairs or groups of three. This is a warm-up discussion and it gives everyone a chance to air their views and talk about their fears. Perhaps remind everyone that they can discuss both phone calls in English and in their own language, and both personal and business calls.

## Sample answers

- It gives me a chance to talk to people and explain things to them better than I can in a letter or fax.

- (Especially in a foreign language) it's stressful trying to communicate with someone you don't know well on the phone, and there's always the feeling that the phone bill is mounting up.

- Mobile phones can ring at awkward times and reception can be poor sometimes; with payphones you can run out of coins in the middle of a call; with cordless phones you can forget where you put it down, which is all right if it's ringing but not if you want to make a call.

- Communicating face-to-face is easier because you see the other person's face and what their reactions are, and you can establish a relationship more easily.

**B 1** Arrange the class into pairs or groups of three. It's a matter of opinion what the three most important 'rules' are, but this task encourages the students to read the text carefully and evaluate it.

**2** Play the recording, which demonstrates what not to do on the phone. Pause the recording for a few seconds between each conversation. The task is an easy one but it's important for everyone to realise what the effect of 'bad telephone behaviour' is. It may be necessary to play the recording again to make sure everyone agrees about what's wrong in each conversation.

## Answers

**1** 7: he keeps interrupting **2** 2: she doesn't speak clearly
**3** 5: he doesn't sound efficient

## Transcript  1 minute 49 seconds

**1**

| | |
|---|---|
| RECEPTIONIST: | Hello, Panorama Hotel, how can I help you? |
| CLIENT: | Hello, do you have a room free for next weekend? |
| RECEPTIONIST : | Yes, we do, would you like a single or a double room? |
| CLIENT : | I'd like a double room with a balc… |
| RECEPTIONIST : | With a balcony? I'll just see if we have one available. … Yes, we do. |
| CLIENT : | Oh, good. We'd be arriving on Friday and leaving on the Mond… |
| RECEPTIONIST : | Leaving on Monday? Right, that's fine. |
| CLIENT : | Good. My name's Mary Brown and my phone num… |
| RECEPTIONIST : | Is that B R O W N? |
| CLIENT : | Yes, that's right, and if … |

**2**

| | |
|---|---|
| INFORMATION OFFICER: | Hello, Information Office. |
| TOURIST : | Hello, I'd like some information about trains, please. |
| INFORMATION OFFICER: | Trains, certainly, what would you like to know? |
| TOURIST : | What time is the last train to London? |
| INFORMATION OFFICER: | To London. The last one's at 9.45 but it doesn't arrive till after midnight. The last fast train is 9.30 and that gets in at 11.05. |
| TOURIST : | Sorry, did you say 9.30 or 19.30? |
| INFORMATION OFFICER: | Half past nine. |
| TOURIST: | Oh, I see. OK, thanks. |

**3**

| | |
|---|---|
| RESTAURANT MANAGER: | Hello, Arcadia Restaurant. How can I help you? |
| GUEST: | Can I reserve a table for this evening? |
| RESTAURANT MANAGER: | Yes, certainly … Um…I'll just find the reservations book … Hold on a sec … Um…here we are. Is this for this evening? |
| GUEST : | Yes, this evening at 8, if that's all right. |
| RESTAURANT MANAGER: | For eight people? What time? |
| GUEST : | Not for eight people, at 8 o'clock for three people. |
| RESTAURANT MANAGER: | Oh right, yeah … No, we haven't got any tables at that time, sorry. |
| GUEST : | Oh, oh dear. Well, never mind. OK. Goodbye. |

**3** Play the recording, pausing it for a few seconds between each conversation. In these conversations we hear the same members of staff using the phone more efficiently. Again, the task is easy. The purpose of this exercise is to give the students a good model for their own phone calls.

Play the recording again and ask the students to say what other 'rules' each of the speakers seems to be following (some, such as rule 1, may not be relevant to the type of call).

## Answers

In the first conversation the receptionist doesn't interrupt the client, in the second the information officer speaks more clearly, in the third the restaurant manager sounds more efficient.

## Transcript  2 minutes 6 seconds

**1**

| | |
|---|---|
| RECEPTIONIST: | Hello, Panorama Hotel, how can I help you? |
| CLIENT: | Hello, do you have a room free for next weekend? |
| RECEPTIONIST: | Yes, we do, would you like a single room or a double room? |
| CLIENT: | I'd like a double room with a balcony if you have one. |
| RECEPTIONIST: | With a balcony? I'll just see if we have one available. … Yes, we do. |
| CLIENT: | Oh, good. We'd be arriving on Friday and leaving on Monday morning. |
| RECEPTIONIST: | Leaving on Monday? Right, that's fine. |
| CLIENT: | Good. My name's Mary Brown and my phone number is 555 9876. |
| RECEPTIONIST: | 555 9876. And is that B R O W N? |
| CLIENT: | No, B R O W N E, with an E. |

**2**

| | |
|---|---|
| INFORMATION OFFICER: | Hello, Information Office. |
| TOURIST: | Hello, I'd like some information about trains, please. |
| INFORMATION OFFICER: | Trains, certainly, what would you like to know? |
| TOURIST: | What time is the last train to London? |
| INFORMATION OFFICER: | To London. The last one is at 9.45 but it doesn't arrive till after midnight. The last fast train is 9.30 and that gets in at 11.05. |
| TOURIST: | Half past nine. Fine, thanks a lot. |
| INFORMATION OFFICER: | You're welcome. |

**3**

| | |
|---|---|
| RESTAURANT MANAGER: | Hello, Arcadia Restaurant. How can I help you? |
| GUEST: | Can I reserve a table for this evening? |
| RESTAURANT MANAGER: | Yes, certainly. A table for this evening, what time would that be? |
| GUEST: | At 8, if that's all right. A table for three people. |
| RESTAURANT MANAGER: | I'm afraid we don't have a table at that time. But we do have a table at 7.15, or at 9.15. Would one of those times be suitable? |
| GUEST: | Um…yes, OK. 9.15. Yes, that would be all right. |
| RESTAURANT MANAGER: | So that's a table for three at 9.15 this evening. |
| GUEST: | Yes. |
| RESTAURANT MANAGER: | Could I have your name, please? |
| GUEST: | Yes, it's … |

**PHOTOCOPIABLE** © Cambridge University Press 2005

**1** Arrange the class into groups of three. If the number of students isn't divisible by three, you may decide to have as many groups of three as possible — plus one or two groups of four (and allow time for a fourth go in Step 4 below) or plus one or two pairs (who'll dispense with the observer role).

If any groups are lacking inspiration, you may have to join in with some suggestions, or the ideas for questions could be brainstormed as a whole-class activity and the best questions written up on the board.

## Suggestions

Where is a good place to stay?

What's the best way to get there from the airport?

How long does it take to get there from the airport?

What's the most popular tourist attraction?

When is the main tourist season?

What is the busiest time of all in the year?

Are all the hotels and restaurants open out of season?

What's the weather like in January/August/March?

What kind of excursions are there that I could go on?

## 2 Role play

Keep the same groups of three. This role play is intended to be reassuringly predictable, with no unexpected questions being fired, so that everyone can focus on following the 'rules' on SB page 28. If necessary, remind everyone what the observer is supposed to do.

Explain to everyone that the reason why the two speakers should sit back-to-back is so that they can't see each other's faces — this simulates a phone call, where you can't see the other person's reactions to what you're saying. The observer may need to lean in or move his or her seat to get close enough to the speakers to be able to hear them.

If the students are sitting in rows and it's impossible to move the chairs, they should at least turn their heads away from each other.

**3** The same role play is repeated with changed roles.

**4** And then it's done a third time with changed roles. If there are any groups of four, they may need to have a fourth go.

## Finally …

**1** Draw everyone's attention to the Advice box.

**2** Remind everyone what the aims of this Lesson were. Have they been achieved?

# 12 How may I help you?

## Aims

Begin by explaining to the class the aims of Lesson 12, which are to improve their ability to:

- use vocabulary connected with telephones
- use appropriate phrases on the phone
- exchange information over the phone.

## Vocabulary

| | |
|---|---|
| desk lamp | phone card |
| dial | receiver |
| extension | repair |
| fax phone | replace |
| hold the line | sort something out |
| leave a message | vehicle registration number |

**A1** Play the recording, pausing between each conversation for a few seconds to give the students time to answer. The first listening helps everyone to get the gist of each conversation before they listen again.

### Answers

**1** dinner tonight **2** change his booking **3** bring an extra lamp

**2** Play the recording again and ask the class to describe the impression they get from the way each receptionist deals with the client and say which one is best, and why.

### Suggested answers

The receptionist in the first conversation sounds rather bored, but she isn't exactly rude.

The receptionist in the second conversation sounds helpful and friendly.

The receptionist in the third conversation sounds friendly enough but she isn't very helpful.

### Transcript  2 minutes 12 seconds

**1**

FIRST CLIENT: Hello, is that Reception?

RECEPTIONIST: Yes, how can I help you?

FIRST CLIENT: This is Tony Attwood in room 428. I've tried phoning the restaurant but there's no reply.

RECEPTIONIST: Well, they're not there this early in the morning. Try them at lunchtime.

FIRST CLIENT: Well, I want a table for this evening and I'm not going to be able to contact them before then. Can I reserve a table through you?

RECEPTIONIST: Yes, I can leave them a message.

FIRST CLIENT: Oh, good. Well, it's a table for six at 8 o'clock.

RECEPTIONIST: So that's 8pm this evening, a table for six people. Could I have your name and room number again, please?

FIRST CLIENT: Yes, it's …

**2**

RECEPTIONIST: Hello, Eldorado Hotel. How can I help you?

SECOND CLIENT: Hello, my name's Alvarez. I've got a room booked for tonight.

RECEPTIONIST: Mr Alvarez … Ah, yes, that's right, a single room for two nights.

SECOND CLIENT: Well, the thing is I'd like to stay longer if that's possible — until Saturday.

RECEPTIONIST: I think that'll be fine … Er…let me just check the computer … Yes, yes, that's absolutely fine, Mr Alvarez. I've entered that onto the computer.

SECOND CLIENT: Oh good, thanks very much.

RECEPTIONIST: You're very welcome. We look forward to seeing you this evening, Mr Alvarez.

SECOND CLIENT: Thank you. I'll be arriving at about …

**3**

RECEPTIONIST: Hello, Reception, how can I help you?

THIRD CLIENT: This is Anna Berti in Room 332.

RECEPTIONIST: Hello, Ms Berti.

THIRD CLIENT: I've got a problem with the lighting in my room. I have to do some work and I want to use the desk but there's not enough light.

RECEPTIONIST: There are two lamps over the bed. You could try turning them on.

THIRD CLIENT: I have, and one of them doesn't work. Anyway, I don't want light on the bed, I want to use the desk.

RECEPTIONIST: I see. Well, I don't know what to suggest, I'm afraid.

THIRD CLIENT: Can I have a desk lamp, please?

RECEPTIONIST: Oh! Yes, I see. I'll call the housekeeper and ask her if she has a spare one. If she has, would you like someone to bring it to your room?

THIRD CLIENT: Yes, I would, please, and could you …

**B1** Arrange the class into pairs. If you anticipate that your students will find this exercise difficult, play the recording once through to give them some ideas of what to write. Most of the phrases in the speech balloon may come in handy. See the Transcript below for a model version.

## 2 Pronunciation

Play the recording through as a key to the exercise. Reassure everyone that there are many different ways of completing the dialogue.

After discussing alternatives from the class, arrange the class into pairs. Then play the recording again and ask everyone to practise the dialogue together. Ask them to concentrate on sounding as polite as possible, especially when playing the role of the travel agent.

## Transcript  1 minute 39 seconds

| | |
|---|---|
| TRAVEL AGENT: | Hello, Transworld Travel, this is Sally speaking. |
| CLIENT: | Hello, my name's David Green. |
| TRAVEL AGENT: | Hello, Mr Green, how can I help you? |
| CLIENT: | Well, I bought a flight ticket from Frankfurt to Mexico City from you last week and now I need to change the outward flight date. |
| TRAVEL AGENT: | All right, I'll just get your file. Could you hold the line for a moment, please? |
| CLIENT: | All right. . . . |
| TRAVEL AGENT: | Yes, here it is. Could you tell me the flight number and the date of travel, please? |
| CLIENT: | Yes, the flight number is LH 414 and the date of travel is May 13th. |
| TRAVEL AGENT: | And what change would you like to make? |
| CLIENT: | I want to depart on May 15th now by the same flight. |
| TRAVEL AGENT: | All right, Mr Green. I'll have to make a call to Lufthansa to sort this out. |
| CLIENT: | I see. How long do you think it will take you to sort it out? |
| TRAVEL AGENT: | It may take a while. Could I call you back later? |
| CLIENT: | Yes, certainly. My number is 555 6789 — extension 449. |
| TRAVEL AGENT: | I'm sorry, could you say that again, please? |
| CLIENT: | Yes, it's 555 6789 — extension 449. |
| TRAVEL AGENT: | That's 555 6789 — extension 499. Is that right? |
| CLIENT: | No, it's four four nine. And can you call me back before 3 o'clock, please? |
| TRAVEL AGENT: | Yes, certainly. I'll call you as soon as I've sorted it out. |
| CLIENT: | Good. I'll hear from you soon, then. Thank you very much. |
| TRAVEL AGENT: | You're welcome, Mr Green. Goodbye. |
| CLIENT: | Goodbye. |

## C Role play

Keep the same pairs as before but this time they should sit back-to-back, or turn away from each other. The information they give can be their own real personal information and their family's car, or it could be imaginary information about, for example, a celebrity. Allow enough time for both partners to have a go. Clients should check that the information written down on the form by the members of staff is correct.

## Finally …

Remind everyone what the aims of this Lesson were. Have they been achieved?

# 13 Answering enquiries

## Aims

Begin by explaining to the class the aims of Lesson 13, which are to improve their ability to:

- say and understand numbers (not only on the phone)
- answer enquiries on the phone.

## Vocabulary

| | |
|---|---|
| *estate* | *post code (US zip code)* |
| *information officer* | *sleeper (train)* |
| *lodge* | |

## First of all …

1  Ask some students to tell the others their phone number (including dialling code) in English — the others should write it down. Can they say it clearly and without hesitation?

2  Then ask others for their post code and their family's car registration number (if they have one) — the others should write those down, too.

3  Explain that this Lesson focuses on understanding numbers in English because understanding numbers is harder than understanding conversations. If you miss one digit, the whole thing is wrong, whereas if you miss a few words in a sentence, you can still make sense of what's being said.

 **A**  Before you play the recording ask the class if they can guess approximately what the missing times in the timetable might be. This will encourage them to look at it carefully before they hear the conversations.

In case people ask, the train types in the timetable are:

TGV = Train à Grand Vitesse (high-speed train)
CIS = Cisalpino express
IC = InterCity express
EN = EuroNight sleeper train

Play the recording, pausing it between the conversations. It'll probably take two listenings for everyone to get all the information.

## Answers

| train type | TGV | CIS | TGV | IC | TGV | IC | EN | EN | EN | EN | EN |
| train number | EC21 | 35 | EC23 | 335 | EC29 | 329 | 213 | 223 | 215 | 219 | 217 |
|---|---|---|---|---|---|---|---|---|---|---|---|
| Paris Lyon    d | 0714 | | 1218 | | 1548 | | 1930 | 2004 | 2007 | *2010* | 2209 |
| Lausanne      a | 1106 | | *1607* | | 1945 | | | | | | |
| Lausanne      d | | 1113 | | *1613* | | 1953 | | | | | |
| Milan Centrale a | | 1417 | | *1950* | | 2345 | | | | 0604 | *0845* |
| Venice Santa  a Lucia | | | | | | | | 0845 | | | |
| Florence SMN a | | | | | | | | | 0938 | | |
| Rome Termini  a | | | | | | | | 1005 | | 1126 | |

## Transcript   2 minutes 12 seconds

**1**

CLERK: Hello, Information. How can I help you?

CLIENT: I'd like some information about trains from Paris to Rome, please.

CLERK: Certainly. What would you like to know?

CLIENT: Well, is there a sleeper train?

CLERK: Yes, actually there are two. One leaves Paris Gare de Lyon at 19.30 and it arrives in Rome at 10.05 the next morning.

CLIENT: Leaving at 19.30 and arriving at 10.05?

CLERK: That's right. Alternatively, there's another at 20.10 which arrives in Rome at 11.26.

CLIENT: Did you say 11.26?

CLERK: Yes.

CLIENT: Oh, well, that one sounds better, thank you very much.

CLERK: You're welcome.

**2**

CLERK: Hello, Information. How may I help you?

CLIENT: I want to travel from Paris to Milan. What time are the trains?

CLERK: What time of day do you want to travel?

CLIENT: I want to get there in the evening.

CLERK: I see. Well … there's a TGV train from Paris Gare de Lyon at 12.18 to Lausanne in Switzerland, arriving there at 16.07. That connects with a train to Milan, leaving at 16.13, which will get you to Milan at 19.50. So, you'd leave Paris at 12.18, change trains in Lausanne, and arrive in Milan at 19.50.

CLIENT: I see. That's over seven hours. Is there a sleeper?

CLERK: Yes, there are two in fact. And you wouldn't have to change trains on either of them.

CLIENT: Tell me about them.

CLERK: One leaves Paris at 20.10, arriving in Milan at 6.04 the next morning. Or there's another at 22.09 arriving at 8.45 in the morning.

CLIENT: Oh, right. Thank you very much. Goodbye.

CLERK: You're welcome. Goodbye.

# If there's time …

Arrange the class into pairs. Ask the students to play the roles of an information officer and a tourist who asks questions about other trains in the timetable.

 Play the recording, pausing it between each conversation to give everyone time to write their answers. Again, it may be necessary to play the recording more than once.

## Answers

1   32 567 012346

2   28010

3   7.30 to 9.45

4   1 39 143691

5   $85 to $95 (or $105, if a junior suite is just a more luxurious double room)

6   711 66 470   711 62 59 62

## Transcript   2 minutes 55 seconds

**1**

RECEPTIONIST: Hello, Carlton Hotel, this is Maria speaking, how may I help you?

CLIENT: I want to send you a fax. Do you have a fax number?

RECEPTIONIST: Yes, it's 32 567 012346.

CLIENT: 32 567 012364?

RECEPTIONIST: No, the last two numbers are 46, not 64.

CLIENT: Oh, OK, thank you.

RECEPTIONIST: You're welcome, sir.

**2**

CLIENT: … and my address is General Arrando 42, 28010 Madrid.

TRAVEL AGENT: Sorry, could you say the post code again, please?

CLIENT: It's 28010.

TRAVEL AGENT: 28010, fine, thanks. All right, Mr Garcia, I'll put the tickets in the post this afternoon.

CLIENT: Thanks very much.

TRAVEL AGENT: Not at all. Goodbye.

**3**

RECEPTIONIST: Reception, can I help you?

CLIENT: Yes, can you tell me when I can get a meal in the hotel restaurant this evening?

RECEPTIONIST: Yes, certainly. The service of dinner starts at half past 7 and last orders are taken at a quarter to 10.

CLIENT: I see. Er…do I need to book a table?

RECEPTIONIST: No, that's not really necessary …

**4**

CLIENT: … so could you phone me when you know, please?

TRAVEL AGENT: Certainly, Ms Bradford. What's your number?

CLIENT: It's 1 39 14 36 91.

TRAVEL AGENT: 1 39 14 36 91.

CLIENT: That's right. And could you possibly phone …

**5**

| | |
|---|---|
| CLIENT: | ... could I reserve a room for myself and my husband for two nights? |
| RECEPTIONIST: | For two nights? Yes, we have several rooms available. |
| CLIENT: | What's the price per night? |
| RECEPTIONIST: | It depends what kind of facilities you require: a basic double with shower is $85, a larger double with balcony is $95 and a junior suite is $105. All those prices are for the room, not per person. |
| CLIENT: | And does that include ... |

**6**

| | |
|---|---|
| RECEPTIONIST: | ... thank you, sir, and what's the phone number, please? |
| CLIENT: | It's 711 66 47 0. |
| RECEPTIONIST: | 711 66 47 0. And your fax number? |
| CLIENT: | 711 62 59 62. |
| RECEPTIONIST: | 711 62 59 62. |
| CLIENT: | That's right. |
| RECEPTIONIST: | Fine, oh, thank you very much, Mr Klett, I'll send you a fax to confirm this as soon as ... |

**PHOTOCOPIABLE** © Cambridge University Press 2005

## C1 Pronunciation

To set the scene, ask everyone to look at the photos: what kind of places do they seem to be? Arrange the class into pairs. The pronunciation practice is also preparation for the role play in

Step 2. Ask the students to practise each call twice, changing roles each time.

## 2 Role play

Keep the same pairs: one student looks at **Activity 8** on SB page 111, the other at **Activity 23** on SB page 119. Explain that many of the New Zealand place names will need spelling out — just as local place names may have to be spelt out to foreigners who don't speak your language. Explain that a lodge is a kind of country inn, patronised by people who enjoy outdoor activities like hiking, fishing and hunting.

Draw everyone's attention to the phrases in the speech balloons, many of which will be useful during their conversation. Make sure the students sit back-to-back or avoid looking at each other. They should also avoid looking at each other's information during the role play.

At the end ask everyone to compare what they've written with their partner's information to make sure they've noted everything down correctly.

## Finally ...

1  Draw everyone's attention to the Advice box.
2  Remind everyone what the aims of this Lesson were. Have they been achieved?

# 14 Taking Messages

## Aim

Begin by explaining to the class the aim of Lesson 14, which is to improve their ability to:

* take messages over the phone.

## Vocabulary

*answer machine*  
*expiration date (GB expiry date)*  
*handwriting*

*relevant/irrelevant*  
*weekend break*

## First of all ...

Find out if any members of the class have experience of taking messages over the phone in their work. What is difficult about it? And how do they feel if they have to leave a message on an answer machine?

**A**

Before playing the recording, ask everyone to look at the notes to see if they can find any places which might contain a mistake.

Play the recording as the students check that each point is correctly noted down and try to spot the mistakes. This may require more than one playing.

## Answers

| | |
|---|---|
| The missing information is: | He doesn't mind paying more. |
| The phone number should be: | 234 9856 (not 324) |
| The last but one line should read: | The return flight can be 19.30 or 22.55 (not 09.30 or 22.25). |

## Transcript  1 minute 23 seconds

| | |
|---|---|
| TRAVEL AGENT: | Hello, Horizon Travel, this is Georgia speaking, how can I help you? |
| CLIENT: | Hello, can I speak to Gemma, please? |

| | |
|---|---|
| TRAVEL AGENT: | I'm afraid she isn't here today. Is there anything I can do? |
| CLIENT: | No, not really, no. When will she be back? |
| TRAVEL AGENT: | Tomorrow morning. |
| CLIENT: | Oh, well, could you give her a message then, please? |
| TRAVEL AGENT: | Yes, certainly. |
| CLIENT: | My name's Boyle, B O Y L E. My phone number is 234 9856. |
| TRAVEL AGENT: | Right, Mr Boyle, what's the message? |
| CLIENT: | Well, I've booked a weekend break in New York with Atlantic Holidays and the thing is I want to change the dates if I can. |
| TRAVEL AGENT: | All right. |
| CLIENT: | The day I've booked to travel is October 2nd and the flight is at 14.00, and I want to change that to the 16th if that's possible. |
| TRAVEL AGENT: | OK. |
| CLIENT: | We're booked into the Rotterdam Hotel, but if the Metro Hotel has a room available, well, that would be better. Oh, I don't mind paying a bit more. The return flight could be either 19.30 or 22.55, I don't mind. |
| TRAVEL AGENT: | All right. |
| CLIENT: | Could she call me on Friday? Oh, not tomorrow — I won't be here tomorrow. |
| TRAVEL AGENT: | Right, now let's just see if I've got all that, Mr Boyle. You want to change your weekend break from October the 2nd to October the 16th … |

**B1** Before playing the recording, draw everyone's attention to the way in which the information in the Horizon Travel message pad has been noted down. These notes are for someone else to read and understand and only the main information is noted down.

Play the recording, pausing between each message. At least two playings will be necessary, probably more — pausing during the messages might help on the second and subsequent playings.

(Model notes are in **Activity 37** on SB page 125 — but don't let anyone know until they've finished Step 3.)

**2** Working now in pairs, the students compare their notes.

### Transcript  2 minutes

| | |
|---|---|
| GUEST: | My name's Katherine Woodford — that's KATHERINE WOODFORD: Woodford. And…um…I'd like to book two rooms for February the 14th, and that'll be for two nights. That's two double rooms for two nights, both with showers and balconies. Oh, and can you send me a fax to confirm that that's OK? My fax number is…um…er… 893 34 56 25. Or you could phone me before 9pm at this number: 893 89 82 40. Thank you. Bye. |
| TOURIST: | Hello, this is Tim Hughes — that's TIM HUGHES. And I have a booking for February the 12th. I'm going to be arriving very late, probably after midnight, and I want to make sure that you hold the room for me. You may |

need my Visa card number to guarantee the room — it's 7777 1902 2867 3456. The expiration date is 12/02. Oh, and could you send a copy of your hotel brochure to a colleague of mine, please? Her name and address is: Sonia Blake — SONIA BLAKE — 1232 Forest Drive, Fargo — FARGO— ND 58105. Thanks very much. Goodbye.

## 3 Writing

This Writing task should be done in class — but only if there's time. Then, when everyone's ready, ask them to look at Activity 37 to see the model notes.

If, by any chance, the notes everyone made earlier are neat and easily understandable, there's no need to do this task.

## C Role play

This role play is in four parts, so allow plenty of time for it. Arrange the class into pairs with one student looking at **Activity 9** on SB page 112 and the other at **Activity 24** on SB page 120. Each student has two messages to give, and two to note down.

## Finally …

**1** Draw everyone's attention to the Advice boxes, if you haven't already done so.

**2** Remind everyone what the aim of this Lesson was. Has it been achieved?

# Phone calls: Vocabulary puzzle

Photocopy the vocabulary puzzle on page 104 for everyone to do in pairs in class, or for homework.

## Answers

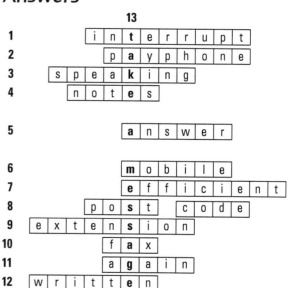

**Phone calls**

# 15 Good morning!

This Module (Lessons 15–20) covers food and beverage service and dealing with clients in a bar, café or restaurant.

## Aims

Begin by explaining to the class the aims of Lesson 15, which are to:

- introduce the topic of food and drink
- introduce some food vocabulary (breakfast dishes and fruit)
- improve their ability to take an order face-to-face and over the phone.

## Vocabulary

| | |
|---|---|
| *boiled eggs* | *marmalade (= bitter orange jam)* |
| *doorknob* | *poached eggs* |
| *fried eggs* | *regular (GB normal)* |
| *hang* | *sausage* |
| *jam* | *scrambled eggs* |

**A**

Arrange the class into groups of three or four for this discussion.

Reassemble the class and ask them how a breakfast menu in their country would differ from the American/Japanese menu on SB pages 36–37. Find out if everyone agrees on what a typical breakfast in their country consists of and what they themselves have.

**B**

Play the recording — twice if necessary — of the guest in Room 213 calling room service to place his breakfast order.

(This and the following recording for the guests in Rooms 121 and 305 constitutes one track on the CD.)

## Answers

Room 213   *Mr Kennedy*

1      beside AMERICAN BREAKFAST

✓      beside orange, scrambled, bacon, breakfast rolls, coffee and milk

1      beside CONTINENTAL BREAKFAST

✓      beside grapefruit, breakfast rolls, tea and lemon

## Transcript    47 seconds

WAITRESS:    Good morning, room service.

GUEST:    Hello, this is Bill Kennedy in Room 213. Can I have breakfast in my room, please?

WAITRESS:    Certainly, Mr Kennedy, what would you like to have?

GUEST:    Er…well, can I have one American breakfast with orange juice, um…scrambled eggs with bacon, breakfast rolls and coffee with milk. A…and one continental breakfast with grapefruit juice,

um…breakfast rolls and tea with lemon.

WAITRESS:    Right, thank you, Mr Kennedy. So that's one American breakfast with orange juice …

**PHOTOCOPIABLE** © Cambridge University Press 2005

Play the recording of the guests in Rooms 121 and 205, pausing it between the two calls. Again, it may be necessary to play it more than once for everyone to note all the information on the form.

## Answers

| | | |
|---|---|---|
| 121 | 7:45 | 2 continental: 2 orange juice, 1 black coffee, 1 tea with lemon + Guardian newspaper |
| 305 | 8:15 | 1 continental: grapefruit juice, rolls, hot chocolate + Financial Times |

## Transcript    2 minutes 4 seconds

**1**

WAITER:    Good evening, room service.

GUEST:    Good evening. Can I order breakfast for tomorrow morning, please?

WAITER:    Certainly, madam. Could I have your name and room number, please?

GUEST:    My name's Mrs Johnson and it's Room 121.

WAITER:    121, right, Mrs Johnson. Now, what time would you like your breakfast served?

GUEST:    A quarter to 8.

WAITER:    7.45, right. And what would you like?

GUEST:    Two continental breakfasts, both with orange juice. One with black coffee and one with tea with lemon.

WAITER:    Two continental breakfasts with orange juice. One black coffee, one tea with lemon.

GUEST:    Right.

WAITER:    Would you like a morning newspaper too?

GUEST:    Oh, yes, please. Er…can I have the *Guardian*, please?

WAITER:    *Guardian*, certainly. Thank you very much, madam. Good night, Mrs Johnson.

GUEST:    Good night, thank you.

**2**

WAITER:    Good evening, room service.

GUEST:    Oh, this is Mr Brown, room 305. Can I order breakfast for tomorrow, please?

WAITER:    Certainly, sir. Er…what time would you like your breakfast served?

GUEST:    Er…quarter past 8?

WAITER:    8.15, certainly. And what would you like?

GUEST:    I'd like a continental breakfast, that's with…um…grapefruit juice, the rolls … Oh…er…can I have…um…er…hot chocolate?

WAITER:    Yes, certainly. Is that just the one breakfast?

GUEST:    Yes, please.

WAITER:    So that's…er…one continental breakfast with grapefruit juice, rolls and hot chocolate.

| | |
|---|---|
| GUEST: | Right. |
| WAITER: | Er…would you like a morning newspaper too, sir? |
| GUEST: | Oh, yeah. Do you…er…do you have any English language papers? |
| WAITER: | Er…yes, we do, we have the…er…*Herald Tribune* and the Financial Times, sir. |
| GUEST: | Right…er…*Financial Times,* please. |
| WAITER: | Certainly, sir. Well, thank you very much, Mr Brown, good night. |
| GUEST: | Er…good night. |

## C1 Pronunciation

Play the recording and ask the students to repeat the words *in bold italic type*. Do this several times. The recording already contains silences during which the students should repeat the words. Explain that it's the intonation that's important here.

### Transcript 36 seconds

| | |
|---|---|
| MALE GUEST: | I'd like some tea, please. |
| WAITRESS: | ***Would you like it with milk or lemon?*** |
| *pause* | |

| | |
|---|---|
| GUEST: | With milk, please. |
| FEMALE GUEST: | Can I have some fruit juice, please? |
| WAITRESS: | ***Would you like orange juice or grapefruit juice?*** |
| *pause* | |
| GUEST: | Orange juice, please. |

## 2 Role play

Arrange the class into pairs for the role play. Tell them when to change roles.

## D Role play

Change the pairs, so that the students have someone different to talk to for this role play. Again, make sure both partners have time to play each role.

## Finally …

Remind everyone what the aims of this Lesson were. Have they been achieved?

# 16 Explaining dishes

## Aim

Begin by explaining to the class the aim of Lesson 16, which is to improve their ability to:

- explain how dishes are prepared, including ingredients and methods of cooking.

## Vocabulary

| | | |
|---|---|---|
| bake(d) | layers | simmer |
| bitter | mousse | sour |
| creamy/rich | mussels | spices |
| curry | oven | spicy/hot |
| deep fry | paella /pɑːelja/ | squeeze |
| flavour | prawns (US shrimp) | steam |
| garlic | saffron | stir-fry |
| grill (US broil) | seafood | stirred |
| herbs | shellfish | stock |
| ingredients | | |

### A1

Do this as a warm-up activity with the whole class. Depending on the nationality and experience of the students, they may already know plenty about *paella* — or nothing!

### 2 Play the recording at least twice.

## Answers

| | |
|---|---|
| The rice is cooked first. | ✗ |
| The basic ingredients are stir-fried | ✓ |
| A *paella* is baked in the oven. | ✗ |
| It must be stirred all the time it's cooking. | ✗ |
| The rice takes about 20 minutes to cook. | ✓ |

### Transcript 1 minute 49 seconds

LEO: Well, in Spain when they make *paella* they use a special *paella* pan — but any large frying pan or a wok will do, a wok's quite good as well.

First of all, you stir-fry a chopped onion and a sliced red pepper in some olive oil, and then you add tomatoes, fresh tomatoes and garlic and you go on cooking for a little longer. Then you add some prawns and some pieces of cooked chicken — or if you like, you can use cooked pork or…er…some Spanish sausage. And you carry on stir-frying for a few more minutes. Um…you can also put in some peas, or some green beans, or other vegetables, too, if you like. Then, next thing you do is you put in some saffron, that's very important, some paprika, some parsley, and a little bit of pepper, a little bit of salt and you mix them all in together. And now it's the time to put in the rice. For each cup of rice that you use, you add two cups of stock or water. Then you bring the whole thing to the boil. When it's come to the boil, you put the cover on the pan and you simmer everything for about ten minutes. But don't stir it, just let it simmer away under the cover.

Then after ten minutes you take some mussels, er…or some other shellfish like prawns, and put them on top of the rice, and put the cover back on and carry on cooking everything for another ten minutes or so until all of the liquid has been absorbed.

Then have a taste — and if the rice is cooked, you put the pan on the table. And everyone can help themselves from the pan and take as much as they want. And if you cut up a couple of lemons and put them on the table too, squeeze lemon juice on top, it's really nice.

**PHOTOCOPIABLE** © Cambridge University Press 2005

**3** Arrange the class into pairs or groups of three. Afterwards, reassemble the class so that everyone can compare their ideas — experts in paella-making may want to criticise the recipe!

**B1** Arrange the class into groups of three or four. When everyone's ready, reassemble the class to check their answers.

## Answers

The pictures show: **1** deep frying   **2** baking   **3** steaming
**4** grilling/broiling   **5** stir-frying   **6** roasting

**2** Arrange the class into an even number of pairs. It may be necessary to point out that people can only recognise four basic flavours — sweet, sour, bitter and salty — plus different textures (creaminess is a texture). Plainness is a lack of flavour.

## Suggested answers

The lemon sorbet is sour and perhaps sweet.

The risotto is creamy and perhaps bitter.

The mousse is creamy and sweet.

The curry is spicy and perhaps creamy.

The bread is plain and perhaps salty.

**3** Combine the pairs into groups of four or five. Ask them to think of at least two examples of each taste. (Although some people confuse *sour* and *bitter*, they are distinctly different taste sensations.)

## Sample answers

| | |
|---|---|
| spicy: | chillies, cayenne pepper, pepper |
| creamy: | cream, coconut milk |
| plain: | rice, potatoes, white bread |
| sweet: | sugar, honey, ripe fruit |
| salty: | fish sauce, dried fish, potato crisps (US chips) |
| sour: | lemons, limes, unripe fruit |
| bitter: | strong coffee, strong tea, cocoa powder, beer (the hops make it taste bitter) |

**C1** This can be done alone or by students working together in pairs. If it's done in pairs, *both* students need to write the menu out.

## 2 Role play

Arrange the class into pairs (with different pairs from the previous Step, if that was done in pairs). Draw their attention to the speech balloons at the foot of the page, which show how dishes can be explained. If possible, encourage the waiters/waitresses to stand up so that the situation feels more realistic.

## Finally …

Remind everyone what the aim of this Lesson was. Has it been achieved?

# 17 May I take your order?

## Aim

Begin by explaining to the class the aim of Lesson 17, which is to improve their ability to:

● take orders for appetizers and main courses.

## Vocabulary

| | |
|---|---|
| **appetizers (GB starters)** | **melon** |
| **asparagus** | **oysters** |
| **double-check** | **port wine** |
| **draught beer (US draft beer)** | **rare/medium rare/well-done** |
| **eggplant (GB aubergine)** | **specialities (US specialties)** |
| **entrées (GB main courses)** | **spinach** |
| **French fries (GB chips)** | **vegetarian** |
| **garlic** | |

+ see Suggested questions and answers for A1 below

## First of all …

Ask everyone to remember the last time they had a meal in a full-service restaurant:

● What did you order?

● How good was the service?

● How good was the food?

● How important is good service in a restaurant?

**A1** Arrange the class into pairs. The missing items in the menu will be added in Section C2. Ask everyone to look back to the foot of SB page 39 for some examples of how to explain items on a menu. (In Britain, *appetizers* are sometimes called *starters* and *entrées* are sometimes called *main courses*.)

### Suggested questions and answers

What's Waldorf salad?
— That's a salad composed of apples, celery, walnuts and mayonnaise.
Can you tell me what tagliatelle is?
— It's thin pasta strips.
Can you tell me what venison is?
— It's the meat of a deer.

Soup of the day — Every day the chef prepares a different soup: today it's …
Cream of asparagus soup — soup made with asparagus and cream
Melon with port wine — half a cantaloupe filled with port wine
Six oysters — shellfish served raw
Grilled sardines with lemon juice and garlic — small fish marinated in lemon juice and garlic, then broiled

Smoked salmon — large fish which has been cured by smoking, served in thin slices
Waldorf salad — (see above)

Entrées — main courses
Grilled fillet steak served with French fries — a beef steak broiled with fried potatoes
Pan-fried trout served with tagliatelle — fish cooked in a pan and served with fresh pasta (see above)
Venison steak with pepper sauce served with roast potatoes — deer's meat steak cooked in a pepper sauce and served with potatoes cooked in oil in the oven (see above)
Veal schnitzel with new potatoes — a thin piece of veal (meat from a calf) served with steamed/boiled potatoes
Grilled lamb chops with sauté potatoes — pieces of lamb broiled and served with sliced, fried potatoes

Vegetables of the day — Every day the chef prepares different vegetables, depending what is fresh and good in the market. Today, as the first waitress explains, these are broccoli, carrots and baby sweetcorn.

Today's specials — special dishes prepared today by the chef
Tomato, spinach and eggplant casserole — a vegetarian stew made with tomatoes, spinach and aubergine
Poached salmon with a ginger and lime juice sauce — fish gently cooked in liquid and served with a spicy sauce

**2** Play the recording, pausing it between each conversation. Point out that although vegetables of the day are offered with each main course, some of the guests may prefer a side salad instead, which isn't on the menu.

## Answers

(The changes each guest asks for are underlined.)

**1**

| |
|---|
| 1 Waldorf salad |
| 1 veal schnitzel + <u>French fries</u> + vegetables |

**2**

| |
|---|
| 1 grilled sardines |
| — |
| 1 trout + <u>new potatoes*</u> + <u>side salad</u> |

    * The waiter says sauté potatoes, but he made a mistake.

**3**

| |
|---|
| 1 oysters |
| 1 asparagus soup |
| — |
| 1 vegetable casserole + <u>side salad</u> |
| 1 salmon + <u>side salad</u> |

**3**  Arrange the class into pairs or groups of three and then play the recording again. The answers to the questions may be a matter of opinion, so allow time for the pairs to compare their answers when you reassemble the class. It may be necessary to play the recording yet again to sort out any disagreements.

## Suggested answers

The waiter in the second conversation made a mistake — he wrote down sauté potatoes instead of new potatoes.

Both the first waitress and the waiter sounded polite.

Both waitresses were efficient (the waiter seemed efficient until he made the mistake).

The friendliest was the first waitress. The second waitress sounded quite hostile.

## Transcript    2 minutes 52 seconds

**1**

| | |
|---|---|
| FIRST WAITRESS: | Are you ready to order, sir? |
| MAN: | Yes, I think so. Oh, but first, can you tell me what a Waldorf salad is? |
| FIRST WAITRESS: | Yes, it's a salad of apples, celery and walnuts with a creamy dressing. |
| MAN: | Oh, right, well, I'll have that first, then the…er…veal schnitzel. Oh, what are the vegetables of the day? |
| FIRST WAITRESS: | Broccoli, carrots and baby sweetcorn. |
| MAN: | Fine, I'll have them. Oh, is it possible to have French fries instead of new potatoes with the veal? |
| FIRST WAITRESS: | Yes, certainly. |
| MAN: | Good. |
| FIRST WAITRESS: | So, that's one Waldorf salad followed by veal schnitzel with French fries and vegetables of the day. And what would you like to drink? |
| MAN: | Mm…I think … |

**2**

| | |
|---|---|
| WAITER: | Are you ready to order, madam? |
| WOMAN: | Mm…yes. But first can you tell me what the soup of the day is? |
| WAITER: | Yes, it's carrot and potato. I'm sure you'd enjoy that, it's really delicious. |
| WOMAN: | Mm…oh, well, I don't know. I'll have the grilled sardines, please. |
| WAITER: | Grilled sardines, good. And as a main course? |
| WOMAN: | Mm…I don't know. Well, I can't decide … |
| WAITER: | May I recommend the…er…pan-fried trout? It's one of the chef's specialities. |
| WOMAN: | Oh, yes. All right. But could I have the new potatoes instead of tagliatelle? |
| WAITER: | Certainly, madam. Er…would you like the vegetables or a side salad? |
| WOMAN: | Oh, I'll have the salad. |
| WAITER: | Good, so that's grilled sardines followed by trout with sauté potatoes and a side salad — is that right? |
| WOMAN: | Yes. |
| WAITER: | And what would you like to drink? |
| WOMAN: | Oh, er…could I have a glass … |

**3**

| | |
|---|---|
| SECOND WAITRESS: | Are you ready to order? |
| MAN: | Oh, sorry, yes, yes, of course. Um…oh, I'll…I'll start with the oysters. |
| SECOND WAITRESS: | Oysters. Right and to follow, sir? |
| MAN: | Um…er…I'll have today's special: er…the vegetable casserole. Can I have it with…um…er…salad, please? |
| SECOND WAITRESS: | Tomato, spinach and eggplant casserole, fine. And for you, madam? |
| WOMAN: | Well, I…I'll have the asparagus soup to start with and the other special to follow, please. With salad. |
| SECOND WAITRESS: | So that's one oysters and one cream of asparagus soup, one tomato, spinach and eggplant casserole and one poached salmon, both with side salads — is that right? |
| MAN: | Yes. |
| SECOND WAITRESS: | And to drink? |
| MAN: | Oh, just a beer for me. |
| WOMAN: | And I'd like … |

**B 1** This can be done by students working in pairs, or alone. As with all these one-sided dialogues, there may be several plausible questions that could be asked (see Transcript below for suggested answers ***in bold italic type***).

## 2 Pronunciation

Play the recording and then discuss possible variations. Then arrange the class into pairs and play it again as a model for the pronunciation exercise (and for the role play in C2 that comes later).

## Transcript    1 minute 2 seconds

| | |
|---|---|
| WAITER: | Are you ready to order, sir? |
| CUSTOMER: | Yes. I'd like a steak, please. |
| WAITER: | Certainly. How ***would you like your steak cooked?*** |
| CUSTOMER: | Medium rare, please. And can I have it with rice instead of French fries? |
| WAITER: | Yes, of course. Would ***you like a salad or vegetables with that?*** |
| CUSTOMER: | Yes, a mixed salad would be nice. |
| WAITER: | Fine, sir, and would ***you like an appetizer or soup to start?*** |
| CUSTOMER: | Oh, yes. Let's see … What's the soup of the day? |
| WAITER: | Today we have cream of asparagus — it's made with fresh asparagus. |
| CUSTOMER: | Good. OK, I'll have that. |
| WAITER: | And would ***you like some wine?*** |
| CUSTOMER: | No, I'll have a beer I think. Do you have local draught beer? |
| WAITER: | No, I'm afraid not. Would ***bottled beer be all right?*** |
| CUSTOMER: | Yes, OK, never mind. That'll be fine. |

| WAITER: | So, that's a medium rare steak with rice and a mixed salad. And cream of asparagus soup to start with. Is that right? |
|---|---|
| CUSTOMER: | Yes, that's right. And can I have some bread, please? |
| WAITER: | **Yes, certainly. I'll bring you some right away.** |
| CUSTOMER: | Thanks very much. |

**C 1** Arrange the class into pairs and ask them to add three more items to the menu on SB page 40. These could be local specialities or their own favourite dishes. The complete menu will be used in the role play that follows, so everyone needs to complete it.

## 2 Role play

Go through the phrases in the speech balloon and make sure everyone knows when to use them and what they all mean. Then arrange the class into groups of three or four. Again, to make the situation seem realistic, the waiters/waitresses should be standing, if possible. Allow enough time for everybody to have a turn at taking the order and for feedback on each waiter's/waitress's performance from the rest of the group.

**3** Arrange the class into pairs for this exercise. Reassemble the class for everyone to pool ideas — but see the extra activity below, which may be relevant.

## If there's time …

If your students are particularly interested in food, or if food and beverage are important for them, brainstorm some typical local dishes and write them on the board. Then decide with the class how they'd explain each one to a foreign guest who hasn't tried it before.

As homework, ask the students to write a recipe for one of the local specialities of their region — or a typical national dish that's popular all over their country.

## Finally …

1 Draw everyone's attention to the Advice box.
2 Remind everyone what the aim of this Lesson was. Has it been achieved?

---

# 18 Drinks, snacks and desserts

## Aims

Begin by explaining to the class the aims of Lesson 18, which are to improve their ability to:

- take orders for snacks, desserts and beverages
- give the bill to the client, including adding up the total.

## Vocabulary

| | | |
|---|---|---|
| aggressive | cocktail | picky |
| barman/barmaid | dessert | pot |
| carafe | freshly squeezed juice | profiteroles |
| carton | jar | snack |
| celebrate | jug | whipped cream |
| club sandwich | | |

## First of all …

Ask everyone what their favourite drinks are:

- with dinner
- with lunch
- with friends in a café or bar
- when they get home after college or work
- on a special occasion if they want to celebrate.

**A** Arrange the class into pairs and ask them to label the beverages and discuss the questions.

### Suggested answers

The beverages shown are:  red/white wine   beer   tea   orange juice   coffee

Some common beverages not shown are:  iced tea   coca-cola   milkshake   cider   whisky   hot chocolate   fizzy lemonade   orange juice

**B** Keep the same pairs for this exercise. Begin by making sure everyone is aware of the pronunciation of the phrases, where the word *of* is pronounced /əv/ or /ə/ — not /ɒv/.

Perhaps also point out that *a beer glass* is a glass suitable for serving beer, *a beer bottle* is usually an empty bottle that once contained beer, and *a beer can* is an empty one.

### Suggested answers

| a glass of | beer | wine | milk | lemonade | orange juice |
|---|---|---|---|---|---|
| a bottle of | beer | wine | milk | lemonade | orange juice |
| a carafe of | wine | (or water) | | | |
| a carton of | milk | | | | |
| a can of | beer | lemonade | | | |
| a jar of | honey | | | | |

| a jug of | beer milk lemonade orange juice |
| a pot of | tea |
| a cup of | tea |

**C1** Arrange the class into pairs and ask them to add three more items to the menu together with appropriate prices (probably in their own currency, or possibly in dollars). The menu is going to be used in the role play that follows. Discuss the kind of questions that a customer might ask when you reassemble the class.

## 2 Role play

Rearrange the class into new groups of three or four. Go through the useful phrases in the speech balloons at the foot of SB page 42 before everyone begins. Allow enough time for everybody to have a turn at taking the order and for the customers to give feedback.

**D1** Play the recording, pausing it between each speaker. Reassure everyone that they don't need to understand every word as long as they can get the main points each speaker makes. At least two listenings will be necessary.

### Answers

**Helen** enjoys being busy, dealing with complaints, explaining what things are, meeting people from other countries, recommending drinks.
She doesn't enjoy not being busy.

**Fiona** enjoys not being too close to the customers.
She doesn't enjoy large orders which cause delays for other tables.

**Sam** enjoys hard work, late nights, long shifts (or at least he's learnt to live with that).
He doesn't enjoy alcohol making people behave badly, asking noisy customers to be quiet.

### Transcript  3 minutes 18 seconds

**1**

PRESENTER: Helen is a wine waitress in a fancy restaurant.
HELEN: Well, actually it's really a nice job. I mean, the best thing is really meeting all sorts of different people from around the world. I mean, we get a lot of tourists in here, from all sorts of different walks of life, so I get to meet an enormous range of people, so I like that. Yes, I suppose one of the nice things too is…is when I have to recommend something suitable, a…a good drink to accompany a dish, er…because people don't always know exactly what they want and…um…they just like to have something recommended to them. So I feel I use my knowledge then.
Of course it's much better when it's busy. I don't like it when it's empty, it gets terribly boring when it's empty, so in fact it's best when it's really buzzing, and actually I don't mind dealing with problems, it's quite enjoyable, it's more of a challenge. People say they don't like the wine perhaps, if they've ordered something and it turns out wrong, but I…I like that. Funny, but the more expensive the wine, the more likely people are to complain about it! No, on the whole it…it's fun, I like it here.

**2**
PRESENTER: Fiona Bowers works in a restaurant. Fiona, what's it like working behind the bar?
FIONA: It's quite nice because you've got a bit of distance from the customers. You deal with them in as much as … it's a service bar so you take the drinks over to the table and if they're waiting for a table at the bar, you get to serve them drinks but you don't have to deal with complaints very much and you are in your own little world a bit behind the bar, but you don't make as much money.
There's nothing really I don't like about the bar. I suppose just little things like when you get huge coffee orders through, that can be really difficult, or huge cocktail orders through like if you have a party of twenty and they all want cocktails, that can take ages and then it kind of puts you back with the other smaller tables.

**3**
PRESENTER: Sam Wilkinson is the manager of the restaurant where Fiona works. Sam, is there anything you don't enjoy about your work?
SAM: Alcohol, in a word. The way alcohol changes the way people behave negatively. Makes 80% of people lovely, really pleasant, really chatty, really nice, but there's 20% of people that don't like…or don't…shouldn't be drinking alcohol. It makes them aggressive, it makes them picky, it makes them noisy, it makes them loud, which is a discomfort for everybody else in the restaurant. And dealing with these people and asking them to be quieter or to leave is my main hate of the job. We probably get one…one difficult customer a month, or one difficult table a month…um…which is too much, you know. But we are a very busy restaurant and we are considered…we do a lot of our trade on the weekend is big parties, where it's birthdays, stag nights, hen nights, that's where we get a lot of our trade from. So obviously you're dealing with people who are out to celebrate…um…and that does involve alcohol unfortunately.
I do find the majority of the things in the job enjoyable. Um…it can be hard work, it can be late nights, long shifts…um…but I've learnt to live with that.

**2** Arrange the class into pairs to begin the discussion, continuing it as a whole-class activity if there's time.

## Finally …

**1** Remind everyone what the aims of this Lesson were. Have they been achieved?

**2** Ask everyone to read through the two texts on SB page 44 before the next Lesson. This will save time in class.

# 19 Eating habits

## Aims

Begin by explaining to the class the aims of Lesson 19, which are to improve their ability to:

- find information in a newspaper article
- understand people talking about what they eat
- talk about what they eat themselves.

## Vocabulary

| | | |
|---|---|---|
| *allergic/allergy* | *free range* | *a sweet tooth* |
| *convenience food* | *junk food* | *wheat* |
| *dairy products* | *microwave* | *wholemeal bread* |
| *digestion* | *noodles* | |

in article 1:

| | | |
|---|---|---|
| *beans and pulses* | *endorse* | *measure* |
| *cereals* | *intake* | *moderate* |
| *claim* | *legumes* | *reduction* |
| *consumption* | *lifestyle factors* | *researcher* |

in article 2:

| | | |
|---|---|---|
| *at risk* | *Danes* | *harmful* |
| *bowel cancer* | *dietary factors* | *protect* |
| *cholesterol level* | *emerge* | *spirits* |
| *clear-cut* | *evidence* | *study* |

in article 3:

| | | |
|---|---|---|
| *boost* | *insulin* | *over-stimulate* |
| *conventional* | *investigation* | *participant* |
| *cut out* | *limited* | *pseudo-science* |
| *data* | *long-term effects* | *set alarm bells ringing* |
| *focus* | *meaningful* | *starchy* |
| *gamble* | *negligent* | *weight gain* |

## First of all ...

Ask the class what they already know about the Mediterranean and the Atkins diets.

**A1** The articles can be prepared by everyone at home before the Lesson.

If they haven't done this, ask them to read the articles in class and then answer all the questions.

The articles are a starting point for a discussion about diets and eating habits, so allow time for the discussion in Section A2.

As with any authentic text, there's no need to understand every word to get the gist of the articles. Moreover, many of the unfamiliar words can be guessed from their context.

## Answers

1 It can help you to live longer.
2 Wine, garlic and olive oil.
3 There is no long-term evidence that it works.

**2** Arrange the class into groups for the discussion. Reassemble the class for everyone to share their ideas.

**B1** Play the recording, pausing for a short while between each speaker to give everyone time to write their answers. (With Peter we can probably *assume* he eats the things ticked below, even though he doesn't actually mention them.)

## Answers

| | |
|---|---|
| **Sally** | beef ✗  cheese ✓  chicken ✗  dairy products ✓  eggs ✓  nuts ✓  pulses ✓  vegetables ✓ |
| **Tim** | cheese ✓  commercial meat products ✗  free range meat ✓  garlic ✓  pasta ✓  spicy foods ✓  vegetables ✓ |
| **Peter** | bread ✗  cakes ✗  eggs ✓  fish ✓  meat ✓  vegetables ✓  wheat flour ✗ |
| **Steve** | chicken ✓  chocolate ✓  convenience foods ✓  desserts ✓  fish ✓  nuts ✗ |

**2** Arrange the class into pairs — their suggestions from the menu on SB page 40 may include the dishes they added themselves.

## Suggested answers

Cream of asparagus soup, followed by Tomato, spinach and eggplant casserole might be suitable for Sally.

Grilled sardines with lemon juice and garlic, followed by Poached salmon might be suitable for Tim.

Six oysters, followed by Grilled lamb chops might be suitable for Peter.

Melon with port wine, followed by any main course might be suitable for Steve — with a sweet dessert to follow!

## Transcript  3 minutes 21 seconds

| | |
|---|---|
| INTERVIEWER: | First, Sally, what do you eat? |
| SALLY: | Well, I'm vegetarian, so mainly I eat, obviously, lots of vegetables, fruit, pulses, nuts…um… quite a lot of eggs and cheese, dairy products. |
| INTERVIEWER: | Why don't you eat meat? |
| SALLY: | I don't like the taste of it and I don't like the idea that animals are being killed in order for people to eat. |
| INTERVIEWER: | What about you, Tim? |
| TIM: | I eat a lot of meat, I eat a lot of vegetables. Um…and I cook both…um…both meat and vegetarian foods for me and my friends. I rear all my own meat, which is something that I've been doing for a few years. It's important to me because I don't like the way that…er…commercial meat is…is processed and…er…the way that commercial animals are treated. Um…and so I cook a lot of pork, a lot of lamb, um…chicken. I buy only free range meats because I think it…it's fairer. Cheese: cheese is |

great, you can do so much with it, you can eat cheese in so many different guises and so many different forms — there are so many different cheeses. Italian foods, pastas. I grow all my own herbs and so whenever I cook Italian food…er…or anything that requires flavouring, then er… the herbs from the garden go in. Garlic, I like eating lots of garlic. Anything that's strong and spicy. I like to drink with my food too.

INTERVIEWER: What about you, Peter?

PETER: The thing is that…er…I've had a problem for some years with my life, with my digestion and I couldn't understand it. And then I read an article about a woman, actually, who'd had much the same sort of problem and she went and had an allergy test, and discovered that she was allergic to wheat. Um…and in fact the term for it is a coeliac, and I've now discovered that what I am is a coeliac. Er…it's an extremely difficult diet, actually, because it means you have to cut out things like, er…bread, cakes, biscuits — anything that's got wheat in. Er…you have to constantly check when you're on a diet like this. When you're in a supermarket, you have to look on labels, you have to see what is in wheat…what has wheat flour in it. For instance, egg noodles…er…very often have egg but they also have wheat flour.

INTERVIEWER: And finally, Steve, what do you eat?

STEVE: Yeah, I can eat pretty much anything. I tend to snack quite a lot, and eat things from…eat convenience food quite a lot, I suppose. Quite a lot of microwave foods, that kind of thing. It's not terribly healthy, I suppose, but…um…I suppose convenience for me is the main thing. I enjoy all sorts of food except for nuts, that's the only thing really I don't like too much. But anything else, especially chocolate I love. I particularly like sweet foods, I've got a very sweet tooth as well, um…so I'm sure I eat far too much sugar but…um…I do enjoy it and I don't seem, luckily to put weight on too much, so that's OK. Um…I enjoy meat, I enjoy chicken and fish particularly, and almost anything really.

**PHOTOCOPIABLE** © Cambridge University Press 2005

**C1** Arrange the class into groups of four or five. (If any of the categories seem outlandish to some students and/or they've never eaten any of them, their answer will be 0 (zero) for that category.)

**2** Reassemble the class for the groups to compare their results. Allow time for the groups to work out the results of their survey.

## Finally …

**1** Remind everyone what the aims of this Lesson were. Have they been achieved?

**2** Ask everyone to read through the text *Chez Fred* on SB page 47 before the next Lesson. This will save time in class. They should also answer the questions about it in A1 on SB page 46.

---

# 20 Welcome to our restaurant!

## Aims

Begin by explaining to the class that this Lesson includes an extended role play / simulation. The aims of the Lesson are to improve their ability to:

- talk about different kinds of places that serve food
- write menus
- behave efficiently as waiters/waitresses.

## Vocabulary

*flowers*
*fridge/refrigerator*
*lay the tables*
  (US *set the tables*)

*opening night*
*photocopy*
*set meal (table d'hôte)*
*showcase*

in the leaflet:
*à la carte menu*

*scrumptious*

*batter*
*fish and chips*
*mouth-watering*
*premises*
*refit*
*reputation*

*takeaway food (US food to go)*
*tempt*
*undergone*
*unlock/lock*
*value-for-money*
*wrapped*

## First of all …

Find out if anyone has eaten British-style fish and chips — what was it like? It's the favourite British takeaway food — what's the favourite takeaway food in their country?

**A1** If everyone has read the leaflet and answered the questions before the Lesson, there'll be more time in class for the simulation / role play in Section C. If not, this will need time in the Lesson.

As with any authentic text, there's no need to understand every word. Moreover, many of the unfamiliar words can be guessed from their context. Demonstrate this to the class by asking them to look at the leaflet, and ask them to guess what *undergone*, *refit* and *outstanding* mean (*had*, *redecoration* and *excellent*). Then get them to do the same with other unfamiliar words (*accomplished*, *formulated*, *scrumptious*, *breading*, etc.).

## Answers

1 the style of the decor (Edwardian) and the taste of the food (a taste of long ago)
2 the up-to-date frying equipment
3 fifty
4 yes
5 chicken
6 in newspaper

**2** Arrange the class into pairs for this discussion. Then reassemble the class for everyone to share their views.

## B Grammar

Arrange the class into pairs again and make sure everyone understands what they have to do. There are many different ways in which the questions can be answered. The suggested answers below are all *Yes* answers.

### Suggested answers

Have you put the drinks in the fridge?
— Yes, I have. I put them in the fridge a couple of hours ago.

Have you unlocked the door?
— Yes, I have. I unlocked it a minute ago.

Have you photocopied the menus?
— Yes, I have. I photocopied them this morning.

Have you bought flowers for the tables?
— Yes, I have. I bought them after breakfast.

Have you put today's menu in the showcase outside?
— Yes, I have. I put it there ten minutes ago.

Have you cleaned the floor?
— Yes, I have. I cleaned it last night.

Have you prepared the reserved tables?
— Yes, I have. I prepared them half an hour ago.

**C** This simulation / role play needs plenty of time to do it justice. If necessary, later parts could be done in the next Lesson.

Arrange the class into an even number of teams (4–6 students in each team). Start by making sure everyone understands the instructions set out on SB page 46.

**1** Although the teams are producing a joint menu, they'll need several copies of it so everyone should write out the completed menu. (If it's possible for you to photocopy the menus that the students produce, that will save time and seem more realistic.)

## 2 Role play

Pairs of teams join up to be guests or restaurateurs. Set up the room as an imaginary restaurant with couples or threes sitting at separate tables.

**3** The same pairs of teams do the same with roles reversed.

Then reassemble the class and find out if the opening nights were successful — what would they do differently if they could do it all again?

## 4 Writing

This is a homework task, but if possible spend a few minutes in class brainstorming ideas.

## If there's time …

The menu-writing exercise could become a full-scale project: Ask everyone to compose and design a full menu of local dishes with appropriate artwork.

## Finally …

1 Remind everyone what the aims of this Lesson were. Have they been achieved?
2 To save time in the next Lesson, ask everyone to read page 48 and find the mistakes in the letter and fax, as explained in A1.

## Food and drink: Vocabulary puzzle

Photocopy the Vocabulary puzzle on page 104 for everyone to do in pairs in class, or for homework.

### Answers

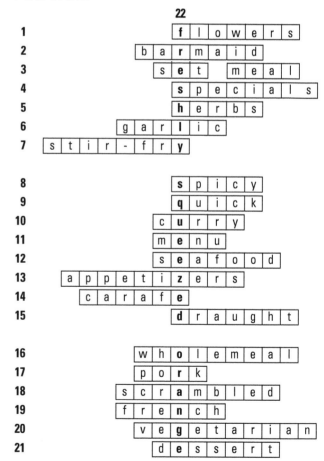

1 flowers
2 barmaid
3 set meal
4 specials
5 herbs
6 garlic
7 stir-fry

8 spicy
9 quick
10 curry
11 menu
12 seafood
13 appetizers
14 carafe
15 draught

16 wholemeal
17 pork
18 scrambled
19 french
20 vegetarian
21 dessert

# 21 Responding to enquiries

This Module (Lessons 21–24) covers the different kinds of correspondence that the students may have to write in their work.

Some of the letter- and email-writing tasks in this Module should be set as homework if possible, rather than using up class time.

## Aims

Begin by explaining to the class the aims of Lesson 21, which are to improve their ability to:

- lay out letters and emails correctly
- understand the information given in a letter, fax or email.

## Vocabulary

| charged | luxurious | suggest |
|---|---|---|
| confirm in writing | one star/five star | suitable |
| enclosed | party | variations |
| grateful | | |

## First of all ...

Find out what kind of letters and emails members of the class have had to write in their work experience. What do they find difficult about writing this kind of correspondence? What kind of impression should a letter or email to a client give?

 **A1** To save time in class, this task can be set as homework to be done before the Lesson. Looking for the mistakes encourages everyone to read the documents carefully.

## Answers

The mistakes are <u>underlined</u> in these extracts.

**Magnolia**

For a party of ten people our price per person would be $45, including 15% service. <u>Wine will be charged extra</u>.
(Mr Harris wants to know the price including wine.)

I would be grateful if you could confirm this booking in writing by the end of this <u>month</u>.
(This would be too late.)

**Bougainvillaea**

If you wish to suggest any variations, please let me know <u>please</u>.
(repetition)

Please confirm this booking in writing by June <u>27</u> at the latest.
(This would be too late.)

**2** Arrange the class into pairs or groups of three. There are no definitive answers to these questions about the style of the two documents, so make sure there's time for everyone to compare ideas when you reassemble the class afterwards.

## Suggested answers

The letter looks smarter and is easier to read than the email. A letter seems more 'permanent' than an email, which seems rather scruffy and 'disposable', so it seems more impressive and gives a better impression of a high-class restaurant. However the email, which would have arrived sooner, may give a better impression of the restaurant's efficiency. Being shorter, the email can be read more quickly.

The client might prefer the permanence of the letter to the relative scruffiness of the email.

**B** Keep the same pairs or groups of three for this exercise, which focuses on the layout of a business letter. Draw everyone's attention to the details of the layout and the formulaic phrases that are used in the letter.

## Answers

The correct sequence is:
6  7  11  2  1  10  4  5  9  (or 9  5)  3  8

**C1** Play the recording at least twice. Arrange the class into pairs for them to check that they've noted down all the requested information.

## Model notes

---

MESSAGE FROM   Stephen McKinley

Wants info about the city:

How many hotels?
Most luxurious hotel? +
address, phone & fax numbers
Most expensive restaurant? +
address, phone & fax numbers
How far to airport? + route from there
Fax answers to 84 948 38789

---

## Transcript  1 minute 14 seconds

CALLER:   Hello, er…my name's Stephen McKinley — that's S-T-E-P-H-E-N-M-C-K-I-N-L-E-Y. Er…I'd like some information about your city. Well, first of all, er…how many hotels are there altogether in the city? Er…and can you tell me what the most luxurious hotel is — the best hotel in town? Er…and what is the most expensive restaurant in town? I'd like the names and addresses of the hotel and the restaurant, please. Oh, and…er…can you let me know their phone and fax numbers, too?

Oh, and one other thing: er…how far is the nearest international airport to the city — er…what's the best way to get there from the airport?

Well, I'd appreciate it if you could fax me this information. Er…my fax number is 84 948 38789. Thank you very much.

## 2 Writing

This should be set for homework. If a reply about their own town or city seems irrelevant, they should write about the place they're working or studying in — or another large place they're familiar with. (If necessary, brainstorm the information that's requested in class before asking everyone to write the fax as homework.)

### Model fax

```
FAX
From:    Newtown-on-Sea Tourist Information Centre    01 pages
To:      Mr Stephen McKinley    84 948 38789
Date:    [today's date]

Dear Mr McKinley,

Thank you very much for your telephone message.

In answer to your questions:
1 There are over 120 hotels in Newtown, ranging from one star
  guest houses to the most luxurious five star hotels.
2 The leading hotel is the Imperial Hotel (100-120 Marine
  Drive, Newtown-on-Sea, NT1 9JM — fax 0133 890 1000, phone
  0133 890 1234).
3 The most expensive restaurant is the Golden Pagoda (24
  Station Road, Newtown-on-Sea, NT2 8QT — fax 0133 890 7081,
  phone 0133 890 4910).
4 The nearest international airport is London Gatwick,
  approximately 50 miles from here. There is an hourly train
  service from 6am until 11pm and the journey takes 55
  minutes.

If you would like to fax me your address, we would be pleased
to send you our latest Holiday Guide and Accommodation
brochures.

Thank you for your enquiry. If you have any other questions
about Newtown, please let me know.

Yours sincerely,
Your signature
(Your name)
```

## Finally …

1 Draw everyone's attention to the two Advice boxes.

2 Remind everyone what the aims of this Lesson were. Have they been achieved?

# 22 Confirming reservations

## Aims

Begin by explaining to the class the aims of Lesson 22, which are to improve their ability to:

- write confirmatory letters and emails
- write a friendly letter rather than a cool unfriendly one.

## Vocabulary

adjoining rooms
buffet lunch/sit-down lunch
conference room
connecting door
draft (of a letter)
facilities
further requests

half board (modified
 American plan)
overhead projector (OHP)
participants
pastries
style of address
VCR (video cassette recorder)

## First of all ...

Before collecting the homework that was set in the previous Lesson (C2), arrange the class into small groups and ask them to read each other's faxes. Ask them to suggest improvements to each other before you collect the work for marking.

**A1** This can be done in pairs or as a whole-class activity. The second letter is clear and to-the-point, but one phrase is too direct (You must let me know ...) and another undersells the hotel (In case you are interested ...). The first letter is friendly and effective.

**2** Arrange the class into pairs. Although they only have to highlight four phrases, five are underlined in the model answer below, which refers to the first letter — the one the students are more likely to prefer.

### Suggested answers

Thank you very much for your telephone call. I am writing to you now to confirm your reservation for two adjoining double rooms with bath for the nights of July 14 to 23. Both rooms have a sea view and are on the fourth floor of the hotel.

The cost for half board (modified American plan) is $85 per person per night, including taxes and service.

I enclose two brochures describing our hotel and its facilities. If you have any questions, we shall be pleased to answer them.

Please let us know if you are arriving at the hotel later than 7pm.

We look forward to welcoming you to the Bellevue on July 14. We hope you will enjoy your stay with us.

Yours sincerely,

**B1** Play the recording at least twice. The second time it may be helpful to pause it from time to time so that everyone has time to 'catch up' while they're writing or checking their answers.

## Answers

### ROYAL SUITE CONFERENCE ROOM BOOKING

CLIENT'S NAME  Jane Barratt

COMPANY NAME  Priceworth plc

COMPANY ADDRESS  100 London Avenue,
                 Newtown, NT4 9PW

PHONE  0345 334455 extension 321

FAX  0345 778899

TOTAL NUMBER OF PARTICIPANTS  60

Date 14 Feb

Starting time 09.00

Coffee break from 11.00          to 11.30

Lunch break from 13.00          to 14.00

Finishing time 16.00

| CATERING | | EQUIPMENT | |
|---|---|---|---|
| coffee | ☑ | overhead projector | ☑ |
| tea | ☑ | VCR | ☐ |
| pastries | ☑ | TV | ☐ |
| sandwiches | ☐ | cassette player | ☐ |
| buffet lunch | ☑ | microphone | ☑ |
| sit-down lunch | ☐ | data projector | ☐ |

## Transcript   2 minutes 33 seconds

RESERVATIONS CLERK:   Imperial Hotel Reservations. How can I help you?

CALLER:   My name's Jane Barratt, I'm with Priceworth plc. I'd like to book the Royal Suite for a conference, please.

CLERK:   The Royal Suite, certainly. When would you like the room?

CALLER:   I'd like it from 9am on Friday the 14th of February. Is it available?

CLERK:   I'll just check for you ... Ah, yes, but only till 5 in the afternoon. We have a wedding party to prepare in the evening.

CALLER:   Oh, that's just perfect, we only need it till 4.

| CLERK: | Good. Can I ask you how many people there will be and what kind of facilities you'll require? |
|---|---|
| CALLER: | Yes, there will be about sixty people. And we'll need an overhead projector and a microphone. |
| CLERK: | What about refreshments and so on? |
| CALLER: | Let's see … Could we have coffee and tea with pastries mid-morning? |
| CLERK: | Yes, certainly, what time? |
| CALLER: | Let's say from 11 o'clock till 11.30. |
| CLERK: | Fine, and how about lunch? |
| CALLER: | Can you do us a buffet lunch from about 1 o'clock? We'll break for lunch for about an hour. |
| CLERK: | Certainly. And you'll be finishing at 4pm? Is that right? |
| CALLER: | Yes, that's right. We've dealt with you before so you'll be able to send us an invoice afterwards, won't you? |
| CLERK: | Yes, of course. I'm new here, so can I just make sure I've got the company details written down correctly? |
| CALLER: | Yes, it's Priceworth plc — that's PRICEWORTH — and the address is 100 London Avenue, Newtown, post code NT4 9PW. I'm Jane Barratt — that's JANE BARRATT. |
| CLERK: | And your phone and fax numbers? |
| CALLER: | The phone is 0345 334455 — extension 321. Oh, and the fax is 0345 778899. |
| CLERK: | Fine, I've reserved the Royal Suite for you for the 14th of February from 9am till 4pm. |
| CALLER: | That's right. |
| CLERK: | I'll confirm this in a letter, which I'll send to you today. |
| CALLER: | That's great. Thanks very much. |
| CLERK: | You're very welcome. Goodbye, Ms Barratt. |
| CALLER: | Goodbye. |

**PHOTOCOPIABLE**

**2** Arrange the class into an even number of pairs. Each pair only needs to draft one joint letter. Draw everyone's attention to the useful phrases at the foot of SB page 50, as well as the ones they've highlighted in the Bellevue Hotel letter above.

**3** Combine the pairs into groups of four (or five). This activity gives everyone the chance to share ideas — it also means that the letter in B2 has been written for someone else to read, it's not just a one-sided exercise.

## 4 Writing

Go through the 'Golden Rules' on SB page 51 and make sure everyone understands them. Allow time for questions and objections.

Set the task of writing an improved draft as homework.

## Finally …

**1** Draw everyone's attention to the Advice box, if you haven't already done so.

**2** Remind everyone what the aims of this Lesson were. Have they been achieved?

*Model letter*

# Imperial Hotel

Ms Jane Barratt
Priceworth plc
100 London Avenue
Newtown    NT4 9PW

[today's date]

Dear Ms Barratt,

Thank you very much for your telephone call today.

I am writing to you to confirm your reservation of our Royal Suite for a conference of about sixty participants on Friday February 14 from 9am till 4pm.

There will be an overhead projector and microphone in the conference room, both of which will be checked by our staff before your arrival.

Coffee, tea and pastries will be served at 11am. A buffet lunch will be served at 1pm.

Please let us know if any of the details above are incorrect or if you have any further requests. If you have any further questions, please let us know and we shall be delighted to help.

Thank you for choosing our hotel.

Yours sincerely,

*Your signature*
(Your name)
Reservations Department

**PHOTOCOPIABLE**

# 23 Avoiding mistakes

## Aims

Begin by explaining to the class the aims of Lesson 23, which are to improve their ability to:

- avoid mistakes in spelling, punctuation and grammar when writing emails or letters
- check drafts for mistakes in spelling, punctuation and grammar and correct them.

## Vocabulary

| | | |
|---|---|---|
| *chambermaid* | *portable iron* | *unpack* |
| *deducted* | *provisionally* | *wake-up call* |
| *overall discount* | *refurbishment* | |

## First of all ...

Before collecting the homework that was set in the previous Lesson (B4), arrange the class into small groups and ask them to read each other's letters. Ask them to suggest improvements to each other before you collect the work for marking. In particular, they should look for mistakes in spelling and punctuation in each other's work.

 **1**

Each email contains a different type of mistake:
7 typing mistakes in the email to Mr Anderson,
12 grammatical mistakes in the one to Mrs Lee
and
12 mistakes in punctuation and capitalisation in the one to Mr Harris.

Perhaps tell everyone how many mistakes to look for in each email.

This exercise can be done in pairs or small groups. But if it's done by students working alone, make sure there's time for everyone to compare what they've spotted with a partner before you reassemble the whole class to go through the answers.

## Answers

The mistakes are <u>underlined</u>.

**1**

> Dear Mr Anderson,
>
> Thank you for your email. I am pleased to say that we have six <u>doulbe</u> rooms and <u>and</u> two single rooms available on January 17 and I have provisionally reserved them for you.
>
> Our rates for <u>bedd</u> and breakfast are £25 per person in a double room and £35 per person in a single room. You, as leader of the party, can stay free of charge. Alternatively, an overall <u>dicsount</u> of 10 per cent can be deducted from each guest's bill if you prefer.
>
> Please <u>confrim</u> this reservation in writing within two days.
>
> I look forward to hearing <u>form</u> you.
>
> Yours <u>sincerly,</u>

**2**

> Dear Mrs Lee,
>
> <u>Thanks</u> you for your letter of 24th June. I <u>be</u> pleased to reserve a double room for you from July 4th to July 7th <u>including</u>.
>
> The room <u>have</u> a balcony with a sea view. It is <u>full</u> air <u>condition</u> and it <u>is having</u> a bathroom with shower.
>
> The price of the room <u>are</u> $50 with continental breakfast and $40 per person with half board.
>
> We <u>looking</u> forward to <u>welcome</u> you <u>at</u> July 4th. Thank you for <u>choose</u> our hotel.
>
> Yours sincerely,

**3**

> Dear <u>mr harris!</u>
>
> Thank you<u>,</u> for your letter. I am sorry to inform you<u>,</u> that we do not have a room available on December 25<u>TH</u> <u>.</u> Because two floors of the hotel will be closed for re <u>furbishment.</u>
>
> As part of our continuing programme of improvement, all our <u>Rooms</u> are being completely redecorated with air conditioning and new cable <u>tv</u>s.
>
> We are sorry that we are unable to serve you on this occasion. <u>from</u> january 1st the hotel will be fully open and we shall be pleased to welcome you at any time after that date.
>
> Yours sincerely<u>?</u>

## 2 Writing

As the first email is the easiest to rewrite, perhaps recommend that everyone chooses one of the others. But if the students work in groups of three, each person could rewrite a different email.

**B1** Arrange the class into pairs. Explain that they should make notes of the information they'll give in their email.

## 2 Writing

This should be done in class, with everyone working alone.

**3** Arrange the class back into the same pairs as in B1. Make sure everyone corrects the mistakes that are spotted.

**4** Rearrange the class into different pairs. The purpose of this activity is to get a reaction from someone who wasn't involved in the note-making earlier — in the role of client.

### Finally ...

1 Draw everyone's attention to the Advice boxes.

2 Remind everyone what the aims of this Lesson were. Have they been achieved?

3 To save time in the next Lesson, ask everyone to read the letter and the replies on SB page 54 before the Lesson.

## Model letter

```
From:  (your name)    Seaview Hotel   01 pages
To:    Ms Susan Duckworth — 01254 776667
Date:  15 August

Dear  Ms Duckworth,

Thank you for your letter.

I am very pleased that you contacted me. We
have been trying to reach you by phone since
your departure, but there has been no reply.

The chambermaid found the portable iron and
the address book in your room, but we were not
sure if they belonged to you or to a previous
guest in the same room.

I am sorry to tell you that there is no sign
of the Walkman. I have spoken to the
chambermaid and she assures me that this was
not left in the room. Perhaps you left this in
another hotel during your trip.

I will send the address book to you by first
class mail, and the iron by parcel post.
Please do not worry about sending us a
cheque, we are happy to pay for the postage.

We look forward to welcoming you at the
Seaview Hotel again in the near future.

Yours sincerely,

Your signature

(Your name)
```

**PHOTOCOPIABLE**

---

# 24 We are very sorry ...

## Aims

Begin by explaining to the class the aims of Lesson 24, which are to improve their ability to:

- deal with complaints and problems in writing
- write tactful emails in potentially tricky situations.

(There's more on dealing with complaints in Lessons 42 and 44.)

## Vocabulary

| | | |
|---|---|---|
| air conditioning | double booked | investigation |
| alternative | emergency | monotonous |
| back yard | escape route | overlook |
| blocked | fire alarm | repeat business |
| boiler room | fire drill | resolve |

| | | |
|---|---|---|
| camp bed | fire stairs/fire escape | sunbeds |
| dissatisfaction | good reputation | voucher |
| dissatisfied | | |

## First of all ...

Ask the class to suggest some things that might go wrong for guests in a hotel — or travellers on a journey. What kind of things do guests *write* to complain about, rather than make an on-the-spot complaint? Has anyone had any first-hand experience of dealing with complaints from guests or clients?

 Play the recording, pausing immediately after the Interviewer asks, 'What are you going to do about it?' and between the two speakers. It'll probably have to be played more than once. This exercise sets the scene for the theme of writing letters of apology, many of which have to be written for things that aren't really your fault.

## Answers

(These are the true statements.)

1  Janine's clients had to pay twice for their accommodation.
2  She is going to write to apologise.
3  Robert's guest's room was cold and the water was cold.
4  He is going to write an apology.

## Transcript   3 minutes 26 seconds

**1**

INTERVIEWER:  Janine is a travel agent.

JANINE:  I've had a case this week with…um…a couple who went to Paris and…um…when they got there, their hotel…the hotel knew nothing about them and that was…um…I've got someone working here in a training position and I don't think they had booked the hotel as he should have done. And they had to pay again…they'd paid us for their hotel accommodation and in order to be able to stay at the hotel, they had to pay again. So I've had quite a lengthy letter of complaint from them this week, which…um…obviously I'll try and resolve by getting our money back from the hotel and then passing that on to the client. Um…and, you know, hopefully apologising to a sufficient level so they'll come back to us again.

Interviewer:  What are you going to do about it?

JANINE:  I've seen them face-to-face and I've apologised to them…um…in the office but obviously, yes, I will…um…be putting my feelings into…into writing, I'll be writing to them to let them know that we are sorry that there was a problem with the short break.

**2**

INTERVIEWER:  Robert is a hotel manager.

ROBERT:  Well, this morning I…er…received a letter from a guest…um…who stayed with us…er…last month. Er…in fact she…she had stayed with us before. And…um…you know, I do take these kind of things quite seriously. Unfortunately what had happened was that…um…on one of the nights she was here there was a…there was a problem with the boiler. Um…not quite sure what happened, there was some sort of fault, an electrical fault in the…in the actual boiler room and…er…unfortunately this started a small fire. Oh, anyway, well, it was small enough…big enough to set the alarm off and…um…we had one of these awful things where all the guests had to get up and leave the building. Um…as it was…as it was so early in the morning — I think it was somewhere about…er…3 o'clock — of course, everybody was in their pyjamas and dressing gowns, etc. It was also freezing outside, which didn't help things. And then we had to wait till the…er…fire brigade had checked everything out, they left and then the guests were allowed back into the building. The only problem was that because it was in a boiler room it meant of course that the heating was off and as the heating was off there

was also no…er…hot water for, you know, washing, showers, etc. Er…but we had a guy came round the next morning, fixed it and…er…I thought that was it, and then unfortunately the whole wretched thing went wrong again the same evening. Um…anyway, the next day everything was…er…put right, but unfortunately this guest who'd sent me the letter…er…had gone, and…er…so her last impression unfortunately wasn't…wasn't…wasn't the best that we'd have wished for.

INTERVIEWER:  What are you going to do about it?

ROBERT:  I'm going to write to her and…er…you know, apo…offer our apologies for what had happened and to explain to her the reasons…er…you know, for the problem about the fire, etc., etc. I think the best thing really is to offer her a…a discount on her room rates or even give her a free night…er…if she wants to come and stay with us again, which of course we'd like. And really it was just that the problem was outside our control and there really wasn't much we could do about it. But, I do take complaints extremely seriously…er…the hotel's got a reputation which we want to keep, and we want people to stay with us, to enjoy their stay and come back.

**B1**  This Step could be prepared at home before the Lesson. The two replies tell Mr Cross that his complaints are being investigated, but that no decisions have been made yet. After everyone has read the email and the two replies, ask them to explain why they prefer one reply over the other. Ask them to highlight the phrases that make one reply better.

## Suggested answers

Both replies are OK, but the second one seems better. It sounds more personal and sincere because the passive isn't used at all and the writer seems to be taking the complaint more seriously.

Compare these phrases from the two emails:

**1**

| |
|---|
| Your email…was forwarded to me |
| The situation is being looked into |
| I assure you that |
| indicates an opportunity for improvement |

**2**

| |
|---|
| Thank you for your email |
| It will take me a few days to look into |
| I would like you to know that |
| gives us a chance to make any improvements |

**2** Arrange the class into pairs to decide what they are going to do about the situation.

**3** Arrange the class into pairs. Explain this isn't a role play — everyone looks at the same letters in **Activity 38** on SB page 126. The style of the letter of apology can serve as a model for the writing task that follows. It's a matter of taste which phrases are highlighted, but reassemble the class and find out what phrases seemed to appeal to everyone.

## 4 Writing

This could be done as homework, rather than using up class time.

### *Model letter*

---

# Phoenix Hotel

J.G. Cross
44 Maple Drive
Rockford   RD5 8PF

[date]

Dear Mr Cross

I apologise for the delay in dealing with your letter. Two key members of staff have been away sick and I needed to talk to them before replying in detail to your letter.

First of all, thank you for informing me about the fire stairs. This could have been very dangerous and I have made sure these stairs are now clear, and I will make sure that all fire escape routes are checked daily.

I have also revised our fire drill procedures. All members of staff have now received special training, which includes keeping guests fully informed of what is going on. This is particularly important when the fire alarm sounds in the middle of the night.

The housekeeper has had the flu and only just returned to work. She tells me that so many people asked for blankets on the day the heating broke down that she completely ran out. I have now made an arrangement with our sister hotel so that we can provide each other with extra blankets if such a situation arises again. I am sorry that you were cold and I hope this did not spoil your stay too much.

Finally, I would like to thank you again for writing to me. I hope that we can welcome you here again in the future. I enclose a voucher giving you a discount of 30% off our normal room rates, which you may use at any time during the next 12 months.

Again I am sorry that your stay with us was less than excellent.

Yours sincerely,

*Your signature*

(Your name)

---

## C Writing

This is quite a substantial writing task, as all the points made by the Wilds need to be answered. If there's time, brainstorm some ideas for the reply as a whole-class activity before everyone writes their letter as homework. (As this is an open-ended task, there's no model letter here.)

## Finally ...

**1** Draw everyone's attention to the Advice box.

**2** Remind everyone what the aims of this Lesson were. Have they been achieved?

## Correspondence: Vocabulary puzzle

Photocopy the Vocabulary puzzle on page 105 for everyone to do in pairs in class, or for homework.

### Answers

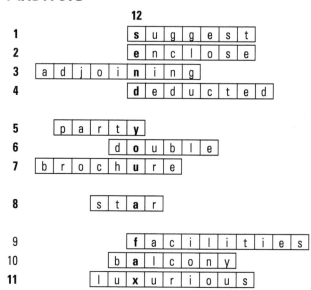

1  **12**
    s u **g** g **e** s t
2    e n c l o s e
3    a d j o i **n** i n g
4    **d** e d u c t e **d**

5    p a r t **y**
6    d **o** u b l e
7    b r o c h **u** r e

8    s t **a** r

9    **f** a c i l i t i e s
10   b a l c o n **y**
11   l u **x** u r i o u s

# 25 Reservations

This Module (Lessons 25-30) covers the procedures involved in dealing with guests in hotels and other aspects of booking accommodation for clients.

- What information is included in the room chart (costs, dates, room numbers, types of room)?
- What information is missing, which would need to be recorded somewhere (guests' addresses, car registration numbers, room facilities, deposit paid, method of payment, etc.)?

## Aims

Begin by explaining to the class the aims of Lesson 25, which are to improve their ability to:

- deal with reservations made over the phone and in writing
- allocate accommodation according to clients' wishes.

## Vocabulary

*continental breakfast*    *full board*
*requirements*    *updated*

## First of all …

Ask everyone to look at the room chart on SB page 56, which is rather simpler than a real room chart (or the equivalent computer display):

**A1** After everyone has read the emails, they see that on the room chart Ms Smith has been allocated a single room and Mr and Mrs Moore have been allocated a room with a double bed.

## Answers

The mistake in the room chart is that Mr and Mrs Moore should have been allocated a room until the 8th, not the 6th.

**Make sure that everyone amends the room chart in their books accordingly.**

The information in the room chart is built up throughout the Lesson. At the *very end* — after *all* the additions have been made in A1, B1 and in the role play in C1 — the chart will be as shown below.

There may be further changes advisable to ensure continuous occupation of some rooms — and this is alluded to in B3 and then discussed in C2.

| room description | 101 twin beds bath, balcony | 102 single bed shower | 103 double bed shower | 104 twin beds bath | 105 double bed shower, balcony |
|---|---|---|---|---|---|
| room price | $92 | $65 | $85 | $88 | $90 |
| Sun May 1 | | Mr Chavez (0171 993 3723) | Mr & Mrs Green (0181 898 9325) (half board) | | Mr & Mrs Moore (full board) |
| Mon May 2 | Mr & Mrs Brown (01303 87 92 31) | | | Ms Davidson (2) (0181 821 4832) | |
| Tue May 3 | | | | | |
| Wed May 4 | | | | | |
| Thu May 5 | | | Mr & Mrs Green | | |
| Fri May 6 | Mr & Mrs Brown Ms Davidson(2) | Mr Chavez Ms Smith (b & b) | Mr Chavez | Ms Davidson Ms Anderson (2) | Mr & Mrs Moore |
| Sat May 7 | | | | (01981 83 21 23) | |
| Sun May 8 | Ms Davidson | Ms Smith | Mr Chavez | Ms Anderson | Mr & Mrs Moore |

**2** This reply (apart from the four mistakes) is a model for the reply to Mrs Moore in A3. Having to find the mistakes encourages everyone to read the text and look at the chart carefully.

# Answers

The mistakes are:

> Dear <u>Mr</u> Smith    **Ms**
>
> The cost of the room with <u>full</u> breakfast is <u>£65</u>.
> **continental    $65**
>
> We look forward to welcoming you ~~both~~ on May 6.

# 3 Writing

This should be set as homework if time is short.

## Model email

> From: (Your name) Royal Hotel
> To: Mrs Mary Moore  0112 555 1234
>
> Dear Mrs Moore,
>
> Thank you very much for your email. I have pleasure in confirming that we have reserved a double room with balcony and shower for you from May 1st to 8th. The room has a double bed, balcony and shower. The price of the room is $170 per day with full board (breakfast, lunch and dinner), making a total of $1,190 for 7 days.
>
> We look forward to welcoming you and your husband on May 1st. If you require any more information, please do not hesitate to contact me.
>
> Thank you for choosing the Royal Hotel,
>
> Yours sincerely,
>
> *Your signature*
>
> (Your name)

**PHOTOCOPIABLE** © Cambridge University Press 2005

## B1

Another guest rings up and he has to be allocated a room. You'll probably need to play the recording more than once. The recording also acts as a model for the role play in C1, showing everyone the way this kind of conversation might go.

## Answers

See the entry for Mr and Mrs Green on the room chart on page 57.

## Transcript 2 minutes 1 second

| | |
|---|---|
| RECEPTIONIST: | Good afternoon, Royal Hotel. How can I help you? |
| MR GREEN: | Do you have any rooms free from the 1st of May. |
| RECEPTIONIST: | May the 1st … Yes, sir, we do. What kind of room would you like? |
| MR GREEN: | Oh, um…well, I'd…I'd like a room with a double bed … oh, and a balcony if possible. |
| RECEPTIONIST: | Let me see, well…er…I'm afraid we only have one room free with a double bed and that hasn't got a balcony. But we have one with twin beds and a balcony — would that be all right? |
| MR GREEN: | Er…no, no, I think I'd prefer the one with the double bed. |

| | |
|---|---|
| RECEPTIONIST: | So that's a room with a double bed and shower from May the 1st. Could I have your name please, sir? |
| MR GREEN: | Oh yes, er…Green…er…Mr and Mrs Green. |
| RECEPTIONIST: | And how long will you be staying with us, Mr Green? |
| MR GREEN: | Right, we'll be leaving on the 5th of May in the morning. |
| RECEPTIONIST: | Fine, Mr Green. Would you like full board, half board or bed and breakfast? |
| MR GREEN: | Oh…um…er…half board, I think. Oh, does that, you know, er…does that mean breakfast and dinner? |
| RECEPTIONIST: | Oh, yes, that's right. Per night that will cost $125 for two people. |
| MR GREEN: | OK, yeah. |
| RECEPTIONIST: | So, right, I've booked you a double room with shower but no balcony from Sunday May the 1st until Thursday May the 5th, is that right? |
| MR GREEN: | Yes, that's right. |
| RECEPTIONIST: | Is there a phone number where we can contact you, Mr Green? |
| MR GREEN: | Yes, of course, it's…er…0181 898 9325. |
| RECEPTIONIST: | Right, that's 0181 898 9325. What time will you be arriving on Sunday, Mr Green? |
| MR GREEN: | About 7. |
| RECEPTIONIST: | Oh, fine. Dinner is served from 7.30 till 9.30. If you're going to be any later than 8pm, would you please telephone us to let us know what time to expect you? |
| MR GREEN: | Sure. |
| RECEPTIONIST: | Thank you very much, Mr Green. We look forward to seeing you both on Sunday May the 1st. |
| MR GREEN: | OK, thanks a lot, bye. |
| RECEPTIONIST: | Goodbye, Mr Green. |

**PHOTOCOPIABLE** © Cambridge University Press 2005

# 2 Pronunciation

Play the recording, pausing it for the students to repeat each phrase in the speech balloon. [1 minute 25 seconds].

They may need to repeat some phrases several times to get them right.

# 3 Grammar

This can be done in pairs or alone. All the *if…* sentences in this exercise are first conditionals. Quite a few variations are possible. (There is more practice in using *if…* sentences in C2.)

## Suggested answers

**2** will have to pay $165 a night for two people.

**3** will have to pay an extra $2 a night each.

**4** have   will also get a room with twin beds.

**5** move   will have to pay more — or we could charge her the single room rate.

**6** has   will have to pay $105 a night.

## C1 Role play

Arrange the class into pairs. In this role play the students take part in four separate phone calls to the Royal Hotel. Each partner has two turns at being the receptionist. Make sure everyone looks carefully at the information in **Activity 7** on SB page 110 or **Activity 22** on SB page 118 *before* the first call begins.

### Answers

See the entries on the room chart on page 57.

**2** Keep the same pairs for this discussion of possible changes. Later reassemble the class so that everyone has a chance to exchange ideas for moving guests around.

## Suggested answers

*If we put the Andersons in 103, the sisters would have to share a double bed. So that's not a good idea.*

*If we put Mr Chavez in 103 for the whole week, there wouldn't be a double room for the Greens. So that's not a good idea.*

*If we put Ms Smith in 103, Mr Chavez could stay in 102 for the whole week — but she must be given the room for $65, not $85. So that might be a good idea.*

*If we put the Andersons in 101, the Davidsons could stay in 104 until Sunday — but they must be charged $88, not $92. So that might be a good idea.*

*If we put the Greens in 101, they wouldn't have a double bed — and Mr Green asked for a double bed in his phone call (see B1). So that's not a good idea.*

## Finally ...

Remind everyone what the aims of this Lesson were. Have they been achieved?

# 26 Checking in

## Aims

Begin by explaining to the class the aims of Lesson 26, which are to improve their ability to:

- deal with guests checking in
- carry out registration procedures.

## Vocabulary

**baggage (GB luggage)**  **leaflet**
**buffet breakfast**  **payment method**
**company account**  **registration card/form**
**fill in/out a form**  **surname/family name**
**forenames**

## First of all ...

Ask everyone to suggest what information a guest is expected to provide when they check in. (Full name, length of stay, credit card, passport number, etc.)

**A1** Play the recording, pausing it at the points marked with stars ★★★ in the Transcript and between the two conversations. Check the answers — if most students still have some details missing, play it again to give them a second chance.

## Answers

| name | Mr Robert Watson |
| --- | --- |
| room number | 414 |
| type of room | twin beds |
| cost | $150 |
| payment method | Visa card |

| name | Ms Emma O'Neill |
| --- | --- |
| room number | 301 |
| type of room | single |
| cost | $95 |
| payment method | MasterCard |

**2** Play the recording again. Listening for mistakes encourages everyone to listen carefully to the recording.

## Suggested answers

(The two mistakes are underlined in the Transcript below.)

She calls him Mr Robert — he's Mr Watson.

He says lunch is served from 8 o'clock which can't be right — he means dinner.

## Transcript   2 minutes 20 seconds

**1**

| | |
|---|---|
| RECEPTIONIST: | Good afternoon, sir. Do you have a reservation? |
| MR WATSON: | No, I don't. Er…do you have a double room for two nights? |
| RECEPTIONIST: | Um… yes we do. |
| MR WATSON: | Oh, good. |
| RECEPTIONIST: | I'll just check what rooms we have available. Just a moment, please. |
| MR WATSON: | Oh, OK, thanks. |
| RECEPTIONIST: | Yes, now, let's see…um…Room 414 is free. It's on the fourth floor and it has a sea view and twin beds. |
| MR WATSON: | Oh, that sounds fine. Er…how much is it? |
| RECEPTIONIST: | Well, the cost is $150 per night, including buffet breakfast. |
| MR WATSON: | Oh, fine. |
| RECEPTIONIST: | Would you fill out this registration form, please? |
| MR WATSON: | Oh, yes, sure, sure … |

★★★

| | |
|---|---|
| RECEPTIONIST: | … thank you very much, Mr Robert. Could I see your passport, please? |
| MR WATSON: | Uhuh, er…here it is. |
| RECEPTIONIST: | Thank you very much. How will you be paying for your room? |
| MR WATSON: | By Visa. |
| RECEPTIONIST: | Mm, may I have your credit card, please? |
| MR WATSON: | Certainly, here you are … |

**2**

| | |
|---|---|
| RECEPTIONIST: | Good afternoon, may I help you? |
| MS O'NEILL: | Yes, I have a room booked. My name's O'Neill. |
| RECEPTIONIST: | Ah, yes, Ms O'Neill. Yes, it's a single room with sea view until Saturday, is that right? |
| MS O'NEILL: | Yes. Um…and a shower. |
| RECEPTIONIST: | Oh, yes, yes, all our rooms have showers. |
| MS O'NEILL: | Um…how much does that cost? |
| RECEPTIONIST: | Well, it's $95 a night but that does include buffet breakfast. |
| MS O'NEILL: | OK. I'll be paying by MasterCard. |
| RECEPTIONIST: | Fine, fine. Would you just fill out the registration form … |

★★★

| | |
|---|---|
| RECEPTIONIST: | … you'll be in Room 301, which is on the third floor. Here's your key and your key card. |
| MS O'NEILL: | Oh, thank you. Oh, and what about my suitcase? |
| RECEPTIONIST: | Your baggage will be taken up to your room for you. |
| MS O'NEILL: | Oh, that's good. |
| RECEPTIONIST: | Have you stayed with us before? |

| | |
|---|---|
| MS O'NEILL: | No. |
| RECEPTIONIST: | Well, this leaflet tells you all about the hotel and the facilities. |
| MS O'NEILL: | Oh, well, thank you very much. |
| RECEPTIONIST: | Lunch is served from 8 o'clock. Would you like to reserve a table? |
| MS O'NEILL: | Oh, yes please. For…um…8.30. |
| RECEPTIONIST: | Fine, and would you like a wake-up call in the morning? |
| MS O'NEILL: | No, thanks. |
| RECEPTIONIST: | OK. The porter will show you to your room. |
| MS O'NEILL: | Oh, that's good. |
| RECEPTIONIST: | If you have any problems, please let me know. |
| MS O'NEILL: | All right, and thank you very much. |
| RECEPTIONIST: | Enjoy your stay with us! |
| MS O'NEILL: | Thanks! |

**PHOTOCOPIABLE**   © Cambridge University Press 2005

**B1** This exercise can be begun in pairs, or simply done as a quick whole-class activity. The unsuitable phrases are:

*Hello, what do you want?* and *Back again, Mr Grey?*

## 2 Pronunciation

Play the recording, pausing it between each phrase long enough for everyone to repeat the phrases. The recording only includes the suitable phrases.

### Transcript 59 seconds

Good evening, how may I help you?

It's good to see you again, Ms Black!

It's nice to see you again, Mrs White.

Hello again, Ms Green, and welcome!

Good afternoon, sir, do you have a reservation with us today?

Good evening, Mr Brown. How nice to see you again!

## C Role play

Arrange the class into pairs. One student looks at **Activity 4** on SB page 109, the other at **Activity 30** on SB page 122. The role play is in two parts. Explain to everyone that they're back again at the Royal Hotel (Lesson 25). The students have to look at their updated room charts on SB page 56. Check that the details are correct.

Reassemble the class to find out if they managed to accommodate the Greens and the Browns — luckily both rooms *were* probably free for the extra night!

Point out that although filling out forms is something clients usually have to do alone, they may well ask for help while they're doing it.

**D** Arrange the class into pairs, but each student should fill out the form individually — but they can ask the other 'guest who is checking in at the same time' for help when necessary.

They might ask each other:

*What are you putting down as 'Purpose of visit'?*
*What does 'Accompanied by' mean?*
*I haven't got a car — what should I put here?*
*What does 'Special requirements' mean?*

Reassemble the class. Point out to everyone that if a client is filling out a form, he or she may ask questions about it — and a member of staff must be able to explain.

Brainstorm some questions that a guest might ask about the form on SB page 59.

Write up some or all of these useful responses on the board:

*Would you just fill out this registration card, please?*

*It's all right, sir, you can leave that blank.*

*Could you just write 'NONE' in that space please?*

*Could you also fill in this information please?*

## Finally …

Remind everyone what the aims of this Lesson were. Have they been achieved?

# Facilities: Enjoy your stay!

## Aim

Begin by explaining to the class the aim of Lesson 27, which is to improve their ability to:

- describe a hotel's facilities and explain them to guests.

## Vocabulary

| | | |
|---|---|---|
| adjust | facilities | sauna |
| car park (US parking lot) | glass door | tennis court |
| closet (GB wardrobe) | housekeeper | towel |
| drawer | remote control | |

+ the words in the Vocabulary list in B1

## First of all …

Ask everyone to think of the last time they stayed in a hotel:

- What furniture and equiment was in the bedroom?
- What public facilities did the hotel have?

**A1** Before playing the recording, point out to everyone that they've already 'met' Mr Watson and Ms O'Neill in Lesson 26. Play the recording, pausing it between each conversation.

### Answers

| | |
|---|---|
| **Mr Watson** | towels + go shopping |
| **Ms O'Neill** | blankets + go for a swim |
| **Mr and Mrs Harris** | TV remote control + go for a drive |

**2** Play the recording again. Then ask the whole class to evaluate the 'performance' of each receptionist.

### Suggested answers

The first two receptionists are both friendly and helpful.

The third receptionist has less patience and isn't so friendly (but she isn't rude).

## Transcript  2 minutes 19 seconds

**1**

RECEPTIONIST: Hello, Mr Watson. How may I help?

MR WATSON: Oh…er…well, er…look, there's only one towel in the bathroom and I, well, I need at least two.

RECEPTIONIST: Oh, I'll ask the housekeeper to put some extra towels in your room right away.

MR WATSON: Oh, thank you. Oh, and…um…I want to go into town to do some shopping. What's the best way to get there? Is it far to walk, or should I take a taxi?

RECEPTIONIST: No, it's only fifteen minutes' walk and the shops are open till 7.30 so you've got plenty of time. You could come back by taxi if your shopping's heavy.

MR WATSON: OK. Thanks.

RECEPTIONIST: You're welcome, Mr Watson. Have a nice afternoon!

MR WATSON: Oh, thank you.

**2**

RECEPTIONIST: Hello, Ms O'Neill. How may I help you?

MS O'NEILL: Oh, well, there…there isn't a blanket on my bed. I…I do think I need one.

RECEPTIONIST: I think you'll find two in the closet, Ms O'Neill. And if there aren't, please let me know straight away and I'll ask the housekeeper to put some on your bed.

MS O'NEILL: Oh, right. I'll look in the closet. And I'm just going for a swim in the pool. Can I rent a towel?

RECEPTIONIST: Ah, no, there's no need to do that. Just ask the pool attendant and he'll give you one. There's no charge.

MS O'NEILL: OK, fine. Thanks.

RECEPTIONIST: You're welcome, Ms O'Neill. Enjoy your swim!

MS O'NEILL: Thank you.

**3**

RECEPTIONIST: Hello, Mr and Mrs Harris.

MR HARRIS: Yeah, look, the television in our room doesn't work.

MRS HARRIS: There's no remote control for it and it won't work without it.

| RECEPTIONIST: | Oh, have you looked in the drawer beside the bed? |
| MR HARRIS: | No. |
| RECEPTIONIST: | Well, the remote control is usually kept there. If it's not, please let me know and I'll make sure you get one right away. |
| MRS HARRIS: | We'll have a look for it later. |
| MR HARRIS: | Yeah, look, there's something else … |
| RECEPTIONIST: | Yes? |
| MR HARRIS: | We're going out for a drive, we won't be back till 8.30. Can we reserve a table for dinner? |
| RECEPTIONIST: | Certainly. Shall I book a table for … 9 o'clock? |
| MR HARRIS: | No, 8.30'd be better. |
| MRS HARRIS: | 9 o'clock's fine. We need time to change and freshen up, won't we, dear? |
| MR HARRIS: | Oh, all right, 9 o'clock. OK, thank you. |
| RECEPTIONIST: | You're welcome. Enjoy your drive! |
| MR HARRIS: | Thanks. |
| MRS HARRIS: | Thank you. |

**PHOTOCOPIABLE** © Cambridge University Press 2005

# B 1 Vocabulary

This can be done in pairs or alone.

The furniture and equipment not shown in the pictures are:

bidet   desk   dressing table   hair-dryer   light switch
mini-bar   radio alarm   radiator   sheets   shower   waste bin

## 2 Grammar

This can also be done alone or in pairs. There are several variations possible.

### Suggested answers

2   It's to the left of the bath tub, in the bathroom.

3   It's in the bedroom above the bed — on the left.

4   They're in the bathroom, on the left of the bath tub.

5   It's in the bedroom on the left, near the window.

6   There's one above the washbasin in the bathroom and one above the dressing table in the bedroom.

## C 1

This can be done in pairs or by students working alone. Play the recording and then reassemble the class to sort out any problems or questions that arise.

### Answers

| ROOMS | CENTRAL HOTEL | BELLEVUE HOTEL |
|---|---|---|
| bath | | ✓ |
| shower | ✓ | ✓ |
| hair-dryer | ✓ | ✓ |
| telephone | ✓ | ✓ |
| desk | ✓ | |
| TV | ✓ | ✓ |
| **HOTEL FACILITIES** | | |
| indoor pool | ✓ | |
| outdoor pool | | ✓ |
| fitness centre | ✓ | |
| sauna | ✓ | |
| car park | | ✓ |
| garage | ✓ | |
| tennis courts | | ✓ |
| garden | | ✓ |
| play area | | ✓ |
| beach | | ✓ |
| water sports | | ✓ |
| restaurant | ✓ | ✓ ✓ |
| night club | ✓ | |
| cocktail bar | | ✓ |
| bar and lounge | ✓ | |
| conference facilities | ✓ | |

## Transcript   3 minutes 22 seconds

CENTRAL HOTEL MANAGER:  Now, in all of our rooms you'll find a bathroom, which has a shower and also a complimentary hair-dryer. We have trouser presses as standard. If you've come to do some work, we have a desk with a desk lamp, a desk chair, that's including an easy chair. And…er…we have a telephone and a socket for your computer modem. And if you've come to relax, we have a remote-controlled satellite television with programmes in English, French and German.

Now, the hotel itself you'll find comes with a restaurant, where we have a…an extensive bar and a lounge. And in the evenings we offer a night club, which is open from 10pm. And if you'd like to relax, we have an indoor swimming pool, which also has a sauna and a fully-equipped fitness centre. And also, if you've got kids with you or…er…you want to just relax even more, we have a games room. We also have an underground garage. Oh, and…er… conference facilities for up to 100 people.

BELLEVUE HOTEL MANAGER:  Welcome to the Bellevue Hotel, we hope you enjoy your stay! Um…let me tell you a little bit about the rooms that we have. Er…they're very well appointed, lots of luxury items, all our rooms in fact have a balcony with either a full or partial view of the sea. Um…you will find in every room that there is a direct dial telephone, if you need to make any urgent calls or to your family. And if you'd like to watch your favourite telly programme, then switch on our remote control televisions. Er…there you'll also find bathroom and it has a bath *and* shower, also an extra hair-dryer in every bathroom, if you need to freshen up.

Now, about the hotel itself: there is…er…a facility for outdoor swimming, we have a lovely outdoor swimming pool and there's a snack bar attached to that if you're feeling like a bit of open air. Also in the same area there's a play pool for small children if you want to bring your family along. And the children's play area is close to that, there's some lovely toys and equipment in there. Er…if you would like to enjoy the sun that we're having, of course we've got a landscaped garden outside and next to that there is a couple of tennis courts for the sporty ones among us. Now, you'll find that there are plenty of spaces for your cars at the back, where there's a car park behind the hotel. And if you make your way down the path at the front, you'll find our private beach, which has watersports available for all our guests — at no extra cost. Er…finally, for those of you who enjoy your food, we have two restaurants, so you have a choice, and both of those have international or local cuisine. And I think … Ah, I ought to tell you one more thing: our cocktail bar — now, if you'd like to relax in the evening, we serve drinks in the cocktail bar until after midnight. We hope you enjoy your stay with us!

 **PHOTOCOPIABLE** © Cambridge University Press 2005

## D Role play

Arrange the class into pairs. Draw everyone's attention to the useful phrases in the speech balloon at the foot of SB page 61 before they begin.

For this to seem realistic, perhaps get everyone to stand up and pretend to enter the room in the photo on SB page 60. Allow enough time for both students to have a turn at being the hotel staff member.

## Finally …

Remind everyone what the aim of this Lesson was. Has it been achieved?

# 28 Giving information

## Aim

Begin by explaining to the class the aim of Lesson 28, which is to improve their ability to:

* give information in a polite and friendly way in many different situations (not just to do with accommodation).

## Vocabulary

| | |
|---|---|
| *associate hotel* | *laundry list* |
| *cabaret* | *overnight train* |
| *concert hall* | *pile* |
| *domestic flight* | *pool attendant* |
| *dry-cleaning* | *sun lotion* |
| *exchange rate* | *symphony concert* |
| *gift shop* | *washing* |
| *hall porter (US concierge)* | |

## First of all …

Ask everyone to suggest what kind of information people ask for in a hotel — and in a restaurant, a tourist information office and a travel agency.

**A 1** Before playing the recording, point out that the illustrations show the five conversations. Play the recording, pausing between each conversation. Note that in the middle of conversations 3 and 4 there is a break to show that time has passed.

## Answers

1 when lunch ends
 reserve a table

2 sun lotion
 doesn't give her a towel

3 find out about today's special
 another dish

4 a concert
 not pay him for the ticket

5 how to get his washing done
 a different bag

 **2** Play the recording again, pausing it between each conversation. Reassemble the class to get a consensus of their evaluation of how the five members of staff sound.

## Suggested answers

| Receptionist | helpful |
|---|---|
| Pool attendant | unhelpful (but not rude) |
| Waitress | inefficient (but friendly) |
| Hall porter | unfriendly (but not rude) |
| Housekeeper | friendly |

## Transcript  3 minutes 13 seconds

**1**

MAN: Excuse me.
RECEPTIONIST: Yes, sir, how may I help?
MAN: Can you tell me when they stop serving lunch in the restaurant?
RECEPTIONIST: Yes, certainly. Well, last orders are at 2 o'clock, but it's probably best not to get there quite so late. It's best if you book a table. I can do that for you if you wish.
MAN: Oh, yes, oh, right, OK …

**2**

Woman: Excuse me.
POOL ATTENDANT: Yes, miss?
Woman: Um…can you tell me where I can buy some sun lotion?
POOL ATTENDANT: Er…yes, certainly, you can buy that at the gift shop just next to the reception in the hotel.

| | |
|---|---|
| Woman: | Oh, good. |
| POOL ATTENDANT: | Oh, and by the way, look, you can help yourself to a towel from that pile over there, if you like. You see, the green ones. |
| Woman: | Oh, fine, thanks … |

**3**

| | |
|---|---|
| MAN: | Excuse me! |
| WAITRESS: | Yes, sir, are you ready to order? |
| MAN: | Mm, ah, but first can you tell me what today's special is? |
| WAITRESS: | Um…I don't really know, I'm afraid. I'll just have to find out. Excuse me a moment. |
| MAN: | Oh, all right … |
| WAITRESS: | … I'm afraid the special's no longer available. Sorry about that. Um…but I think you might like the fish of the day: it's red snapper, pan-fried, and served with lemon. It's very nice. |
| MAN: | Oh, well, that sounds delicious … |

**4**

| | |
|---|---|
| WOMAN: | Excuse me. |
| HALL PORTER: | Yes, Ms O'Neill? |
| WOMAN: | Can you get me a ticket for tonight's symphony concert? |
| PORTER: | Is that one ticket or two? |
| WOMAN: | Just one. It doesn't matter what price. |
| PORTER: | I'll just have to find out if there are tickets still available. Er…just excuse me a moment, please … |
| WOMAN: | … Any luck? |
| PORTER: | Yes, I've managed to get you one at $40. Is that OK? |
| WOMAN: | Fine. |
| PORTER: | If you get to the concert hall before 7.30, you can collect the ticket and pay for it then. It's reserved in your name, Ms O'Neill. Er…the concert starts at 8. |
| WOMAN: | Oh, OK, thanks very much … |

**5**

| | |
|---|---|
| HOUSEKEEPER: | Housekeeper, good morning. |
| MAN: | Oh, good morning. This is Mr Watson in 414. |
| HOUSEKEEPER: | Yes, Mr Watson, how can I help? |
| MAN: | I've got some clothes that need washing. Can you tell me what I should do? |
| HOUSEKEEPER: | Yes, certainly. If you look inside your closet, you'll find a plastic bag and a laundry list. |
| MAN: | OK, I'll just look … Um…oh, yes, here we are. |
| HOUSEKEEPER: | If you put the clothes in the bag and fill out the form, I'll send someone to collect it in about ten minutes. |
| MAN: | Oh, fine, good. All right, thanks. |
| HOUSEKEEPER: | And if you have any dry-cleaning you'd like us to do, we can collect that from you at the same time. But don't put it in the same bag as the washing. |
| MAN: | Oh right, no, I…I, no, well, actually, no, I haven't got anything that…er…needs … |

**PHOTOCOPIABLE** © Cambridge University Press 2005

**B1** Ask everyone to match each phrase in the speech balloon with one situation. There may be some phrases that can be used in more than one situation.

Play the recording which gives the right answers. There's a pause recorded after each one so there's no need to pause it unless there are any questions or problems to sort out.

## 2 Pronunciation

 Play the recording again. Be ready to extend some of the pauses if the students need to repeat any of the phrases again.

### Transcript  1 minute 44 seconds

**1**

| | |
|---|---|
| MAN: | Yes, certainly. Well, … |
| WOMAN: | Certainly, I'll just explain … |

**2**

| | |
|---|---|
| WOMAN: | Excuse me a moment, I'll have to check. |
| WOMAN: | I'll just have to find out. |
| MAN: | Just one moment, please, I'll ask one of my colleagues. |

**3**

| | |
|---|---|
| WOMAN: | I'm afraid I don't know. |
| WOMAN: | I'm not quite sure, I'm afraid. |
| MAN: | I'm sorry, I don't really know. |

**4**

| | |
|---|---|
| WOMAN: | By the way, you might be interested to know that … |

## C Role play

Please familiarise yourself with the instructions in **Activity 11** on SB page 113 and **Activity 26** on SB page 121 before you begin this role play — and allow enough time for all four parts to be done.

**1** First, draw everyone's attention to the phrases in the speech balloons and practise the pronunciation with them.

**2** Arrange the class into two halves: one half should look at **Activity 11**, the others at **26**.

**3** Allow them enough time to study their information. Answer any questions that come up.

**4** Demonstrate what has to be done by playing the role of guest yourself with one of your more confident students who's been looking at Activity 11. Ask him or her:
*How long does it take to get to the international airport?*
*What's the best way of getting there?*
*What's the best way of getting to Granada?*

**5** Ask the receptionists to stand on one side of the room (or, in a large class, in two or three separate places in the room) as if they are standing behind a reception desk. The guests should begin standing somewhere away from the receptionists. Then, in Part 1, they approach *one* of the receptionists to ask for some information. When they've got the information they want, they say thank you and go away.

**6** Then, in Part 2, they approach a *different* receptionist, if possible — this may not be possible if all the other receptionists are busy, but it doesn't really matter if some of them have to ask the same receptionist.

**7** Then the two halves change roles and places. Tell them when to do this so that the groups are coordinated. In Part 3, the guests approach one of the receptionists to ask for some information. When they've got the information they want, they say thank you and go away.

8 In Part 4, they approach a *different* receptionist, if possible — again, this may not be possible if all the other receptionists are busy, but it doesn't really matter if some of them have to ask the same receptionist.

9 Reassemble the class and find out how everyone got on. If everyone found this difficult, ask them to do Parts 1 and 3 again — this time sitting together in pairs rather than standing up.

## Finally ...

1 Remind everyone what the aim of this Lesson was. Has it been achieved?

2 To save time in the next Lesson, ask everyone to read the texts on SB page 65 before the next Lesson. They should also answer the questions in A1.

# 29 The best hotel for you ...

## Aims

Begin by explaining to the class the aims of Lesson 29, which are to improve their ability to:

- compare the facilities at different hotels
- recommend accommodation to suit different clients' requirements.

## Vocabulary

in the accommodation descriptions:

*all inclusive*
*breathtaking view*
*ceiling fan*
*complimentary drinks*
*four poster bed*
*hammock*
*hideaway*
*inhouse movies*
*kingsize bed*

*lush*
*nursery*
*obliging personal service*
*oceanside*
*picnic hamper*
*picturesque*
*plantation*
*porterage*
*rain forest hike*

*secluded*
*semi detached cottages*
*snorkelling*
*sunfish*
*swim-up bar*
*trail*
*venture out*
*wrap around balcony*

## First of all ...

Ask everyone if they'd like to spend a holiday in the Caribbean:

- Why? What are the attractions of the Caribbean, and why is it so popular with tourists?
- What are the advantages of an all-inclusive resort? What are the disadvantages?

### A 1

To save time in class, the students should read the descriptions and answer the questions at home before the Lesson. If this isn't feasible, the students could decide on their answers working together in pairs. Reassemble the class to go through the answers. If anyone has visited a Caribbean resort (or stayed at an all-inclusive resort elsewhere) ask them to share their experiences with the class.

### Answers

| | |
|---|---|
| Anse Chastenet | doesn't charge for excursions |
| Anse Chastenet | has its own dive school |

| | |
|---|---|
| Club St Lucia | has most organised activities |
| East Winds Inn | serves free champagne |
| Club St Lucia | has free water skiing |
| Anse Chastenet | has the fewest rooms |
| Club St Lucia | has the most rooms |
| East Winds Inn | has the best food package |

**2** This should be done alone. Perhaps limit the number of features to the five most attractive.

**3** Arrange the class into pairs for them to compare their ideas. The last question raises a more general issue — in the case of St Lucia it might be better to avoid all the hotels described and find a room in a small guest house where it's easier to meet the local people. All-inclusive resorts isolate tourists from the local people. Reassemble the class and ask everyone to share their views, particularly on the last question.

### B 1

Point out that this question should be considered as a general one: what kind of place (anywhere) would best suit each client — and which of the three hotels in St Lucia would best suit each client? This can be a whole-class activity or done in small groups.

## 2 Role play

Arrange the class into pairs. There's extra 'inside information' for the travel agents in **Activity 36** on SB page 125. Allow enough time for both students to have a turn at playing the travel agent's role.

## If there's time ...

Photocopy the English descriptions of some hotels in your students' region. (You may be able to find these in a local English-language tourist guide, or in a British or American tour operator's brochure.) Ask the students to highlight the most attractive features of each and then decide which to recommend to the four clients in Section B1, and perhaps do the role play in B2 as well.

## Finally ...

To save time in the next Lesson, ask everyone to prepare Lesson 30 Section A1. This involves reading the description on page 67.

#  30 The perfect hotel ...

## Aims

Begin by explaining to the class that this Lesson includes an extended role play / simulation. The aims of Lesson 30 are to improve their ability to:

- discuss the facilities offered by a hotel or resort
- work together as part of an English-speaking team.

## Vocabulary

in the resort description:

| | | |
|---|---|---|
| *budget travellers* | *stilts* | *villas* |
| *ferry* | *suites* | *virgin rainforest/jungle* |
| *outskirts* | *sweeping bays/* | *wilderness* |
| *panoramic views* | *views* | *wildlife* |
| *satellite TV* | *trekking* | |

## First of all ...

Ask everyone about the most luxurious hotel they've ever stayed (or worked) in:

- What facilities did it have?
- How was it different from other hotels you've stayed (or worked) in?
- What were the (other) guests like?
- What were the staff like?

### A1

To save time in class, the students should read the description and write down their answers at home *before* the Lesson. If this isn't feasible, the students could decide on their answers working together in pairs. Reassemble the class to go through the answers.

### Answers

1  Either by private ferry (from Lumut on the mainland) or by plane (to Pangkor Island) and then by boat (across the Straits)

2  None (only guests and staff)

3  125

4  Five  (Palm Grove Café, Samudra Restaurant, Royal Bay Beach Club, Oasis Bar, Chapmans Bar)

### 2

Arrange the class into groups of three or four. The purpose of this activity is to warm everyone up for the simulation that follows in Section B and to give them some ideas to consider. Reassemble the class for everyone to share ideas.

## B

To do justice to this simulation, allow plenty of time. If possible, get hold of some large sheets of plain paper and spare board markers or felt tip pens for Section B3.

Depending on the size of the class, arrange everyone into two, three or four (or more) teams. Each team should consist of around six students (but in a large class, larger teams would be OK too). Before they start, decide as a class how to fill the blanks in 1 and 2 with ideas from the class that are relevant to their local situations. Make sure everyone understands what they're supposed to be doing.

### 1

The teams decide on the location and clientele of their hotel.

### 2

Then they decide on facilities — limit of five in the rooms and five public facilities.

### 3

If possible, provide each team with two large sheets of paper (perhaps from a flip chart) so that they can draw a plan which can be seen at a distance (when they get to Section C). Suggest that they draw the plans first in pencil and then go over them with felt tips later (perhaps using a board marker, if you have one spare).

### 4

The teams prepare their presentation. Perhaps suggest that each member of the team prepares to talk about a different aspect of the hotel.

### 5

This can be done in the same Lesson, but if time is short or if the teams need more time, they could continue Section B4 as homework and then do C in the next Lesson.

Reassemble the class and ask each team to describe their hotel to the others. Voting could be restricted to other teams' proposals, unless there are only two teams.

## C Writing

This should be set as homework, but it may need to be prepared in class.

## Finally ...

Remind everyone what the aims of this Lesson were. Have they been achieved?

# Accommodation:
# Vocabulary puzzle

Photocopy the Vocabulary puzzle on page 105 for everyone to do
in pairs in class, or for homework.

## Answers

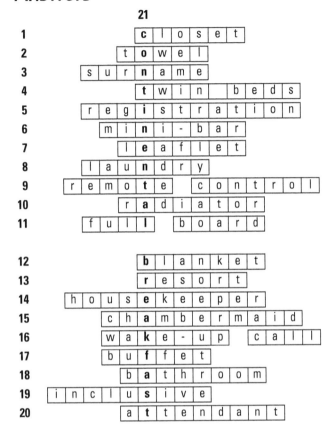

**21**

1. c l o s e t
2. t o w e l
3. s u r n a m e
4. t w i n   b e d s
5. r e g i s t r a t i o n
6. m i n i - b a r
7. l e a f l e t
8. l a u n d r y
9. r e m o t e   c o n t r o l
10. r a d i a t o r
11. f u l l   b o a r d

12. b l a n k e t
13. r e s o r t
14. h o u s e k e e p e r
15. c h a m b e r m a i d
16. w a k e - u p   c a l l
17. b u f f e t
18. b a t h r o o m
19. i n c l u s i v e
20. a t t e n d a n t

# 31 How would you like to pay?

> This Module (Lessons 31-34) covers the important situations where students may have to deal with payments or foreign exchange.

## Aims

Begin by explaining to the class the aims of Lesson 31, which are to improve their ability to:

- understand prices they are told
- say prices aloud clearly and fluently
- compare methods of payment.

## Vocabulary

| | |
|---|---|
| airport tax | house wine |
| altogether | mineral water |
| arithmetic | overcharged |
| note (US bill) | pay by credit card |
| change | pay in cash |
| (pay by) charge card | personal cheque |
| coins | purchases |
| credit card | sterling |
| credit facilities | total |
| currency | traveller's cheque (US traveler's |
| Eurocheque | check) |
| goods and services | voucher |

## First of all ...

Ask everyone to write down the following figures:

- how much they paid for their three most recent purchases (clothes, music, books, magazines, etc.)
- how much they paid for the last drink they had
- the cost of the last meal they had
- how much a new car costs
- how much they paid last time they went to the cinema.

Then ask some of the students to say some of their prices aloud (in no particular order) while the others write them down. Can the others guess what each purchase or expenditure was? There should be no difficulty with the new car, but the others may not be so easy to guess!

**A 1** Play the recording, pausing it between each speaker. More than one playing may be necessary for everyone to get all the information.

## Answers

1 by credit card   currency   coins
2 60   70   by credit card(s)   phone
3 by credit card   cost   credit
4 cash   50   traveller's cheques   change   currency
5 cash   by credit card

**2** Ask everyone to look at the table of payment methods at the top of SB page 68 and ask them if they know the difference between a *credit card* and a *charge card* — explain if necessary. (With a charge card like American Express, customers have to pay the whole bill when it comes each month; with a credit card like Visa, they can pay the bill in full, or defer payment and pay the bank interest on the amount they haven't paid. From a trader's point of view the difference is unimportant.)

Encourage everyone to compare different countries they have experience of — in particular the use of plastic as against cash in different countries. Are there any differences between the way younger and older people pay in their country?

## Transcript   3 minutes

**1**

INTERVIEWER:   Jane is a flight attendant, who sells duty free goods on board. Jane, how do customers pay?

JANE:   I would say most people pay by credit card now and a few with cash. You don't often get people paying with traveller's cheques any more. Um…it's all done by computers on the aircraft so people can give you a handful of this currency and a handful of that currency and you can take that. You can't take coins, any kind of coins at all these days, apart from sterling, so it…it's just notes. Um…and any change that involves coins has to be given in sterling. So I would say credit cards by far and away are the most usual form of payment.

**2**

INTERVIEWER:   Rod is a travel agent. Rod, how do customers pay?

ROD:   It's becoming more and more common for credit cards. The…the proportion of tickets that are actually paid for by cash and cheque has reduced quite substantially over the last three or four years and probably now 60 to 70% of bookings are paid for by credit card, which may be a telephone booking, where they phone us up and make a booking over the phone and pay by card over the phone or they come into the shop and do it.

**3**

INTERVIEWER: Janine is also a travel agent. Janine, how do customers pay?

JANINE: I think most people tend to pay using their credit cards. I mean, we…we accept all sorts of…we accept various methods of payment. Obviously, cash is extremely acceptable, um…people write us cheques, um…we also accept traveller's cheques and Eurocheques. But primarily people pay using their credit cards. Um…I think credit cards give extra protection when you're buying a holiday…um…and possibly people don't always have the funds to buy…um…you know, pay for their holiday in one go with cash so they spread the cost of it using credit facilities.

**4**

INTERVIEWER: Tom works in a sports store. Tom, how do your foreign customers pay?

TOM: We…er…do get a lot of foreign tourists and we always prefer it if they pay cash — a credit card transaction takes up time and it doesn't seem worth the effort for just a few dollars. I'd say most people pay cash when they're spending less than about $50. On the other hand if we insisted on cash all the time, we'd lose sales. We'll also accept traveller's cheques as long as they're in dollars, and then we give them change in cash. But we don't take foreign currency.

**5**

INTERVIEWER: Fiona works in a restaurant. Fiona, how do your foreign customers pay?

FIONA: I think if they're younger, it's usually cash and if they're older, it's probably credit cards.

## B **1** Ask the students to decide on the average prices of the items illustrated. This could be done in pairs or as a whole-class activity.

## 2 Role play

Arrange the class into pairs. Draw their attention to the phrases in the speech balloon before they begin the role play. Allow time for both to have a turn at playing the local person's role.

## C **1** Play the recording at least twice, pausing it from time to time as necessary. The prices quoted are printed **in bold italic type** in the Transcript.

### *Transcript* 1 minute 41 seconds

1 A double room costs **$79** a night including breakfast.

2 A round trip to Melbourne costs **$695** — that's an Apex fare.

3 The set meal costs **$14.95**, not including service.

4 You can get an all day ticket to use on public transport. It costs **$21**.

5 A taxi to the airport will cost you about **$35**.

6 There's an airport tax to pay — it's an extra **$7.50**.

7 A one-way ticket to Tokyo costs **22,000** yen.

8 I'm afraid you've been overcharged by **$24.55**. Sorry about that. I'll give you a refund right away.

## 2 Pronunciation

The prices are all recorded. Play the recording as a model before everyone practises the pronunciation — or afterwards as a key.

Some variations are possible (e.g. *fifteen dollars ninety-nine* or *fifteen dollars and ninety-nine cents*). Instead of *a hundred* or *a thousand* we can say *one hundred* or *one thousand*.

### *Transcript* 1 minute 45 seconds

1 Fifteen dollars ninety-nine cents

2 A hundred and fifteen New Zealand dollars

3 A hundred and fifty Australian dollars

4 A hundred and twenty-five Swiss francs

5 Seventeen dollars and seventy cents

6 Thirty-one thousand two hundred Japanese yen

7 A hundred and sixteen dollars

8 A hundred and sixty Saudi riyals

## D Role play

Arrange the class into pairs. One partner looks at **Activity 14** on SB page 114, the other at **Activity 32** on SB page 123. The role play is in two parts so that both partners have a turn at being the cashier.

Draw everyone's attention to the phrases in the speech balloons before they begin. Explain that they'll not only have to say the prices aloud but also add them up. They may be tempted to do the arithmetic in their own language, but ask everyone to do this in English so that the customer can follow the arithmetic.

## Finally …

1 Remind everyone what the aims of this Lesson were. Have they been achieved?

2 Ask everyone to look at a newspaper before the next Lesson and cut out the section on Tourist Rates, which gives exchange rates. It needn't be an English-language newspaper.

# 32 Changing money

## Aims

Begin by explaining to the class the aims of Lesson 32, which are to improve their ability to:

- deal with currency exchange situations
- deal with clients who want to pay by different methods.

## Vocabulary

| | | |
|---|---|---|
| *25% discount* | *expires* | *plus* |
| *calculator* | *less/minus* | *transaction* |
| *commission* | *local currency* | *wallet* |
| *exchange rate* | | |

+ the names of currencies the students are likely to encounter: Euros, Japanese yen, German marks, Swedish crowns, etc.

## First of all ...

Bring to class:

- a newspaper showing Tourist Rates in your students' currency
- some foreign currency notes and coins.

Show the notes and coins to the students and ask them to say approximately how much each is worth in their currency.

**A1** Arrange the class into pairs. Explain that this isn't a 'test' — just an opportunity to discuss different countries and currencies. Encourage them to guess the ones they don't know.

### Answers

baht /baːt/ — Thailand   dollars — Canada   forints — Hungary francs — Switzerland   pesos — Mexico   rands — South Africa   ringgits — Malaysia   roubles — Russia   rupees — India   yen — Japan

**2** The Euro.

**3** This could also be done in pairs — or combine the pairs into groups. Draw everyone's attention to the exchange in the speech balloon before they begin.

### Suggested answers

dollars — Australia, New Zealand, Singapore, East Caribbean, USA
francs — French-speaking Africa (CFA)
pesos — Argentina, Dominican Republic, Cuba, Chile, Philippines
rupees — Pakistan, Sri Lanka

**4** Use a newspaper showing Tourist Rates in your students' currency — it needn't be an English-language paper. If any students have brought a local newspaper with them, they should consult that.

The chart should be filled out with the rates in the students' own country.

**B1** Play the recording, pausing between each transaction. (Exchange rates fluctuate, so don't be embarrassed if the rates quoted seem out of date!)

### Answers

1   Sfr 500   $371.40

2   ¥20,000   $132.80

3   150 Singapore dollars   40 New Zealand dollars   US$123

4   $200   ¥26,613

### Transcript   3 minutes 11 seconds

**1**

CLERK:   Good morning.

CUSTOMER:   Good morning, I'd like to change some Swiss francs into US dollars, please.

CLERK:   Certainly, how much would you like to change?

CUSTOMER:   500 francs. Here you are.

CLERK:   Thank you. Today's rate is $75.28 for 100 francs ... so that's $376.40. Less $5 commission, so that's $371.40. So that's 50, 100, 150, 200, 250, 300, 350 dollars in fifties. And another 20 makes 370 dollars, and one makes 371 — and forty cents. There you are.

CUSTOMER:   Thank you. Goodbye.

CLERK:   You're welcome, goodbye.

**2**

CLERK:   Good morning.

CUSTOMER:   Good morning. Can I change this Japanese money into dollars, please?

CLERK:   Certainly, that's 20,000 yen, is that right?

CUSTOMER:   Yes — what's the exchange rate?

CLERK:   It's $7.14 for 1,000 yen. So that makes $142.80 altogether. Our commission is $10, so that's $132.80 ... 50, 100, 110, 120, 130, 131, 132 and 80 cents, there you are.

CUSTOMER:   OK, thank you. Goodbye.

CLERK:   Not at all, goodbye.

**3**

CUSTOMER:   Hi.

CLERK:   Hello, sir.

CUSTOMER:   I want to change this money into dollars — I've got 150 Singapore dollars and 40 New Zealand dollars.

CLERK:   Into US dollars?

CUSTOMER:   Yes.

CLERK:   All right, let's see ... that's...er...$98.70 for the Singapore dollars and $31.80 for the New Zealand dollars. That makes a total of $130.50 less commission of $7.50. That comes to $123. Here you are ... 50, 100, 110, 120 and 1, 2, 3 dollars.

Customer:   Thank you.

**4**

| | |
|---|---|
| CLERK: | Good morning. |
| CUSTOMER: | Hello, I'd like to buy some US dollars, please. |
| CLERK: | Certainly, how much would you like? |
| CUSTOMER: | I'd like 200, please. |
| CLERK: | $200 … that's 26,350 yen plus 1% commission, which makes 26,613 yen altogether. |
| CUSTOMER: | Did you say 1% commission? |
| CLERK: | Yes. |
| CUSTOMER: | Hmm. Oh, well, all right. Er…will you take a cheque? |
| CLERK: | Yes, of course, sir, no problem … |

**PHOTOCOPIABLE** © Cambridge University Press 2005

**2** If members of the class have a local newspaper, they should consult it — or use the same paper you consulted in A3. (Photocopy the Tourist Rates information, if possible.)

## 3 Role play

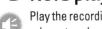

Play the recording again as a model for the role play. Write up the relevant exchange rates on the board from the Tourist Rates in a recent local newspaper.

Note that the students may need calculators. But ask them to assume for the sake of speed that there is no commission — or make it an easy 1% to be subtracted from the total.

Arrange the class into pairs for the role play.

**C1** Arrange the class into pairs. Some of these situations are quite tricky, but encourage the students to use their imaginations and initiative to come up with suitable replies. Draw their attention to the phrases in the speech balloon.

Reassemble the class to pool ideas — there are many different ways of dealing with each situation and two suggested replies for each are given below.

### *Suggested replies*

My Visa card expires tomorrow.
— Well, I'm afraid that makes it rather difficult, you see, because the transaction won't be put through till Monday. Is there any other way you could pay?
— That's quite all right, sir. If I put it through the machine now, it should be all right.

I seem to have forgotten my wallet.
— Could you leave something here as security while you go and get it, perhaps your watch?
— I wonder whether someone else in your party could pay the bill.

Is it all right if I pay you tomorrow?
— Yes, that's no problem at all, sir. You can collect the tickets then.
— Well, no, I'm sorry it has to be paid today if you want to secure the tickets. Could you come back later today — we close at 5.30.

I was expecting a 25 per cent discount on my bill, but you haven't given me any discount.
— I'm sorry about that, madam. I'm afraid you aren't entitled to a discount at weekends.
— Oh, I'm sorry, my mistake. You're quite right. I'll write it out again.

I'm afraid I only have dollars, not local currency.
— That's quite all right, sir, you can pay me in dollars.
— Well, I'm afraid we only take local currency. Or you could use a credit card.

$99? Is that your best price?
— Yes, I'm afraid it's company policy not to give discounts. Sorry about that.
— Well, maybe as a special favour we could make a small reduction. Shall we say $95 for cash?

I can get the same thing round the corner for $10 less.
— Well, I'm afraid that's our price for this item. We can't make a reduction.
— Well, sir, I'll just ask my manager if we can make a reduction — I'll be back as soon as I can.

Do you take sterling traveller's cheques?
— I'm afraid we don't. But there's a bank across the road — you could change some money there.
— Yes, certainly. Could you show me your passport, please?

**2** Arrange the class into *different* pairs. They should take it in turns to be the client and role play the situations they discussed in C1.

## Finally …

Remind everyone what the aims of this Lesson were. Have they been achieved?

# 33 Explaining the bill

## Aims

Begin by explaining to the class the aims of Lesson 33, which are to improve their ability to:

- explain a bill to a client
- explain the various charges on a bill.

## Vocabulary

| | |
|---|---|
| amount | mini-bar |
| balance due | miscellaneous |
| bill (US check) | posting |
| Bermuda Plan (= room and full American breakfast) | postings (= charges sent to the accounts office) |
| charges | receipt |
| Continental Plan (= room and continental breakfast) | reference number |
| | sailboat (GB sailing boat) |
| cover charge | service charge |
| deliberate mistake | shrimp cocktail (GB prawn |
| front desk (GB reception) | cocktail) |
| item/itemise | toiletries |

## First of all …

Bring to class copies of some real hotel and restaurant bills you've collected. Show them to the class and ask the students to say what questions they'd ask if they'd received the same bills (reasons for the charges, meaning of abbreviations, illegible handwriting, whether service is included, etc.).

 **A**
Play the recording. It will take more than one listening for everyone to note down all the information. Explain to everyone that they don't need to repeat their notes for the Summary of Charges at the foot of the bill on SB page 72.

The students should compare their notes in pairs before you reassemble the class and go through the answers. (Computerised bills are often more complicated and impenetrable than this one!)

## Suggested answers

**Sunset**
BEACH RESORT

| DATE | REFERENCE | DESCRIPTION | AMOUNT |
|---|---|---|---|
| 05 Jan | 4668 | PALM BEACH drinks at the bar | 7.50 |
| 05 Jan | 1955 | SPORTS tennis court hire + equipment | 12.00 |
| 05 Jan | R 101 | BERMUDA PLAN room number 101 + full American breakfast | 180.00 |
| 06 Jan | 3891 | POOL SIDE snack | 6.30 |
| 06 Jan | 12345 | TELEX & FAX fax | 18.00 |
| 06 Jan | 3291 | ROOM SERVICE room service | 10.00 |
| 06 Jan | 4668 | PALM BEACH drinks at the bar | 5.50 |
| 06 Jan | 9832 | COFFEE HSE lunch in Coffee House | 12.00 |
| 06 Jan | 1291 | WTR SPORTS rental of sailboat | 15.00 |
| 06 Jan | R 101 | BERMUDA PLAN room + breakfast | 180.00 |
| 07 Jan | 3892 | POOL SIDE snack (?) | 8.00 |
| 07 Jan | 29871 | PALM BEACH drinks at the bar | 9.00 |
| 07 Jan | 12010 | MISCELLANEOUS purchase of guide book from Front Desk | 15.00 |
| 07 Jan | R 101 | BERMUDA PLAN room + breakfast | 180.00 |
| | | BALANCE DUE.... | 658.30 |

## Transcript   2 minutes 14 seconds

GUEST: Can I have my bill, please?

CASHIER: Yes, certainly, Mr Cook, here you are. The individual charges are itemised and the receipts are here.

GUEST: OK … Oh, can you just explain what the extras are?

CASHIER: Yes, certainly, 'Palm Beach' is the name of the main bar, and you had drinks at the bar on the 5th and again on the 6th. Let's see, all…all the receipts are here, yeah, here's the check you signed on the 5th and here's the one from the 6th.

GUEST: OK, what about 'Sports'?

CASHIER: Did you play tennis on the 5th?

GUEST: Yes, that's right.

CASHIER: Well, that charge is for the hire of the court and tennis equipment.

GUEST: I see, what is 'Bermuda Plan'?

CASHIER: That's your room charge — it's the charge for your room and for full American breakfast. R 101 means Room 101.

GUEST: Right. And what about 'Pool Side'?

CASHIER: Did you have a drink at the snack bar beside the swimming pool?

GUEST: Oh, yes, I must have done. And then there's 'Telex and Fax' — I did send a fax. And 'Room Service' — I understand that. And Palm Beach again, and then what's this?

CASHIER: Oh, that's…that's 'Coffee House' — did you have lunch in the Coffee House on the 6th?

GUEST: That's right, I did. OK, what's this next one?

| CASHIER: | 'Water Sports' — that's either renting a windsurfer or a sailboat. |
| GUEST: | Oh, yes. I rented a sailboat — I thought it was free, though. |
| CASHIER: | No, I'm afraid not — according to the receipt here you had it out for two hours. |
| GUEST: | Yes, I did. OK, the rest are the same again — except for this one: 'Miscellaneous'. What do you think that is? |
| CASHIER: | Oh, I've no idea, I'm afraid. I'll just check that receipt for that … Yes, here it is: it's for a guide book, which you bought from the Front Desk. |
| GUEST: | Oh, yes, I remember. Right, good. Here's my Visa card. |
| CASHIER: | Thank you very much, Mr Cook. … Could you just sign here on the dotted line? |
| GUEST: | Certainly yes. … There you are. |
| CASHIER: | Thank you very much, Mr Cook. I do hope you enjoyed your stay with us. |
| GUEST: | I did, yes. Thank you. |
| CASHIER: | And we hope to see you again before too long. |
| GUEST: | I hope so, too. Goodbye. |
| CASHIER: | Goodbye, Mr Cook. Have a good journey… |

## B Role play

Before arranging the class into pairs, perhaps play the recording for A again to give everyone some ideas on how to approach the speech balloons. Draw everyone's attention to the phrases in the speech balloons. Allow enough time for both partners to have a turn at being the cashier and explaining the bill — they should change roles after *11 July* on the bill.

## C Role play

Arrange the class into different pairs. One partner looks at **Activity 10** on SB page 112, the other at **Activity 25** on SB page 120. Draw everyone's attention to the phrases in the speech balloons on page 74 *and* in the Activity before they begin. The role play is in two parts. The reason why the instructions tell the waiter/waitress to make at least one deliberate mistake is so that the customer listens carefully and checks the bill — just as an alert customer would do in real life.

## Finally …

Remind everyone what the aims of this Lesson were. Have they been achieved?

# 34 Is service included?

## Aims

Begin by explaining to the class the aims of Lesson 34, which are to improve their ability to:

- understand native speakers of English talking at their natural speed
- discuss, explain and justify tipping customs.

## Vocabulary

| | |
| --- | --- |
| *approximate* | *incurred* |
| *bus conductor* | *major hotel* |
| *compulsory* | *meter fare* |
| *customary* | *optional* |
| *developed countries* | *percentage* |
| *exact sum* | *round up to the nearest dollar* |
| *hairdresser* | *toilet attendant* |

## First of all …

Ask the students about foreign tourists in their country:

- Do visitors tend to over-tip or under-tip?
- Do some nationalities tip more generously than others?

- What do you do if you haven't received the expected tip from a client? Do you say anything or just grin and bear it?

**A1** Play the recording, pausing it between each speaker. There's a lot of information to note down, so it may have to be played more than twice. (The information about Japan and Australia is dealt with in Step 3.)

### Suggested answers

(including answers for Step 3)

| *Will they expect a tip? How much should I give?* | | | | | |
| --- | --- | --- | --- | --- | --- |
| | USA | UK | France | Japan | Australia |
| Waiter/Waitress | 15–20% | 10–15% | included | included | 10% for good service |
| Barman/Barmaid | 15% | nothing | small change only | nothing | nothing |
| Hotel porter | $1–2 per bag | £1 per bag (only big hotels) | 10–15 francs per bag | nothing | nothing |
| Hotel maid | $2 per night | $2 per night (optional) | 10 francs per night | nothing | nothing |
| Taxi driver | 15% of meter fare | 10% | 10–15% | nothing | |

**2** Discuss the question as a whole-class activity. If your students *are* French, do they agree with what was said about France?

**3** Arrange the class into pairs or do this as a whole-class activity. If done in pairs, reassemble the class to go through the answers. (See chart above.) Ask any Japanese students you may have if they agree with the text.

### *Transcript*  2 minutes 6 seconds

MAN: In the…er…USA…er…often waiters and waitresses they don't actually receive that much money up front, they rely a lot on tips. So…er…if you go to a restaurant, you're looking at about a 15 to 20 per cent tip. And barmen are usually around 15 per cent. Er…if you go into a hotel, a hotel porter, usually give him $1, $2 per bag. Or if it's a hotel maid, they usually expect about $2 for each night of your stay. A taxi driver expects to get around 15 per cent of the meter fare.

WOMAN: Well, in Britain, um…you'd add about, well, 10 to 15 per cent onto a restaurant bill. A barman, well, wouldn't usually expect a tip. In a hotel, um…the person who carries your bags, well, you'd give them around about £1 a bag, but only in a really big hotel. Your maid, your room maid, you'd give her about £2 for each night, but really that's up to you. Taxi drivers, huh, they expect around 10 per cent of the fare.

MAN: Er…in France, eating out at a restaurant: you'll find it's…it's really unusual to leave a tip because the…the service charge would be included in the bill. Um…a barman: well, he wouldn't expect much, maybe…maybe a bit of small change. In a hotel: the…er…porter or whoever's taking your bags upstairs would expect somewhere in the region of between 5 to 10 francs…er…per bag. The chambermaid: um…a little bit more, maybe about 10 francs per night. And…er…taxis: well, a taxi driver is going to expect in the region — or you would expect to pay between 10…add 10 to 15 per cent to the fare.

**PHOTOCOPIABLE**  © Cambridge University Press 2005

**B1** Arrange the class into an even number of groups of three or four. There are four columns in the chart for each member of the group's answers. Make sure everyone understands the system for recording answers before they begin.

**2** Combine the groups into larger groups for them to compare their answers.

## 3 Role play

Arrange the class into pairs for this role play. If time is limited, there's no need for two turns.

## 4 Writing

This should be done as homework. The paragraph should be similar in style to one of the paragraphs on SB page 74. (If your students are Japanese, perhaps ask them to write advice for Japanese visitors to the USA or the UK.)

## Finally …

Remind everyone what the aims of this Lesson were. Have they been achieved?

## Money: Vocabulary puzzle

Photocopy the Vocabulary puzzle on page 106 for everyone to do in pairs in class, or for homework.

### *Answers*

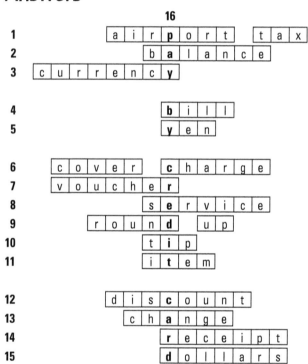

1  a i r **p** o r t   t a **x**  (16)
2  **b** a l a n c e
3  c u r r e n c **y**
4  **b** i l l
5  **y** e n
6  c o v e r   **c** h a r g e
7  v o u c h e **r**
8  s **e** r v i c e
9  r o u n **d**   u p
10  t **i** p
11  i **t** e m
12  d i s **c** o u n t
13  c h **a** n g e
14  r **e** c e i p t
15  **d** o l l a r s

# 35 To and from the airport

This Module (Lessons 35–40) covers public transport, car rental and motoring, as well as giving directions to clients on how to get to different local places.

## Aim

Begin by explaining to the class the aim of Lesson 35, which is to improve their ability to:

• explain and recommend routes by public transport.

## Vocabulary

cab/taxi ride
complicated
downtown
helicopter
internal flight/domestic
  flight
local resident

monorail
shuttle bus
suburban train
subway/metro (GB underground)
transfer

**A1** Ask everyone to read the guide book extract about Tokyo Airport and write *exactly what they'd say* to a client who asked them each of the questions.

### Suggested answers

1  It takes around 1 hour.

2  It costs a small fortune (a lot of money). Public transport is cheaper and quicker.

3  Not really — the train is quicker.

4  You need to allow at least three hours if the internal flight leaves from Haneda.

5  Probably by train: the Narita Express goes direct to downtown Tokyo.

**2** Play the recording, pausing between each conversation. The answers on the right have to be rearranged to match the questions on the left. (There is now a new AirTrain connecting JFK with Jamaica and Howard Beach stations. This has replaced the free shuttle bus to Howard Beach station. It is now quite esy to catch Subway lines J, Z and A.)

### Answers

1  1¹⁄₂ hours

2  1 hour

3  20 mins

4  1¹⁄₄ hours

5  30 mins

6  2 hours

7  15 mins

## Transcript   2 minutes 50 seconds

**1**

| | |
|---|---|
| MAN: | What's the cheapest way of getting to downtown Manhattan from JFK? |
| TRAVEL AGENT: | Mm…well, the cheapest way is by bus and subway, but that's, you know…I don't know … |
| MAN: | But what? |
| TRAVEL AGENT: | Well, it's kind of complicated: you have to get a shuttle bus to Howard Beach subway station and then get a subway train. It's not a good idea, especially if you're tired after your flight and have luggage and…and you're on your own … |
| MAN: | How long does it take? |
| TRAVEL AGENT: | Well, it takes about an hour and a half. But, I mean, even if you take a cab, it might take that long. |
| MAN: | What do you recommend? |
| TRAVEL AGENT: | Well … |

**2**

| | |
|---|---|
| WOMAN: | … so what's the best way of getting into Manhattan? |
| TRAVEL AGENT: | Well, the best way is by cab. |
| WOMAN: | But that's expensive, isn't it? |
| TRAVEL AGENT: | Yeah, but there's also the Carey Airport Express bus, which costs about $10, I think. Well, that's almost as quick as a cab. It usually takes about an hour, depending on the traffic. And they go to Grand Central Station and Port Authority Bus Terminal. |
| WOMAN: | I see, how often do they run? |
| TRAVEL AGENT: | Oh, well, they…they run every 20 minutes. Or you can take a Gray Line Air Shuttle — they'll drop you anywhere between 23rd and 63rd Street. That costs a bit more but they're much more convenient. |
| WOMAN: | And they take about the same time, do they? |
| TRAVEL AGENT: | Yeah, about an hour and a quarter — it all depends. |

**3**

| | |
|---|---|
| MAN: | … when I get to New York, is it easy to get to the centre of the city? |
| TRAVEL AGENT: | Oh, sure, you can just take a cab. |
| MAN: | I see, and about how much will that cost? |
| TRAVEL AGENT: | Well, er…when I last went, it cost about $30 — the rides are metered and you should add another 10 to 15 per cent for a tip. |
| MAN: | I see, and how long will it take? |
| TRAVEL AGENT: | It might take 30 minutes if you're lucky … |
| MAN: | And if I'm unlucky? |
| TRAVEL AGENT: | It could take two hours if you arrive at a busy time. |
| MAN: | Hmm … |

| TRAVEL AGENT: | Or … or you…you could take a helicopter — it's expensive but a wonderful way to arrive in Manhattan. An unforgettable 15-minute flight. It costs two to three times the cab fare. |
| MAN: | Right! That's the way for me! Can I book that now? |
| TRAVEL AGENT: | There's no need. Just go to TWA International Terminal Gate 37. They go every few minutes. |

*PHOTOCOPIABLE* © Cambridge University Press 2005

**B1** Arrange the class into groups of three or four. After they've considered all the questions, reassemble the class and let them compare their ideas.

## 2 Role play

Arrange the class into pairs. Explain that this role play is in four parts because the four visitors may go by different routes, depending on the amount of luggage they have, their budget, their fitness and the amount of time they have. Draw everyone's attention to the instructions and to the speech balloons. Allow enough time for all four parts — or just two if time is short.

## Finally …

Remind everyone what the aim of this Lesson was. Has it been achieved?

# 36 Local knowledge

## Aims

Begin by explaining to the class the aims of Lesson 36, which are to improve their ability to:

- give visitors the benefit of their knowledge of the area they live or work in
- respond to enquiries about their locality.

## Vocabulary

| | |
| --- | --- |
| *a 24-hour ticket* | *network* |
| *baby-sitting/dog-sitting* | *tourist attractions* |
| *bureau de change/exchange office* | *tram* |
| *department store* | *validated* |
| *favour* | *walking stick* |

## First of all …

As it's often difficult for students to realise that their own, familiar city might be strange for a visitor, ask them to remember the first time they visited another city (preferably in another country):

- What was strange about the place?
- How easy was it to find your way around?
- How does the public transport system there work?
- Did anything go wrong while you were there?

**A1** Play the recording, pausing at the places marked with stars ★★★ in the Transcript if necessary.

The task focuses on the questions, but not the answers. If there's time, play the recording again and ask everyone to note down what the speaker does/did or says/said in reply to each question.

## Answers

1 Can you recommend a good hotel near here?
2 How do I get to the rail station?
3 Why do you drive on the left in Britain?
4 Where can I find a shop that sells walking sticks?
5 Can you look after my dog for an hour while I go shopping?
6 Can you book a flight to Tokyo for me?

**2** Reassemble the class and brainstorm further questions.

## Suggested questions

When are the stores open?

Where can I change some traveller's cheques?

Can you recommend a nice day out?

Can I buy a one-day bus/metro pass here?

## Transcript  2 minutes 40 seconds

INTERVIEWER:   What are the most common questions people ask?
FIRST INFORMATION OFFICER:  We aren't allowed to answer the most common question we get asked, that's because we can't favour any particular place. The question is: 'Can you recommend a good hotel near here?' — so we try to narrow down the choices by asking, 'What kind of hotel do you like? What price range are you looking for? What facilities do you want: swimming pool, family rooms and…and…er…so on?'
SECOND INFORMATION OFFICER:  We do get asked all kinds of questions about bus services and rail services, but I suppose the most common question that we get asked is…er: 'How do I get to the rail station?' Well, it's twenty minutes' walk from

here, so if they aren't in a hurry and they don't look too old or unfit, then I show them the route on the map. Or I tell them there's a bus every ten minutes from the main square just around the corner from here.

★★★

INTERVIEWER: What was the most difficult question?

FIRST INFORMATION OFFICER: Mm, yeah, an American came in the other day and the only thing he wanted to know was: 'Why do you drive on the left in Britain?' I said I didn't know. But then I asked him: 'Why do you drive on the right in America?' and he couldn't answer that. And there was a Japanese person waiting behind who said they drive on the left there, too.

SECOND INFORMATION OFFICER: People often ask where they can *buy* various things, you know, like books, umbrellas, and so on, but the most difficult question was: 'Where can I find a shop that sells walking sticks?' Well, I had no idea, but we looked it up in the Yellow Pages and there's a shop two blocks from here — apparently, they're the most famous walking stick makers in the country!

★★★

INTERVIEWER: What was the most unusual question?

FIRST INFORMATION OFFICER: Mm, a man came in with a dog and he asked me: 'Can you look after my dog for an hour while I go shopping?' I said I couldn't: we give information not a dog-sitting service!

SECOND INFORMATION OFFICER: The other day a woman came into the office and she said to me: 'Can you book a flight to Tokyo for me?' Well, I had to explain that we *can* book train tickets and coach tickets but not airline tickets. Anyway, there's a travel agency just opposite, so I told her to go over there.

**B** Play the recording while everyone notes down their answers. Afterwards (or between playings) the students should compare their answers with a partner.

## Suggested answers

| Bus or metro tickets | 3 marks (24-hour ticket 10 marks) ticket machines |
|---|---|
| Bank opening hours | Monday to Friday: 9–6   Saturday: 9–1 Sunday: closed |
| | Other places to change money: main railway station or bureaux de change |
| Department stores | Monday to Friday: 9–8   Saturday: 9–4 Sunday: closed |

## Transcript   1 minute 47 seconds

**1**

INFORMATION OFFICER:   Hello, can I help you?

VISITOR:   Oh, yes, I want to travel on the subway. How much do tickets cost?

INFORMATION OFFICER:   Well, a ticket costs 3 marks and you can go anywhere on the network — subway, elevated trains and buses. But if you're going to make several journeys, I'd recommend a 24-hour ticket and that's 10 marks.

VISITOR:   Oh, I see, and where can I get a ticket?

INFORMATION OFFICER:   From a ticket machine at any station: the machines take notes and coins — and they give change.

**2**

INFORMATION OFFICER:   Hello, can I help you?

VISITOR:   Ah, yes, er…thanks. Um…when are the banks open?

INFORMATION OFFICER:   Well, on weekdays they're open from 9 till 6 and on Saturdays from 9 until 1 o'clock. They're closed on Sundays.

VISITOR:   Oh, well, er…well, where can I change money when the banks are closed?

INFORMATION OFFICER:   You can change money any time at the main railway station. Or one of the bureaux de change.

**3**

INFORMATION OFFICER:   Hello, can I help you?

VISITOR:   Yes, it's Saturday afternoon and all the shops are closed. When are they open?

INFORMATION OFFICER:   Well, on Saturdays the stores are open from about 9am, and they all close at 4pm. It's 4.30 now, so that's why they're closed.

VISITOR:   Oh, I see! What about tomorrow, Sunday? Are they closed then?

INFORMATION OFFICER:   Yes, I'm afraid so, but on weekdays most stores are open from about 9am until 8pm.

VISITOR:   It's a pity I'm leaving first thing on Monday, isn't it?

**C1** Arrange the class into groups of three or four. If your students aren't knowledgeable about their own town or city, this may have to be continued as homework — or prepared before the Lesson.

Reassemble the class in the hope that any missing information can be supplied by another group.

## 2 Role play

Arrange the students into pairs. Draw everyone's attention to the phrases in the speech balloon. If time allows, they should role play several conversations, changing roles after each one. The tourists' questions should mainly focus on the information already discussed in C1 — but they can ask other questions if they like.

## Finally …

Remind everyone what the aims of this Lesson were. Have they been achieved?

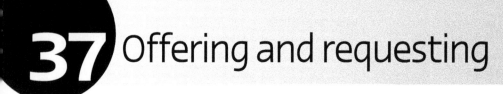

# 37 Offering and requesting

## Aims

Begin by explaining to the class the aims of Lesson 37, which are to improve their ability to:

- offer to do things for clients
- ask clients to do things.

These functions are not restricted to Travelling around situations.

## Vocabulary

| | |
|---|---|
| blocking the exit | light bulb |
| carry-on bag | local newspaper |
| clock-radio | lost property |
| driving licence | maintenance man |
| engaged (US busy) | swimsuit |
| large denomination bank note | |

**A 1** As a warm-up, ask everyone to look at the picture. What do they think the guest wants and what will the receptionist offer to do for them?

Play the recording, pausing after each conversation.

### Answers

phone the railway station for Mr White

lend Mrs Brown a swimsuit

show Miss Green how to operate the fax machine

give Mr Black a wake-up (early morning) call

**2** Arrange the class into pairs and then play the recording again. After the pairs have made their decisions, reassemble the class and pool ideas.

### Suggested answers

She was least polite to Miss Green.

The least sensible idea was asking the maintenance man to fix Mr Black's clock-radio (radio alarm). It would have been better to replace it — they're cheap enough.

### Transcript  1 minute 54 seconds

**1**

RECEPTIONIST: Hello, Mr White.
GUEST: Hello, do you know anything about trains to Manchester? I want to go there next Monday.
RECEPTIONIST: Well, the timetable changes on Sunday and we don't have a copy of the new one yet.
GUEST: Well, I need to get there by lunchtime.
RECEPTIONIST: Would you like me to ring the enquiry office and find out for you?
GUEST: Oh, yes, please.
RECEPTIONIST: All right. … It's engaged, I'll try again in a couple of minutes.
GUEST: All right, er…well, I'm just going for a walk, I'll be back in an hour or so …

**2**

RECEPTIONIST: Hello, Mrs Brown.
GUEST: Hello, I wonder if you could help me.
RECEPTIONIST: Certainly, what can I do for you?
GUEST: Well, I'd like to use the pool but I haven't got a swimsuit.
RECEPTIONIST: Oh. Well, I could look in the lost property box and see if there's one there, if you like.
GUEST: Oh, all right, thanks.
RECEPTIONIST: Let's see … here we are. Do you think this would be all right?
GUEST: Well, it looks the right size but …

**3**

RECEPTIONIST: Hello, Miss Green.
GUEST: Hello, can I send a fax, please?
RECEPTIONIST: Certainly, how many pages are there?
GUEST: Well, it's a bit complicated — can I do it myself?
RECEPTIONIST: All right, come into the office. I'll show you how to work the machine.
GUEST: Great, thanks.

**4**

RECEPTIONIST: Hello, Mr Black.
GUEST: Hello, the clock-radio in my room doesn't seem to work.
RECEPTIONIST: Oh, dear, they're always going wrong. Well, I'll ask the maintenance man to look at it for you. But he may not be able to fix it.
GUEST: Oh, dear, I need it to wake me up in the morning.
RECEPTIONIST: Shall I put you down for an early morning call just in case?
GUEST: That's probably best. At 7 o'clock.
RECEPTIONIST: All right, Mr Black.
GUEST: Thanks.

**3** Keep the same pairs. Some pairs may need input from other students if any of the situations seems to present problems. If necessary, combine the pairs into groups or reassemble the class. There are various ways of helping each of the clients besides the suggestions here.

### Suggested answers

I'd offer to …

look in the local newspaper for the guest or give the guest a local newspaper to look at.

send someone up to replace it.

move him or her to another quieter room as soon as possible.

prepare his or her bill this evening.

order a taxi for him or her.

change it for him or her or get the porter to go to the bank for the guest.

## 4 Role play

Arrange the class into different pairs. Draw everyone's attention to the phrases in the speech balloon. The partners should alternate roles of guest and member of staff.

## B1 Grammar

This can be done in pairs or alone. The students only need to write one sentence for each situation, not two as here. Perhaps point out that the *Excuse me* can be omitted and *please* can be added in most cases.

### Suggested answers

1 Excuse me. Would you mind moving your car?
I'm sorry, but could I ask you to move your car, please?

2 I'm sorry, but could I ask you to pay in cash, please?
Would you mind paying in cash, please?

3 Would you mind showing me your driving licence, please?
I'm sorry, but could I ask you to show me your driving licence, please?

4 I'm sorry, but could I ask you to wait a moment, please?
Would you mind waiting a moment, please?

5 Excuse me. Would you mind not sitting there, please?
I'm sorry, but could I ask you not to sit there, please?

## 2

This can also be done in pairs or alone. If spoken very politely, many of the 'impolite' reasons can sound polite. When the best reasons have been agreed, the students can practise making the request and giving the reasons in a polite and friendly way.

### Suggested answers

1 because it's blocking the exit.

2 because we only accept credit cards for amounts over $10.

3 because I need to make a note of the number.

4 because there are no tables free.

5 because this table is reserved.

Arrange the class into pairs or do this as a whole-class activity.

## C Role play

Arrange the class into pairs. Draw everyone's attention to the phrases in the speech balloon. Reiterate the need to sound polite — and ask the client to correct the member of staff if he or she doesn't sound polite.

## Finally ...

1 Draw everyone's attention to the Advice boxes.

2 Remind everyone what the aims of this Lesson were. Have they been achieved?

3 To save time in Lesson 38, ask everyone to read the text on SB page 83 and find the answers to the questions about it in C.

# 38 Car rental

## Aims

Begin by explaining to the class the aims of Lesson 38, which are to improve their ability to:

- deal with car hire situations

- find specific information within an authentic text — ignoring irrelevant points and unknown vocabulary.

## Vocabulary

| brochure | pick-up location | unlimited mileage |
|---|---|---|
| car hire/rental | return/drop-off location | |

in the text:

| authorised | invoice | steal/stolen |
|---|---|---|
| breakdown | petrol (US gas) | surcharge |
| damage | pre-bookable | theft |
| fuel | refunded | third party cover |
| in advance | rural | unspoilt |
| insurance | secluded | vandalism |

## First of all ...

Find out if anyone has ever rented a car (or been with a friend or family member who rented one):

- What documents had to be shown?

- What forms had to be filled in?

- What information was required on the main form?

- How was payment made?

- Did anything exciting or unfortunate happen during the rental period?

 Play the recording twice, pausing it between the two playings for everyone to compare the answers they've got so far with a partner. The second time through, maybe pause the recording after each important piece of information.

## Answers

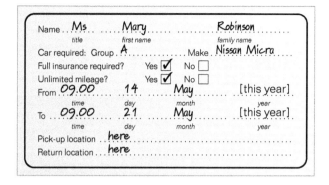

Name ..Ms....... Mary........... Robinson......
         _title_         _first name_         _family name_

Car required: Group ..A.......... Make ..Nissan Micra......

Full insurance required?   Yes ☑  No ☐

Unlimited mileage?   Yes ☑  No ☐

From ..09.00....... 14...... May....... [this year]
      _time_       _day_    _month_     _year_

To ..09.00....... 21...... May....... [this year]
      _time_       _day_    _month_     _year_

Pick-up location ...here......

Return location ...here......

## Transcript   1 minute 14 seconds

WOMAN: Good evening.

RENTAL CLERK: Good evening, madam. How can I help you?

WOMAN: Well, I want to rent a car. Do you have any available?

RENTAL CLERK: Yes, certainly, we've got most groups available now.

WOMAN: Oh, good. Can I have one then?

RENTAL CLERK: Of course, but I've got to take your details first.

WOMAN: Oh, sure.

RENTAL CLERK: Now, first of all your name?

WOMAN: My name's Ms Mary Robinson, that's ROBINSON.

RENTAL CLERK: And what kind of car would you like?

WOMAN: Well, just a small one — it's just for me.

RENTAL CLERK: Ah, group A — er…we've got a Nissan Micra or an Opel Corsa — any preference?

WOMAN: Oh … a Nissan.

RENTAL CLERK: And will you be requiring full insurance?

WOMAN: Yes.

RENTAL CLERK: Good. Do you want unlimited mileage, or do you want to pay for each kilometre you travel?

WOMAN: Oh, no, unlimited mileage.

RENTAL CLERK: Uhuh. And when do you want the car from?

WOMAN: Well, from tomorrow for seven days — can I pick it up at 9am?

RENTAL CLERK: Yes, certainly. So that's 9 o'clock on the 14th of May. Returning the car here?

WOMAN: Yes, at the same time on the 21st of May.

RENTAL CLERK: Fine. So all I need to do now is to take your driving licence details and take an imprint of your credit card.

WOMAN: All right. Here you are.

**PHOTOCOPIABLE** © Cambridge University Press 2005

**B** If your students are likely to find this very difficult, play them the recording of the model version of the dialogue once through before they attempt to fill the blanks. Filling the blanks can be done in pairs or alone.

Play the model version and discuss any possible variations to the suggestions **_in bold italic type_**.

## Transcript   1 minute 1 second

CLERK: Good morning. How can I help you?

CLIENT: Good morning. Can I arrange car rental here?

CLERK: **_Yes, certainly, sir. When would you like the car?_**

CLIENT: For three days, starting tomorrow morning.

CLERK: **_All right. And what kind of car would you like?_**

CLIENT: I don't really mind, but I only need a small one.

CLERK: **_I have a Group B car, a Ford Fiesta, available. Would that be all right?_**

CLIENT: That sounds fine. How much will it cost?

CLERK: **_The cost per day is $35, sir._**

CLIENT: Does that include all the extras?

CLERK: **_Yes, that's with unlimited mileage and full insurance._**

CLIENT: Excellent! Well, can I do the paperwork now, to save time tomorrow?

CLERK: **_Certainly. I'll just need to fill in this form with your details._**

CLIENT: Good. Right, here's my driver's licence and my passport.

CLERK: **_And how will you be paying for the car, sir?_**

CLIENT: By Visa — here's my card …

**PHOTOCOPIABLE** © Cambridge University Press 2005

**C** To save time in class, the students could prepare the text and do this exercise at home before the Lesson. However, if it's done in class it's good practice in scanning a text for specific information — and disregarding irrelevant points and unfamiliar vocabulary.

## Answers

1  No (unlimited mileage)

2  Yes (theft)

3  Yes (subject to an excess, which means you pay for the first £50 or £100 of any claim for such damage)

4  Not unless you want to insure its contents

5  No (except on some extras)

6  No (delivered to your hotel)

7  Yes (approximately 500 drachmas a day)

8  Yes (charges for additional drivers)

9  Not this year (minimum driving age 21)

10  Your driving licence

## **D** Role play

Arrange the class into pairs. One should look at **Activity 13** on SB page 114, the other at **Activity 28** on SB page 122. The role play is in two parts and involves taking a booking for a car. Perhaps play the recording for A again to show everyone how their conversation might go.

## Finally …

1  Remind everyone what the aims of this Lesson were. Have they been achieved?

2  To save time in Lesson 39, ask the class to read the text on SB page 85 before the next Lesson. If you think it might help, explain some of the vocabulary in the text beforehand (see the second Vocabulary list for Lesson 39).

# 39 Motoring

## Aim

Begin by explaining to the class the aim of Lesson 39, which is to improve their ability to:

- give advice to clients about driving rules and regulations, motoring habits and road dangers in their country.

## Vocabulary

*cyclist*
*equivalent*
*freeway/highway (GB motorway)*
*motor vehicle*
*one-way*
*overtake*
*pedestrian (zebra) crossing*

*picnic site*
*(road) sign*
*roundabout*
*seat belt*
*speed limit*
*traffic light*

in the text:
*buckle up*
*call 911 (emergency)*
*claim*
*convertible*
*counter personnel*
*disabled (GB broken down)*
*flashing*
*headlights*

*hitch hiker*
*if applicable*
*malfunctioning*
*prior to*
*service station*
*trunk (GB boot)*
*unattended*
*wave someone down*

## First of all ...

Find out if anyone has driven (or been driven) in a foreign country.

- How was it different from driving or being driven in your country?
- What was the most alarming thing about it?
- Which side of the road do people drive on?

**A1** Ask everyone to look at the photos and discuss the questions. The pictures show a pedestrian crossing in the UK (with cars stopping for people to cross) and a not-very-busy city intersection in Asia.

**2** Play the recording, pausing it between the two interviews. Perhaps point out, if it seems relevant, that each state in the USA has its own driving laws (and speed limits) but in the UK the same laws apply nationwide. The task helps the students to focus on the main points of information the speakers give.

## Answers

| | |
|---|---|
| They drive on the left. | Britain |
| They drive on the right. | USA |
| Drivers do stop at pedestrian crossings to let people cross. | Britain |
| Everyone in the car must wear a seat belt. | Britain |
| Most drivers seem to ignore speed limits. | USA |
| The speed limit is 30 mph in towns. | Britain |
| The speed limit is 70 mph on motorways/ highways. | Britain |
| There are a lot of roundabouts. | Britain |
| There are special lanes for cars carrying passengers. | USA |
| You can overtake on the inside. | USA |
| You can turn right at a red traffic light. | USA |

**3** Arrange the class into groups for them to discuss this question, but reassemble the class if there's any disagreement.

## If there's time ...

Play the recording again. Ask the students to pick up more little bits of interesting information about driving in the USA and the UK, which weren't covered in the task earlier (car sharing, slow driving, honking, whether drivers observe speed limits, etc.).

## Transcript  3 minutes 7 seconds

INTERVIEWER: Richard, have you driven anywhere else, apart from your own country?

RICHARD: Yep, I've actually...er...driven abroad in the States. I've been there a couple of times and both times I hired a car.

INTERVIEWER: And did anything surprise you about driving there?

RICHARD: I think what surprised me about driving in the States was how well they drove, actually. Much better than over here, far more polite.

INTERVIEWER: Was it difficult to get used to?

RICHARD: Um...yeah, it was in a way. The first problem, of course, you drive on the...the other side of the road — that's always a...a bit of a headache to begin with. Um...and also odd things like...er...you can turn right at a red traffic light if nothing's coming the other way, you can just turn right and...like...you'd forget that and you'd get 'honk honk' behind you, getting you to move on. And also on the freeways over there you can overtake on either side. And also they have special lanes...er...for people with more than two people in the car to encourage...er... sharing cars, and above there's a sign saying that if you're in this lane, anybody can report you if you haven't got enough passengers.
Funnily enough the speed limit was something I thought I was going to have trouble with because my brother warned me, he said, 'Look, you know, you've got to keep to the speed limit. If you don't, you'll be booked.' And so I went out the first day crawling along at the speed limit and all these cars going 'zeow zeow zeow' right past me ...

| | |
|---|---|
| INTERVIEWER: | Monica, …um… have you driven anywhere else apart from your own country? |
| MONICA: | I've been driving in…um…the UK, in England. Um…I drove quite a bit there, actually, and…er…it was interesting. The amazing thing about driving in England is that you, you know, first of all you're on the other side of the road and you have to get used to not only being on the other side of the road but the steering wheel being on the other side of the road, and I'm left-handed and everything and so it made it very awkward but…um…at first but then I…I got used to it. I think the thing that really astounded me though were roundabouts, roundabouts, just completely … I didn't understand them at all. |
| INTERVIEWER: | What surprised you about driving there? |
| MONICA: | Well, in England…um…drivers actually stop at…er…at zebra crossings to let pedestrians…er…go across, they…they…er…they do stop, which is not like it is in America — I mean, you can only cross on the lights and things like that and often that's ignored, but…um…in England the drivers really do stop, which I think is civilised. One law that I…I wasn't aware of that…um…is that in England they…they actually wear seat belts not only in front but in the back seats, so…um…you know, you always see people belted in the back as well. |
| INTERVIEWER: | What are the speed limits there? |
| MONICA: | In the built-up areas…er…town situations, the speed limit is 30 miles an hour. Um…and on the motorways…er…it's 70 miles an hour but, you know, everybody seems to do about 80 actually. |

## B1

The international signs shown here wouldn't be seen in the USA. However, many of the signs shown are not truly international — some countries have their own signs or similar signs to American ones.

Arrange the class into pairs for them to discuss the meaning of each sign.

## 2 Grammar

This exercise can be done by the same pairs, or alone. If it's done in pairs, the partners could work individually with one partner writing about the top row of signs and the other writing about the bottom row. Reassemble the class to discuss possible variations.

### Suggested answers

1 This sign means that you have to stop if a pedestrian wants to cross the road.

2 This sign means that you should drive slowly because there's a school ahead.

3 This sign means that you have to drive carefully because you're approaching a crossroads.

4 This sign means that you have to stop until it's safe to drive on.

5 This sign means that you can't drive any motor vehicle on this road.

6 This sign means that you mustn't drive at less than 30.

7 This sign means that you have to keep driving in this direction — it's a one-way street.

8 This sign means that you shouldn't park here.

9 This sign means that you have to observe motorway regulations.

10 This sign means that you mustn't drive over 40.

11 This sign means that you can't drive on this road — only cyclists and pedestrians are allowed.

12 This sign means that you can stop for a picnic.

## C

This is a difficult, unsimplified text. It's a handout given to people who are going to rent a car, and some of the advice it gives may affect your life or safety.

Despite its difficulty, many of the unfamiliar words can be guessed from their context. Demonstrate this by asking everyone to look at the first paragraph of advice and try to guess the meanings of these words: *facility*, *unattended*, *claim*, *assign*, *applicable* (office, unwatched, take/say which are yours, give them the task, relevant).

Then ask them to do the same with the words in the next few paragraphs (*prior to*, *trunk*, *glove compartment*, *malfunctioning*, etc.).

Some of the vocabulary in the text is worth remembering, some isn't. Students may need some advice on this (for example, *malfunctioning* isn't worth remembering, but *claim* probably is).

Even if everyone has prepared this text before the Lesson, arrange everyone into groups of three or four. Depending on how safe their country is (or how cautious or nervous they are) there may be lots of ticks or hardly any. Reassemble the class and find out if everyone shares the same views.

## D1 Role play

Arrange everyone into pairs. Draw everyone's attention to the phrases in the speech balloons before they begin the role play. Allow enough time for both partners to have a turn at being the local resident.

## 2 Writing

This should be done at home, but it may be advisable to brainstorm ideas in class before everyone does it as homework.

## Finally …

Remind everyone what the aim of this Lesson was. Has it been achieved?

# 40 The best way to get there

## Aim

Begin by explaining to the class the aim of Lesson 40, which is to improve their ability to:

- explain to people how to get to different places on foot.

## Vocabulary

| | |
|---|---|
| *art gallery (US art museum)* | *next door* |
| *block* | *opposite* |
| *castle* | *pharmacy* |
| *city hall* | *shortcut* |
| *complicated* | *street plan* |
| *corner* | *viewpoint* |
| *inexpensive* | *zig-zag* |

## First of all ...

Ask some members of the class to explain where the nearest pharmacy, the railway station, City Hall and the art gallery are situated. Then ask some others to explain the best route to get to each place from the main college entrance on foot (or by public transport). Explain that this Lesson is all about giving directions to people who don't know the city as well as you do!

**A 1** Ask everyone to look at the street plan and explain that they're at the Royal Hotel, facing north, looking out of the main door on Central Avenue. Play the recording, pausing it between each conversation. Allow everyone time to compare their answers so far before you play it again. (There are two pharmacies near the Royal Hotel.)

## Transcript  1 minute 45 seconds

| | |
|---|---|
| GUEST: | Excuse me, how do I get to the railway station? |
| RECEPTIONIST: | The railway station? Well, you just go out of the hotel, turn right and when you get to East Street, turn right again. The station is two blocks down on your left. It's quite easy to find. |
| GUEST: | Thank you. |
| | |
| GUEST: | How do I get to City Hall? |
| HALL PORTER: | City Hall? Er…well, you…you go out of the hotel, you turn left and when you get to Main Street you turn left again. Keep walking down Main Street, cross Broadway and you'll see City Hall on your right. It's about five minutes' walk. |
| GUEST: | Oh, thanks. |
| | |
| GUEST: | I need to find a pharmacy — is there one near here? |
| RECEPTIONIST: | Yes, you go out of the hotel, and you turn right and there's a pharmacy on the right. If that one's closed, there's another one that's always open day and night. |
| GUEST: | Where's that? |
| RECEPTIONIST: | OK, you go out of the hotel, turn left and when you get to Main Street, turn right. The pharmacy is just round the corner on the right. |
| GUEST: | Where's the art gallery? |
| HALL PORTER: | Well, it's a bit complicated. Er…first you go out of the hotel and turn right. And then when you get to East Street, you turn left and…and you keep going up East Street all the way until you get to North Street. Right? And then you turn right and you take the second road on your right. The art gallery is at the end of that little road — you…you'll see a sign for it. |
| GUEST: | OK, thanks. |
| HALL PORTER: | It's open late this evening — it doesn't close till 10pm. |
| GUEST: | Oh, good. Thanks. |

**PHOTOCOPIABLE** © Cambridge University Press 2005

**2** Do this as whole-class activity, asking different students to offer suggestions.

## Suggested routes

Just go out of the hotel and turn right and keep walking along Central Avenue. When you've crossed East Street you'll come to **Eaton's** on your right.

Go out of the hotel and turn left. When you get to Main Street, turn left and walk down until you get to Broadway. Then turn left again and you'll soon come to the **Odeon** on your left.

It's quite a long way. First go out of the hotel and turn left. Then keep walking along Central Avenue, cross Main Street and you'll eventually come to West Street. Then turn left and walk down there, cross over South Street and you'll come to the **El Greco** on your right.

Go out of the hotel and turn right. When you get to East Street, turn right and keep walking down there. Just after you've crossed South Street, you'll see **McDonald's** on your left.

## B Role play

Arrange everyone into pairs. Draw everyone's attention to the phrases in the speech balloons. The role play is in two parts, so please allow time for both parts.

One partner looks at **Activity 15** on SB page 115, the other at **Activity 31** on SB page 123. Activity 15 shows the south of the city with more places marked on it; Activity 31 shows the north of the city with different places marked on it. They'll also need to consult the main map on SB page 86.

## If there's time …

Get some street plans of the students' own city (or the place they're studying in). Get everyone to role play giving directions to different hotels in town from the tourist information centre, or from where they are now.

**C1** Arrange the class into groups of three or four. If some students come from villages or small towns, they may need to decide on a suitable larger town to focus on.

Reassemble the class for everyone to share their ideas now, or maybe wait until they've done the next task.

**2** Keep the same groups for this. Afterwards, reassemble the class for everyone to share ideas.

## 3 Role play

Arrange everyone into pairs. The starting point for the route could be where you are now, or the main square, or another agreed point. (Use a local street plan for this role play if possible.)

## Finally …

**1** Draw everyone's attention to the Advice box.

**2** Remind everyone what the aim of this Lesson was. Has it been achieved?

## Travelling around: Vocabulary puzzle

Photocopy the Vocabulary puzzle on page 106 for everyone to do in pairs in class, or for homework.

### Answers

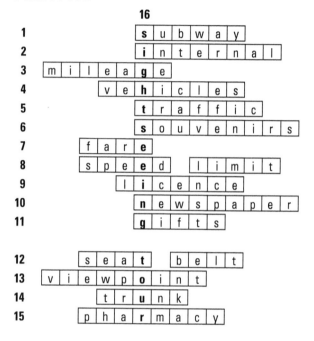

1. s u b w a y
2. i n t e r n a l
3. m i l e a g e
4. v e h i c l e s
5. t r a f f i c
6. s o u v e n i r s
7. f a r e
8. s p e e d  l i m i t
9. l i c e n c e
10. n e w s p a p e r
11. g i f t s

12. s e a t  b e l t
13. v i e w p o i n t
14. t r u n k
15. p h a r m a c y

# 41 Is there anything I can do?

This Module (Lessons 41–44) covers helping clients to solve their problems, dealing with complaints and advising clients how to avoid taking risks.

## Aim

Begin by explaining to the class the aim of Lesson 41, which is to improve their ability to:

- assist clients with their difficulties (i.e. clients' problems, not complaints).

## Vocabulary

| | | |
|---|---|---|
| argument | contact number | oversleep |
| bowls | flat tyre (US tire) | pet store |
| briefcase | food poisoning | replacement |
| bunch of flowers | headache | spill/spilt |
| collected | in a great panic | unaccompanied minor |

**A1**  As a warm-up, ask everyone to look at the pictures, which show clients having problems. What do they think has happened in each situation?

Explain that the speakers are shown in the photos. Play the recording, pausing it between each speaker.

### Answers

| | |
|---|---|
| Jim | picture 3 |
| Tony | picture 2 |
| Anna | picture 4 |
| Karen | picture 1 |

### Transcript  2 minutes 4 seconds

INTERVIEWER: Jim, what happened?

JIM: There was a guest who left his car outside the hotel while he came in to get his luggage and he left his keys in the car. And…er…somebody jumped into the car and drove his car away.

INTERVIEWER: Tony, what happened?

TONY: Well, we had a fairly unusual incident where…um…where a guest turned up and she had two dogs with her and…er…she wanted…er…the dogs to stay in her room. Well, they were fairly nice dogs, they were well behaved. Now, we normally allow dogs in the guest rooms, but…er…not on the ground floor. Anyway, huh, the cheek of the woman! She wanted us to feed the dogs.

INTERVIEWER: Anna, what happened?

ANNA: It was very early, I think it was about nine in the morning, and a client of ours came into the office in a great panic, she was in a terrible state. Well, what she'd done, she'd written the date of her departure down wrong and her flight, the aeroplane had left the day before. She and her husband were frantic, they were supposed to be going on a two-week trip and it was an inclusive tour so it was a charter flight, which was a problem.

INTERVIEWER: Karen, what happened.

KAREN: Well, we had this little boy on board, officially an 'unaccompanied minor'. Anyway, he was about nine, ten, and we were flying into this airport in Africa, where the boy was going to be met by someone — I…I think it was his uncle, yeah, it was his uncle. Anyway, the uncle didn't show. I waited with the boy for over an hour, poor little thing, but the uncle still didn't show up.

**PHOTOCOPIABLE**  © Cambridge University Press 2005

**2** Arrange everyone into pairs to predict how each person dealt with the problems in Step 1.

**3** Play the recording, pausing it after each speaker. It may need to be played more than once. Afterwards reassemble the class and find out if they think each person did the right thing. Do they have any personal experiences of clients with problems?

### Answers

1  The guest drove off in his replacement car the same day. ✓
   The police never found the car. ✗

2  The guest had to go out to buy some dog food. ✗
   The chef prepared a special meal for them. ✓

3  The client managed to get seats on another flight. ✓
   The tour operators were unhelpful. ✗

4  The child shared a room at the airport hotel. ✓
   They waited at the airport until the child was collected. ✗

### Transcript  2 minutes 23 seconds

INTERVIEWER: Jim, what did you do?

JIM: Well, um…er…we called the police right away and they came round and they took a statement. And…er…the guest, I mean, obviously wanted to continue with his trip so…er…we got him a replacement hire car. And…er…he set off a couple of hours later but…And the car…the car didn't turn up for a week — but we found it eventually in a car park completely undamaged.

INTERVIEWER: Tony, what did you do?

TONY: Well, I…I asked her what it is that they like to eat, you know, what kind of dog food and that.

So…um…anyway…um… someone from room service went out, er…bought some cans, er…two plastic dog bowls at a local…er…pet store. And…er…we served it up, took it up to the room on a tray, and…er…well, they ate the same meal…er…twice a day for a week.

INTERVIEWER: Anna, what did you do?

ANNA: Well, first, we got in touch and telephoned the tour operators for her, and luckily they still had two spare seats on another flight to the same destination, and it was supposed to be leaving at about lunchtime that day, but they'd have to check in for it at 10am. So, we called a taxi immediately to take her straight home to pick up her husband and their luggage and then we rushed them to the airport in time for the flight. Amazingly, they made it. And do you know what? They brought us a magnum of champagne after their holiday! It was lovely!

INTERVIEWER: Karen, what did you do?

KAREN: Well, we always take a contact number, so I phoned the uncle. Oh, he was terribly upset, he'd got the wrong date — he was expecting the boy the following day. And he…there was no way that he could get there that evening. So we took the boy with us to our hotel, treated him really well, and he spent the night in my room in fact, very sweet little boy. Following morning: uncle arrives. It was really nice, he'd bought me this huge bunch of flowers, he was so apologetic.

## B 1

Arrange everyone into pairs. Encourage them not only to describe what they'd do, but also decide what they'd say — the actual words they'd use. The Suggested answers are just suggestions (not necessarily the best solutions) — your students may well come up with much better ideas.

## Suggested answers

**I've locked myself out of my car. The keys are inside and so is my wallet. I'm afraid someone might break into it if I leave it unattended.**

The only thing we can do is call a locksmith. I'll let you know when he gets here. Meanwhile I'll ask the car park attendant to keep an eye on your car. Or, if you like, you can sit by the window over there and watch the car yourself.

**I've lost my airline ticket. I'm booked to fly on the 11am flight to London. It's already 9.30 and I still have to get to the airport.**

I'll phone the airline to see what they suggest. I think they can issue you with another ticket at the airport, but it's best to arrange this in advance to make sure.

**My car has two flat tyres. I've got to drive to a meeting and I'm due there in an hour.**

I'll call the garage to see if they can come and fix them, but that may take some time. I think the best thing to do may be to rent a car for today. I'll just check if the car rental desk has one available right away.

**I've turned on both taps in my bath and I can't turn them off. They are completely stuck and the bath is about to overflow.**

I'll send the maintenance man up right away. Can you keep trying to turn them off until he gets there, please?

**My room is on the ground floor and someone keeps looking into my window.**

Would you like me to move you to another room on the second floor? Otherwise, the only thing I can suggest is that you pull the curtains/close the shutters, and I'll call the police.

**I feel terrible: I've got a terrible headache and I feel sick. I think I've got food poisoning.**

Would you like me to call a doctor? Or would you like me to send someone to the pharmacy round the corner for you?

**2** Rearrange the students into different pairs for the role plays. Draw everyone's attention to the phrases in the speech balloon.

## C Role play

Arrange everyone into pairs. One partner looks at **Activity 27** on SB page 121, the other at **Activity 34** on SB page 124. Explain that they'll be taking part in eight separate short conversations, and that they should change roles for each one.

## Finally …

Remind everyone what the aim of this Lesson was. Has it been achieved?

There's quite a lot to get through in this Lesson. If you don't manage to get through it all in one classroom session, what's left can be postponed until the next Lesson. (Lesson 43 is likely to take less long than usual.)

# 42 Dealing with complaints

## Aim

Begin by explaining to the class the aim of Lesson 42, which is to improve their ability to:

* respond to complaints and to apologise.

## Vocabulary

| | | |
|---|---|---|
| *air conditioning* | *duty manager* | *piped music* |
| *apologetically* | *excuses* | *shortly* |
| *appetite* | *fault* | *sightseeing tour* |
| *blame* | *heating* | *TV channels* |
| *caterpillar* | *high expectations* | *unjustified* |
| *cross/aggrieved* | *inevitable* | *unreasonable* |
| *dishwasher* | *leaking* | |

## First of all …

Ask the class to think of some things that clients or guests complain about. Have any of them had cause to complain themselves as guests? If so, what happened?

**A** Play the recording, pausing it between each speaker. The purpose of this exercise is to encourage everyone not to take complaints personally but to take them seriously. Don't spend too long on it because there's more listening to do in Sections B2 and B3.

### Answers

**1** hotel general manager  **2** restaurant manager  **3** receptionist
**4** travel agent  **5** waitress

### Transcript  2 minutes 41 seconds

RECEPTIONIST:  People complain. It's…er…not nice to deal with that…um… especially at reception, you're the front line and it's you that people complain to. Um…you just have to not sort of take it personally and just apologise to them and, you know, pass on comments or get the duty manager to help them.

WAITRESS:  It would be easier if you could all blame each other but, you know, you're a hotel, you're a team, you know, if the kitchen goes wrong…the…it's…it affects us. Likewise if I take the wrong order, it affects the kitchen, so it's all a bit give and take and you just can't blame people. If they're that cross, you know, you need to get the manager to speak to them and…er… and also you haven't really got time to be making long excuses.

GENERAL MANAGER:  The complaints we do get are people on the whole that are quite reasonable, just bringing things to our attention because they don't feel they're quite right and they just want us to have the opportunity to a) say why it's not happened and b) make sure it doesn't happen again for another guest.

RESTAURANT MANAGER:  And you're never going to please everybody all the time. But you have to try and make sure that at least they feel when they've left that something has been tried…they've been given some help, they haven't just been ignored. But you've just at least got to give them a sense of feeling that they just haven't been ignored — just going over and…and saying a few words to them helps.

TRAVEL AGENT:  Holidays are very important to people and…um…if they go wrong…um…then the level of complaint is quite high, people have high expectations from their holidays, it's quite a responsible job in that way in that you're dealing with the thing that people look forward to for the most…the majority of the year and if when they get to the…they've saved all year and they get on holiday and there's something wrong with it, they feel particularly aggrieved about it. In an ideal world everything would go completely smoothly but actually sometimes there are problems and, I mean that…in the travel industry that's always going to be part of the job. It's unfortunate but it's inevitable.

**B1** This is a warm-up for the students to do in pairs before they hear the recordings. It also gives everyone a chance to say what they'd do, so that they can compare their ideas with what the members of staff in the recording said.

**2** Play the recording, pausing between each conversation. This demonstrates what *not* to do. Ask everyone to pitch in with comments on what each person did wrong — and what they should have done instead. The 'bad behaviour' is probably obvious enough for everyone to spot that it's wrong.

## Suggested answers

**1** She didn't sound sincere and she implied that the guest was at fault, not the staff.

**2** His excuse wasn't very good and he wasn't apologetic enough.

**3** She treated the complaint as a joke.

**4** He made the guest wait for him to finish on the phone.

## Transcript  1 minute 48 seconds

**1**

GUEST: Look at the bed!

MEMBER OF STAFF: Oh, I'm sorry about that. The chambermaid must have missed your room.

GUEST: Yes.

MEMBER OF STAFF: Well, did you have a 'Do not disturb' sign on your door?

GUEST: Yes, but only during the morning.

MEMBER OF STAFF: Well, that explains it. The rooms are cleaned before lunch. Make sure you change the sign to 'Please make up my room' when you leave tomorrow, otherwise it won't happen …

**2**

GUEST: Excuse me, look at this plate!

MEMBER OF STAFF: Oh, dear. Um…sorry about that. We've been having problems with our dishwasher, I'm afraid.

GUEST: I see.

MEMBER OF STAFF: I'll see if I can find you a cleaner one.

GUEST: Thank you!

**3**

GUEST: Look at this insect!

MEMBER OF STAFF: Oh, yes, it's a caterpillar. I think I'd better get you another salad.

GUEST: Well, I'm not sure that I …

MEMBER OF STAFF: I'll make sure the new salad is insect-free!

GUEST: I don't think I want to risk another one.

MEMBER OF STAFF: Don't worry, it was only a caterpillar. It could have been a …

**4**

RECEPTIONIST: (on the phone) … OK, certainly, I'll just have to check that for you.

GUEST: Um…how long are you going to be?

RECEPTIONIST: (on the phone) Sorry, could you hold on a moment? (to the guest) I'm just on the phone. I'll be with your shortly.

GUEST: But I'm in a hurry.

RECEPTIONIST: (on the phone) Can I call you back? All right. Goodbye. (to the guest) Right, Mrs Brown, what can I do for you?

GUEST: I just want to check out. I've got a train to catch.

**3** Play the recording, which demonstrates better ways of dealing with the same complaints. Each one is better because the members of staff put themselves in the guests' shoes, treating them with respect.

## Transcript  1 minute 53 seconds

**1**

GUEST: Look at the bed!

MEMBER OF STAFF: Oh, I'm terribly sorry about that. The chambermaid may have thought you were sleeping late and she didn't want to disturb you.

GUEST: Well, what are you going to do about it?

MEMBER OF STAFF: I'll call the housekeeper right away and make sure the room is cleaned by the time you've had dinner.

GUEST: Good, thank you.

MEMBER OF STAFF: Could you make sure the 'Do not disturb sign' isn't on your door, please, if you're not in your room?

GUEST: Oh, yes, yes, all right. Thank you …

**2**

GUEST: Excuse me, look at this plate!

MEMBER OF STAFF: Oh, dear, I'm really very sorry about that. I'll get you a clean one right away.

GUEST: Thank you.

MEMBER OF STAFF: Is everything else all right?

GUEST: Oh, good. I'm very sorry about the dirty plate. I'll make sure it doesn't happen again …

**3**

GUEST: Look at this insect!

MEMBER OF STAFF: Oh, dear, I'm terribly sorry about that. I'll take it back to the kitchen.

GUEST: I think you'd better.

MEMBER OF STAFF: Shall I bring you another green salad?

GUEST: No, I don't think so, I've lost my appetite.

MEMBER OF STAFF: All right, I'll speak to the chef and make sure it doesn't happen again, sir, and I'm terribly sorry …

**4**

RECEPTIONIST: (on the phone) … I'll just have to check that for you.

GUEST: How long are you going to be?

RECEPTIONIST: (on the phone) Sorry, could you hold on a moment? (to the guest) I'm terribly sorry, Mrs Brown, I didn't realise you were waiting. I'll just ask my colleague to help you. (to colleague in back office) Max, could you come to the front desk, please? (to the guest) He's just coming, Mrs Brown. I'm very sorry you were kept waiting.

GUEST: That's all right.

RECEPTIONIST: (on the phone) Hello. I'm sorry to keep you waiting …

## C1 Pronunciation

 Play the recording, pausing it for everyone to repeat the sentences in the speech balloon. [1 minute 12 seconds]

**2** Arrange everyone into pairs. Make sure everyone not only decides how to deal with each complaint in the speech balloons but also exactly what to say. Encourage them to use the phrases they practised in Step 1. Point out that the only thing they might be able to say in some cases is something like this:

*I'm very sorry about that, sir, but I'm afraid there's nothing I can do about it.*

*I'm really very sorry that happened, madam. I'm not sure what I can do about it.*

## 3 Role play

Rearrange everyone into *different* pairs to role play some of the situations in Step 2. (There probably won't be time to do them all.)

## D1 Role play

Arrange everyone into pairs. One partner looks at **Activity 12** on SB page 113, the other at **Activity 35** on SB page 124. Each partner has six complaints to make. Make sure everyone changes roles after each short interaction.

## 2 Writing

Refer everyone back to the letter of apology in **Activity 38** on SB page 126 as a model for this task.

## Finally …

1  Draw everyone's attention to the Advice box.

2  Remind everyone what the aim of this Lesson was. Has it been achieved?

3  To save time in the next Lesson (especially if you haven't completed all the role plays in this Lesson), ask everyone to read the *Traveler Safety Tips* on SB page 92 before the next Lesson.

---

# 43 Better safe than sorry

## Aim

Begin by explaining to the class the aim of Lesson 43, which is to improve their ability to:

- advise clients on safety precautions and how to avoid risks.

## Vocabulary

| | | |
|---|---|---|
| carelessly | locking devices | safe deposit box |
| criminal | observant | securely |
| displaying | precautions | suspicious activity |
| employee | risks | verifying |
| jewelry (GB jewellery) | | |

## First of all …

Draw everyone's attention to the title of this Lesson — what is the equivalent expression in their language? Do they agree with the sentiment — or do they prefer to take risks and live dangerously?

### A1

The text is a handout issued by the American Hotel and Motel Association — hence the American spellings of *traveler* (GB *traveller*) and *jewelry* (GB *jewellery*). Depending on how safe their country is, it may be quite difficult for the students to choose the three most important tips.

### 2

Arrange everyone into pairs. Draw everyone's attention to the phrases in the speech balloon and encourage them to use the first conditional with *might*. Afterwards reassemble the class to exchange ideas.

### Suggested answers

2  If you don't use the main entrance late at night, someone might follow you into the hotel. If you aren't careful in parking lots, someone might attack or mug you.

3  If you don't close the door securely, someone might come into your room while you're asleep.

4  If you leave your room key somewhere, it might get stolen.

5  If someone sees your cash or jewellery, they might steal it.

6  If you invite strangers into your room, they might attack you or rob you.

7  If you put your valuables in the safe deposit box, no one can steal them.

8  If you leave valuables in your car, it's easy for someone to break a window and steal them.

9  If your doors or windows aren't locked, it's easy for someone to get into your room.

10  If you report suspicious activity to the management, we can stop crimes happening.

## B1

Arrange the class into groups of three or four for this activity. Encourage everyone to make notes on their discussion to use in Step 2 and in Section C later.

Reassemble the class for everyone to share their ideas for a few minutes.

## 2 Role play

Arrange everyone into pairs. They should take it in turns to play each role.

## C Writing

The notes everyone made in B1, as well as the advice for tourists on SB page 92, can be the starting point for this writing task.

## Finally …

Remind everyone what the aim of this Lesson was. Has it been achieved?

## If there's time ...

Photocopy the leaflet below from another hotel.

Ask the students to choose the three most important precautions from the ALWAYS list and the three most important from the NEVER list:

- What are the differences between the set of advice below and the one in the Student's Book?
- What tips are given in the one below that aren't given in the one in the Student's Book?

---

# HOTEL SECURITY AND SAFETY PRECAUTIONS

## ALWAYS

1. Keep your luggage in sight when checking into a hotel. DO NOT leave it unattended even for a minute.
2. Place all valuables in the hotel safe deposit box as soon as possible, preferably when you check in.
3. Close the door of your hotel room by hand when leaving to make sure it is locked. Then try to open the door to make certain it is locked.
4. Keep the door locked while you are in your hotel room.
5. Lock your door by hand even if leaving your room for a short period of time.
6. Lock your luggage when not in use and place in a closet. If the luggage has a lock, always use it.
7. Protect your room key. Be sure to give it DIRECTLY to the desk clerk when you go out of the hotel; DO NOT simply leave it on the counter. Always return your key when checking out.
8. Notify the manager immediately of any unusual occurrences such as: persons loitering in the corridor, repeated phone calls from persons who do not identify themselves, knocking on your door by persons unknown to you, or finding no one at the door when you answer it.
9. Our hotel safety committee requests that you extinguish all cigarettes and cigars before retiring.

## NEVER

1. Never display jewelry, money or any valuables in your room.
2. Never invite strangers to your room.
3. Never permit repairmen, window washers etc. into your room without checking first with hotel management.
4. Never allow persons in your room with unsolicited deliveries.
5. When socializing, do not reveal the name of your hotel or hotel room number to strangers.
6. Never discuss specific future plans for a day away etc. in public.
7. Never carry hotel keys outside of the hotel.

AMBASSADOR
HOTEL
★ ★ ★ ★

---

**Problems**

# 44 Difficult customers?

## Aims

Begin by explaining to the class the aims of Lesson 44, which are to improve their ability to:

- deal with awkward clients
- cope with not understanding what people say (in unfamiliar accents or unclear voices).

## Vocabulary

| | | |
|---|---|---|
| accommodate | handcuff | repatriating |
| anticipate | illegal | security (guard) |
| awkward | lose your temper | spare ribs |
| burst (into) | null and void | use my initiative |
| calm people down | pestering | violent and abusive |
| difficult/hard to please | pyjamas | work outing |
| embassy | remain calm | |

## First of all ...

1 Ask the class if any of them have had any experiences with difficult-to-please, awkward clients? If so, what happened? Why are some people hard to please, and others easier to please?

2 Explain that this Lesson will help them to cope with clients who are difficult to please or awkward (in A and C) — and also with clients who are difficult to understand (in B).

**A1**  Play the recording, pausing it between each speaker — and also before some or all of the the presenter's questions. Although this recording is quite long, don't spend too long on it — there's more listening in B1 later. Explain to everyone that they don't need to understand everything — just the main points.

# Answers

1 ✓  2 ✓  3 ✗  4 ✓  5 ✗  6 ✓  7 ✓  8 ✓
9 ✓  10 ✗

## Transcript  5 minutes 17 seconds

PRESENTER: Jane Sparkes is a senior flight attendant. When do passengers complain?

JANE: Gosh, you get the situations where people are being difficult a lot of the time, it depends on the degree of difficulty. Usually you can calm people down, dissuade them from carrying on with what they're doing quite easily. The problem really gets bad when, for example, people have had too much to drink, or are under the influence of some kind of drugs, either legal or illegal. I had a situation fairly recently on a flight where a…a young man was pestering people. He insisted on smoking cigarettes and it was a no-smoking flight. And then he became quite violent and abusive, in fact he actually knocked me around.

PRESENTER: So what did you do?

JANE: We had to get the restraint kit from the flight deck, which is a pair of handcuffs and tape, and lash him to the seat. And the aircraft was met by security and he was hauled off to the cells for the night. He wasn't allowed back on a British Airways flight and he was banned from Qantas as well, and his ticket was made null and void. And he had to spend a few uncomfortable nights in Bangkok until he could get home. I think his embassy probably ended up repatriating him.

PRESENTER: But presumably most problems are less serious than that?

JANE: I suppose a…a small mundane problem is somebody who's maybe ordered a special meal and it hasn't turned up. Well, we're not a supermarket, I can't just nip out and get what they want. Um…I can't change the fact that the meal isn't there for them. Um…you could say that a special meal not on board isn't really a big deal, but if somebody's paid a lot of money and they've ordered it, they think that they should actually have that meal.

PRESENTER: So what do you do in that situation?

JANE: All I can do is talk to people, try and pacify them, assure them that it won't happen next time, use my initiative, have a damn good look around the aircraft, see what there is there and bring them something that's suitable. A lot of the time, little problems like that, as I say you can't change the fact that you haven't got the thing there for them, but it's talking to people and I suppose in a way making them feel important.

PRESENTER: Fiona Bowers is a waitress. Fiona, have you had any difficult customers recently?

FIONA: Yeah, Friday night. Um…we had a party of fifteen turn up three-quarters of an hour late, very drunk, and it was one of those situations where when they'd arrived and sat down, it was quite difficult to then ask them to leave. So we carried ahead with the service and they were just very difficult, I mean it was difficult to get the order out of them and they were just difficult in general and one man at the end who was paying for the meal clicked his fingers at me a lot and shouted at me across the restaurant for service and things like that, which is quite difficult to be polite in situations like that. They were an insurance company on a…on a work outing. Yeah, it's always the work outings! I hope I'm not painting a bad picture because we get lovely customers as well.

PRESENTER: Sam Wilkinson manages a Mexican restaurant. What kind of complaints do your customers make?

SAM: Well, we deal with Mexican food and we do get a surprising amount of customers coming in who have never had Mexican food. And so a common complaint is that the food is too spicy for them, or they don't know what they've ordered and they've thought, 'Ooh, that sounds nice! We'll try that,' and then they've got it and they've not liked it.

PRESENTER: So what do you do?

SAM: We always try to give somebody a meal that they will enjoy, so we'll give them an alternative… alternative dish to the one they've had, so hopefully they leave having eaten and being happy. If the customer says to you, 'I've never eaten Mexican before, can you point something out to me?' you can then ask them questions like: what do they like, do they like spicy chicken, do they like seafood, do they like this, that…then you can sort of anticipate what drinks…sorry, what food they may enjoy and guide them towards making a good choice.

PRESENTER: What about difficult customers?

SAM: For example — it's a very small example — we had a group of…er…five women come in just last night and…and they wanted Chinese barbecue spare ribs. This is what they wanted. Well, one of them decided, 'Well, I don't like Mexican' and the others were like, 'Oh you'll enjoy it, you'll enjoy it, you'll have it'. 'But I want barbecue Chinese spare ribs' and I was like, 'Well, we do our ribs' and she was like, 'No, we don't want your ribs I want this'.

PRESENTER: So what do you do?

SAM: There's not a lot you can do, if they want something which you haven't got, then OK we try and accommodate, like everything can come without this or without that, you can have no chilli, you can have no cheese. Basically if it's on the menu, then they can have it in one form or another but if it's not, then they can't, especially during the busy periods we…we do tend to stick quite rigidly to the menu.

**2** Arrange everyone into groups of three or four. If not many members of the class have already worked, there may not be much to say.

## B 1

Begin by explaining that 'a difficult customer' means a client who is awkward or hard to please. In these conversations the clients are not being difficult — but it *is* difficult to understand them. Students must be able to cope with this kind of difficulty, too!

Play the recording, making sure you pause it after each interaction to give everyone time to reflect on what was said. Then play it again from the beginning, again pausing between the interactions.

Ask the class what they do if they have to deal with clients who are hard to understand because they speak unclearly, fast or in an unfamiliar accent. Then move on to Step 2 (see below the Transcript).

### Answers

1  for 3 nights from 4 July

2  apart

3  6pm

4  58930, ext 16

5  a table at 8 o'clock for 7 people

6  the opera house tour

7  6.50

8  wants someone to help her with them (She pronounces *can't* in the American way.)

### Transcript   1 minute 54 seconds

**1**

RECEPTIONIST:    Yes, Mr Adams, how can I help you?

MR ADAMS:    I'd like to make a reservation, please. Do you have a double room with shower and balcony for three nights from the 4th of July?

**2**

RECEPTIONIST:    Yes, Mrs Butler?

MRS BUTLER:    The two beds in my room are too close together. Can you send someone to move them apart and put them on different sides of the room, please?

**3**

RECEPTIONIST:    Yes, Mr Cohen?

MR COHEN:    I have to change my travel plans. I was going to leave tomorrow mid-morning, but I've got to leave earlier at about 6 in the morning. Could you have my bill ready this evening at 6?

**4**

RECEPTIONIST:    Yes, Ms Daniels?

MS DANIELS:    Hi, yeah, could you phone my office and let them know I'll be there very soon? I'm just leaving now. Er...the phone number's 58930 — extension 16.

**5**

RECEPTIONIST:    Yes, Mr Edwards?

MR EDWARDS:    Can you book a table for me in the restaurant this evening? I want a table for seven people at 8 o'clock.

**6**

RECEPTIONIST:    Yes, Mrs Foster?

MRS FOSTER:    Can you help me? I want to see the opera house. Can you arrange for me to have two tickets to go round it tomorrow?

**7**

RECEPTIONIST:    Yes, Mr Graham?

MR GRAHAM:    Can you give me an early morning call at about...er...6.50, please?

**8**

RECEPTIONIST:    Yes, Ms Hughes?

MS HUGHES:    Oh, er...I've got two bags, I can't carry them to my room myself.

## 2  Pronunciation

Play the recording, pausing it for everyone to repeat the sentences in the speech balloon. [42 seconds]

## C  Role play

**1**  Arrange everyone into pairs. Make sure they read the instructions before they begin the role play.

**2**  Everyone changes roles for the second role play.

Afterwards reassemble the class to find out how everyone got on.

## Finally ...

1  Draw everyone's attention to the Advice box.

2  Remind everyone what the aims of this Lesson were. Have they been achieved?

## Problems: Vocabulary puzzle

Photocopy the Vocabulary puzzle on page 107 for everyone to do in pairs in class, or for homework.

### Answers

**19**

1  s a f e  d e p o s i t

2  k e y

3  k e y c a r d

4  a p o l o g i s e

5  w i n d o w

6  s u s p i c i o u s

7  f a u l t

8  h o t  w a t e r

9  o v e r c h a r g e d

10  c o n t a c t

11  s w i m m i n g  p o o l

12  p o l i t e

13  i l l e g a l

14  m a n a g e r

15  v e r i f y

16  u n d e r s t a n d

17  v i s i t o r s

18  s t r a n g e r

# 45 Seeing the sights

This Module (Lessons 45–50) covers recommending what clients can do during their stay, describing the attractions and history of the region, and the effects of tourism in general.

## Aim

Begin by explaining to the class the aim of Lesson 45, which is to improve their ability to:

- describe local tourist attractions.

## Vocabulary

| all the year round | lake | palace |
| avoid the crowds | monument | public holidays |
| castle | national park | theme park |
| dome | out of season | viewpoint |
| entertainment | | |

+ the descriptive words in B2

**A** Arrange everyone into groups of three or four. This warm-up discussion is an introduction to the theme of this Module. The sights shown are a Mexican pyramid, the Statue of Liberty, Ayers Rock (Uluru) in Australia and the Great Wall of China. Allow everyone enough time to discuss all the questions.

Reassemble the class and get a sample of everyone's views on the last question.

**B1** Arrange the class into pairs. Draw everyone's attention to the phrases in the speech balloons. This is an open-ended vocabulary activity — not a test.

### Suggested answers

A theme park is a place where you can go on rides and have fun. A national park is a place where nature is protected and which you can visit to experience beautiful scenery.

A castle is an old building that is usually on a hill (it may be ruined). The old city is the oldest part of a city with historic buildings and narrow streets, popular with tourists.

A mountain is very high. A hill is lower than a mountain. (British mountains might be considered to be hills by the Swiss!)

A monument commemorates a famous person or a historic event. A viewpoint is a place, usually at the top of a hill, where you can see over a wide distance.

A market is a place where people sell fresh vegetables, fruit and other goods very cheaply. A shopping centre is the part of a town where most of the big shops and stores are.

## 2 Vocabulary

This can be done by the same pairs as before. The answers here are only suggestions — many variations are possible, and you may disagree with some answers. *Nice* and *lovely* can be used to describe most of the places but they haven't been included *below* — and so can great, which isn't in the list on SB page 96.

### Suggested answers

| | ✓ | ✓ | ✗ |
|---|---|---|---|
| art gallery | fascinating | worth visiting | enjoyable |
| historical museum | interesting | wonderful | dull |
| mountain | impressive | beautiful | high |
| hill | worth the trip | lovely | interesting |
| theme park | enjoyable | exhausting | charming |
| national park | wonderful | worthwhile | charming |
| monument | impressive | interesting | pretty |
| viewpoint | worth the trip | unforgettable | charming |
| castle | attractive | unusual | enjoyable |
| old city | charming | worth visiting | enjoyable |
| market | fascinating | interesting | large |
| shopping centre | interesting | worth visiting | beautiful |

## If there's time ...

Ask everyone to explain the differences between these pairs:

shopping mall ↔ department store

palace ↔ castle

hotel ↔ guest house

restaurant ↔ café

main road ↔ motorway or freeway (US)

suburbs ↔ city centre or downtown (US)

### Suggested answers

A shopping mall is a place where there are lots of shops gathered together. A department store is a large store with different departments.

A palace is a large house (formerly) lived in by royals. A castle is an old building, often built on a hill, surrounded by strong walls to protect it from enemies.

A hotel is a building where guests are accommodated, usually with its own restaurant. A guest house is much smaller and may not have its own restaurant, offering guests bed and breakfast only.

A restaurant serves full meals, usually lunch and dinner. A café serves drinks and snacks or light meals.

A main road carries all types of traffic between towns, it usually has two lanes. A motorway or freeway only carries cars, buses and trucks (not bicycles or tractors) and it has four or more lanes — two or more lanes in each direction.

The suburbs are the outer parts of a town where most of the houses are family houses with their own gardens. The city centre or downtown is the main business district, where the shops and offices are, as well as blocks of flats.

**C1** Play the recording, pausing it between each speaker. The task isn't too difficult — but there are only three correct reasons! The recording is intended mainly as a model for what everyone will have to do in the role play in Step 3.

## Answers

The Lake District    1

Futuroscope    5

The Royal Pavilion    2

## Transcript   2 minutes 51 seconds

**1**

PRESENTER: I'm staying in Manchester and I've got a free day. What should I do?

WOMAN: Well, the Lake District is really very popular, and it's a national park. It's in the north. It's a very beautiful area with mountains and lakes, there's lots of lovely walks up the mountains or beside the lakes. You can get there in about an hour from Manchester on the motorway. Actually, it's much nicer in the winter because there are fewer people there. It's really very crowded on public holidays in the summer.

**2**

PRESENTER: I'm staying in Poitiers and I've got a free day. What should I do?

MAN: Most visitors spend at least a day at Futuroscope — it's the…er…European theme park of the moving image…er…near Poitiers. You'll need a whole day at least because there's so much to see there: there are lots of different cinemas, each housed in a fantastic modern building. It's quite large and…er…well, you'll have to walk from one cinema to the next, which can be extremely tiring, especially on a hot day. Now, each cinema gives you a different e…experience, a different cinematic experience: such as…um…a 360-degree screen where all the action is going on around you. Er…there's a huge screen where you feel as if you're part of the action, a three-dimensional film, and so on. Each film is quite short, but the waiting times can be long, so it's best to go out of season, and certainly try and avoid weekends. And…er…it is extremely popular. Now, getting there: you can get there on the motorway or there's a shuttle bus from the main rail station. And the…the best part is: it's open all the year round.

**3**

PRESENTER: I'm staying in Brighton and I've got a free day. What should I do?

WOMAN: Well, the Royal Pavilion is well worth a visit — it was a royal palace. When King George III went mad in 1812, his son became Prince Regent and he had the palace built in the style of an Indian palace, with lots of smaller domes and…er…one huge one. Er…inside you can see the royal apartments and the amazing Chinese decorations. It's open to the public every day, and it…it's really popular because it's completely unlike other palaces or famous buildings. It's right in the centre of town, as well, quite close to the station.

# If there's time …

Play the recording again and ask everyone to note down the main attractions of each place not already covered in the task in Step 1.

**2** Arrange everyone into pairs. This and the role play in Step 3 may take quite a while to do — if time is short, it could be continued in the next Lesson.

Reassemble the class for everyone to share ideas. Suitable questions depend on what the attractions are. The suggested questions below are about a historic building.

## Suggested questions

When was it built?

How much does it cost to get in?

Have you been there yourself? What did you think of it?

**3** Role play

Rearrange the class into different pairs. Draw everyone's attention to the phrases in the speech balloon. Allow enough time for both partners to have a turn at being the local resident.

**4** Writing

This may need preparing in class before everyone writes the letter as homework.

# Finally …

Remind everyone what the aim of this Lesson was. Has it been achieved?

# 46 Making suggestions and giving advice

## Aims

Begin by explaining to the class the aims of Lesson 46, which are to improve their ability to:

- make suggestions to clients
- give advice to clients.

These functions are not restricted to describing attractions and activities.

## Vocabulary

| | | |
|---|---|---|
| *below freezing* | *heavy rain* | *temperature* |
| *coast* | *humid* | *thunder(storm)* |
| *coat* | *jogging* | *walking boots* |
| *foggy* | *open-air swimming pool* | *weather forecast* |

**A1** Do this warm-up as a whole-class activity. Maybe point out that the weather is very important to someone on holiday — more than it is to someone who's working indoors all day, like a member of the hotel staff.

Encourage more than one remark for each kind of weather shown:

*It's going to be windy. It's going to be very windy today.*
*There's going to be a strong wind today.*
*It's going to snow. It's going to snow soon.*
*I think it may snow later.*
*It's going to rain heavily.*
*There's going to be a lot of rain this morning.*
*It's going to be hot and sunny. It's going to be very warm today.*

**2** Play the recording, pausing between each forecast.

### Answers

| | |
|---|---|
| **March 1st** | sunny but very cold all day |
| **April 1st** | heavy rain later |
| **May 1st** | sunshine and showers |
| **June 1st** | thunderstorms in the afternoon |
| **July 1st** | sunny and warm all day |

### Transcript 1 minute 42 seconds

**1**
FEMALE FORECASTER: … and after an unexpectedly warm February, here we are on March the 1st and it's going to be below freezing all day, but it will be sunny. Tomorrow we can expect …

**2**
MALE FORECASTER: … April the 1st today and another fairly warm and dry morning, but later this afternoon rain will spread from the west and there will be quite a lot of rain lasting into the evening …

**3**
FEMALE FORECASTER: … and the weather today, May the 1st, is going to be a bit of a mixture: there may be a little rain during the morning but most of the day it will be quite sunny — though even this afternoon there may be the odd spot of rain.

**4**
MALE FORECASTER: … and the morning of June the 1st is going to be very hot and quite humid, but…er…after about lunchtime there's likely to be some thunder. Most parts of the area will be affected by a storm some time during the afternoon …

**5**
FEMALE FORECASTER: … and a very nice day today, the 1st of July: the sun's going to be shining all day and the temperature's going to be around 22 this morning, rising to about 24 this afternoon, and then on …

**PHOTOCOPIABLE** © Cambridge University Press 2005

**3** The cartoons refer to the same weather as above, so some people are inappropriately dressed. This can be begun in pairs before it becomes a whole-class activity. Encourage everyone to use the phrases in the speech balloon and ask for several ideas for each situation illustrated.

### Suggested answers

| | |
|---|---|
| **March 1st** | It might be a good idea to wear a warm coat today — although it's sunny, it's going to be very cold. |
| **April 1st** | I think you should perhaps take a raincoat or an umbrella with you today — it's probably going to rain this afternoon. |
| **May 1st** | It might be a good idea to take an umbrella today — there may be some rain later. |
| **June 1st** | I think you should perhaps take an umbrella— there may be a thunderstorm later. |
| **July 1st** | I don't think you should stay out in the sun for too long — it's going to be sunny all day. Perhaps you should use a stronger lotion than factor 4. |

## 4 Role play

Arrange everyone into pairs for this role play and remind them to change roles after each conversation. They should begin each conversation by saying 'Good morning'.

## If there's time ...

Video two real weather forecasts in English or in your students' language. Show them to the class and ask them what they'd say to a tourist (in English) about what kind of weather to expect that day.

Discuss these questions with the class:

- Do *you* regularly read or watch the weather forecast? Why/Why not?

- What difference does the weather make to the way you feel?

- How do you feel on:
  a sunny spring day
  a hot and humid summer night
  a cold and wet autumn (US *fall*) day
  a dry and cold winter day?

**B1** Arrange the class into pairs. The answers depend on what place your class are talking about and what kind of activities are available there: skiing, museums, beaches, country walks, shops, boat trips, etc. Reassemble the class to pool ideas.

## 2 Role play

Arrange everyone into *different* pairs. Draw everyone's attention to the phrases in the speech balloons before they start the role play.

**C1** Arrange everyone into pairs. These questions refer to the students' own home town — or to the place they're working in. It's a warm-up for the role play that follows.

## 2 Role play

 Keep the same pairs. One partner looks at **Activity 16** on SB page 115, the other at **Activity 29** on SB page 122. The role play is in two parts, so please allow time for both parts.

## Finally ...

1  Draw everyone's attention to the Advice boxes.

2  Remind everyone what the aims of this Lesson were. Have they been achieved?

3  To save time in class in Lesson 47, ask everyone to read the advertisement for Spain on page 100 and the one for Thailand on page 101 before the next Lesson. They should also find the answers to the questions in A1.

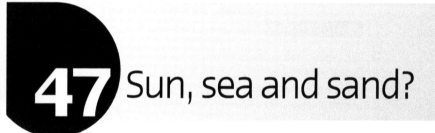

# 47 Sun, sea and sand?

## Aims

Begin by explaining to the class the aims of Lesson 47, which are to improve their ability to:

- read and understand advertisements

- understand members of the public describing their holidays

- describe the attractions of their own country or region.

## Vocabulary

in the Spain advertisement:

| | | |
|---|---|---|
| *coincidence* | *natives (local people)* | *soaking up* |
| *energetic* | *reluctantly* | *stroll* |
| *horizon* | *sibilant* | *synonymous* |

in the Thailand advertisement:

| | | |
|---|---|---|
| *boat trip* | *options* | *silk* |
| *coral reef* | *outlying* | *spectacular* |
| *deserted* | *pristine* | *stretch out* |
| *in equal measure* | *rejuvenating* | *succulent* |

+ the adjectives of description in A2 and B1

## First of all ...

Ask the class what they know about the attractions of Spain and Thailand as tourist destinations:

- Why is each country popular?

- Do they appeal to different kinds of tourists?

- What can visitors do there?

- Which of them would you rather go to on holiday? Why?

**A1** If this has not been prepared at home before the Lesson, it can be done in pairs before everyone compares answers when the class is reassembled.

There's likely to be some disagreement about the answer to the first question.

## Suggested answers

At least six:   sun, sea, sand, summer   [soaking up the sun]
[soaking up the sea]
water sport (on the sea and under the sea)
*sangria* (= red wine with orange juice)
*siesta* (a sleep in the afternoon)   [satisfaction]

Only one:   nightlife

**2** Play the recording, pausing it between each speaker. Point out that all the points are probably *true*, but they aren't all actually *mentioned* by the speakers.

It may help if you write up on the board the names of the places that the speakers mention:

Formentera   Madrid   Segovia   the Prado   Canary Islands
Tenerife   the Costa Brava

## Answers

| | |
|---|---|
| It used to be very unspoilt. | ✓ |
| There are lots of parks to walk in. | ✓ |
| The food is delicious. | |
| The weather is hot and sunny. | ✓ |
| The nightlife is brilliant. | ✓ |
| You can get everywhere easily by public transport. | |
| The beach was beautiful with white sand. | ✓ |
| The people are really friendly. | |
| It's a great place for a relaxing holiday. | ✓ |

## Transcript 2 minutes 52 seconds

**1**

INTERVIEWER: Jane, you've been to Spain on holiday, haven't you?

JANE: The first time I went was to the island of Formentera, and that was a long time ago — it was over twenty years ago when there was very little tourism there and I think I appreciated it because it was so unspoilt. I don't know what the island's like now. Um…and I've also been to Madrid and Segovia — not terribly keen on big cities these days but I…er…did find Madrid to be a particularly nice city and Segovia was really interesting as well.

INTERVIEWER: What did you do in Madrid?

JANE: We were staying with friends who lived there, so we went to visit some of their friends, we went to the Prado [*art gallery*] which I enjoyed very much, we hung around in various bars, walked around in various parks that were there — I can't remember any of the names of them — and I suppose really we just went sightseeing.

**2**

INTERVIEWER: Emma, which part of Spain have you been to?

EMMA: Canary Islands … I've been there the last three years because 1) the weather and 2) the nightlife and I love it so I go back. Sunbathe all day, be lazy, have a sleep from about 5 till 8 o'clock at night and then get ready and go out all night. I enjoy it because I really like it and I do want to go to other places, but at the moment I keep going back to Tenerife, and my friends that I go with really like it as well.

INTERVIEWER: Which resort did you go to?

EMMA: Playa de las Americas. Basically all it is is a tourist town…um…not a lot to do by day but a lot to do at night time and everyone goes for the same thing: the weather and the night time.

**3**

INTERVIEWER: Sally, did you enjoy your holiday on the Costa Brava?

SALLY: Oh, I had a wonderful time. Yes, it was really, really good. It was lovely and hot and sunny, and the beach was beautiful, great stretches of white sand, beautiful waves, lovely swimming. We stayed in a nice little hotel right on the beach. We used to get up in the morning, have breakfast, sometimes we'd have a swim before breakfast, um…and then spend most of the morning on the beach in and out of the water, sunbathing, reading, going for little strolls. Um…and then a light lunch and then back to the beach for the afternoon, sometimes a stroll round the town. Um…and then a nice meal in the evening and a nice walk. Um…it was a nice cheap holiday: sun, sea, fresh air, it was very enjoyable and relaxing.

**3** Arrange everyone into an even number of pairs. Depending on the size of your students' country, decide whether they should talk about their region or the whole of their country. Many of the reasons may coincide with the reasons listed in Step 2 above.

**4** Combine the pairs into groups. At the end of the discussion reassemble the class for them to compare their ideas.

## B1 Vocabulary

This can be begun in pairs, and then gone through as a whole-class activity.

### Suggested answers

Probably all except: *cloudy*, *depressing*, *dusty* — and maybe also *fertile* and *remote*

**2** This can be done in pairs or small groups before the class is reassembled.

## 3 Writing

The advertisement for Thailand could be a model for this. Agree together whether this should be about the whole country, or just their region.

## Finally …

**1** Remind everyone what the aims of this Lesson were. Have they been achieved?

**2** In preparation for Lesson 48, ask everyone to look at the banknotes in their wallets and find out more about the famous people or historic buildings shown on them. (Not all countries have famous people or buildings on their banknotes, however.)

**3** Also, to save time in the next Lesson, ask them to look at the history of Mexico on SB page 103 and find the answers to the questions in B1.

# 48 History and folklore

## Aims

Begin by explaining to the class the aims of Lesson 48, which are to improve their ability to:

- talk about the history of their country and historical figures well-known there
- recommend places to see local folklore and places of historical interest.

## Vocabulary

| | | |
|---|---|---|
| commanded | handicrafts | pianist and composer |
| defeated | laboratory | published |
| folklore | experimentalist | statue |
| | magnetism | |

in the text:

| | | |
|---|---|---|
| civil war | cultures | republican |
| civilization | invaded | ruled |
| constitution | prisoner | sacrifices |
| converted | reconquered | spring water |

### A1

Begin by asking the class if they can guess which country each banknote comes from. (They are from Great Britain, Germany, Japan and the USA.) And what do they know about the people depicted on each of them?

Play the recording, pausing between each speaker.

### Suggested answers

1 electricity  magnetism
2 wife  composer
3 writer  Heart
4 first  Independence

### Transcript  1 minute 46 seconds

TOURIST: Who was Michael Faraday?
MAN: Michael Faraday was a 19th-century chemist and physicist. He's best known for his experiments with electricity and magnetism. He discovered the concept of lines of magnetic force. Scientists still honour him as the greatest laboratory experimentalist who ever lived.

TOURIST: Who was Clara Schumann?
WOMAN: Clara Schumann was a 19th-century pianist and composer. Um…she married the composer Robert Schumann and she performed his works. After his death she became one of the great pianists of the time. She was a good friend of…um…Johannes Brahms and performed his piano works, as well as composing many piano works herself.

TOURIST: Who was Natsume Soseki?
JAPANESE WOMAN: Natsume Soseki was a famous Japanese writer, born in 1867. He studied and taught English literature. Many of his novels are very amusing, but his most famous book *Kokoro* (which means 'The Heart') is very sad. It was published in 1914.

TOURIST: Who was George Washington?
MAN: George Washington was the first president of the United States. Um…he commanded the American army which defeated the British in the…er…War of Independence, and that was at Yorktown in 1781. The capital of the USA was named after him, as was the state in the Pacific North West: Washington State.

**2** Arrange the class into groups of three or four. Some of these questions require some thought and may need some research — perhaps make sure you know something about the people on the banknotes in your own wallet and decide on some famous historical figures from *your* country too.

Reassemble the class for everyone to compare ideas. Did they think of the same five people?

### Suggested answers

Five important historical figures from British history (not necessarily the five *most* important):

Henry VIII — he had six wives and broke away from the Roman Catholic church. He reigned from 1509 to 1547.

Winston Churchill (1874–1965) — he was prime minister during the Second World War.

Oliver Cromwell (1599–1658) — he led the Roundheads during the English Civil War and was leader of the country after King Charles I was beheaded in 1649.

Queen Victoria — she was queen for most of the 19th century, when Britain became the world's leading industrial and colonial power. She reigned from 1837 to 1901.

William the Conqueror — he led the Norman invasion of England in 1066 and was King William I from 1066 to 1087.

### B1

This can be done alone or in pairs. The illustration shows a mural painted by Diego Rivera showing Tenochtitlán as it may have looked at the time of Moctezuma II. Reassemble the class to go through the answers.

## Suggested answers

1 Moctezuma II (also known as Montezuma) was the emperor of the Aztecs when the Spanish invaded Mexico. (He was put to death by the Spanish in 1621, but this isn't stated in the text.)

2 600

3 300 years (from 1521 to 1821)

4 California, New Mexico, Arizona, Texas

5 He was an Austrian who became emperor of Mexico in 1863. (He was executed by firing squad in 1867, but this isn't stated in the text.)

**2** Arrange everyone into pairs. There may be disagreement about the three most important dates.

## Suggested answers

Some important dates in British history (not necessarily the three *most* important):

55bc — Julius Caesar invaded England and it became part of the Roman Empire.

1066 — William the Conqueror invaded England from Normandy and became king of England

1649 — King Charles I was executed and England became a republic (but only until 1660).

1825 — The British army defeated Napoleon's army at Waterloo.

1914–18 — The First World War, in which millions of young men were killed in France.

## If there's time ...

Ask everyone to think of two well-known historical places in your country:

- Why are the places famous?
- Why do people enjoy visiting them?
- If someone only had time to visit one of the places, which would you recommend, and why?

**C** Arrange everyone into groups of three or four for them to discuss the questions. Reassemble the class to pool ideas at the end. The photos show: folk dancing in Madeira; umbrella painting in Thailand; a historical reenactment in the USA.

## Finally ...

1 Remind everyone what the aims of this Lesson were. Have they been achieved?

2 To save time in Lesson 49, tell everyone they *must* read the guide book descriptions on SB page 105 before the next Lesson. They should also answer the questions in A2 on SB page 104.

3 Also, see if some students can bring a local map to class in the next Lesson.

And, if possible, collect up some brochures and maps yourself in preparation for the extended role play / simulation in Lesson 49 — see C1 below.

# 49 A nice day out

## Aims

Begin by explaining to the class that Lesson 49 includes an extended simulation in C1 and 2. The aims of the Lesson are to improve their ability to:

- recommend excursions and days out
- arrange a personalised programme for a day out.

## Vocabulary

in the guide book extracts:

| | | |
|---|---|---|
| **demolish** | **inside-out** | **sculptures** |
| **designed** | **pavement cafés** | **setting** |
| **displayed** | **piazza (open area)** | **tomb** |
| **dominates** | **queues** | **unpretentious** |
| **gargoyles** | **restore** | **works of art** |
| **housed** | | |

## First of all ...

Find out what everyone already knows about Paris:

- What is there to see there?
- If you've been there, what did you do? What was the best thing you did?
- Are organised sightseeing tours a good idea?
- Or is it better to discover a place for yourself with or without a guide book?

**A1** These guide book extracts will be helpful for the discussion and role play in Sections B and C, suggesting the kind of information that is relevant and useful for tourists.

Ask everyone to read the extracts and then discuss their answers in pairs before reassembling the class for them to share ideas.

**2** This can be done in pairs or individually.

## Suggested answers

1 No, it's closed on Tuesdays. But any other evening would be fine.

2 Yes, there is. You have a nice view over the rooftops of Paris from there.

3 The Picasso Museum, a short walk from the Pompidou Centre.

4 In the Musée d'Orsay — but Monet's water lilies are in the Orangerie nearby.

5 It's a former railway station converted into a museum.

6 The best time is any day in the morning. It opens at 10am.

7 Cruises start near the Pont Neuf, which is near Notre-Dame.

8 Yes, but the top floor closes at 8pm, so don't leave it too late. The lower levels are open till 11pm or midnight in summer.

9 If it's very busy, it may take two hours. You could walk up, if you're very energetic, but there are 1,642 steps!

10 Plenty: you can walk to the church where Napoleon is buried or visit the Rodin Museum.

**B** Arrange everyone into pairs. This is a warm-up for the extended role play / simulation in C.

**C 1** Try to collect up some local maps and brochures (in English) on local tourist attractions and make them available for the groups to consult during this activity.

Arrange everyone into an even number of small groups. This activity will require a fair amount of time to do justice to. Tell everyone to make notes because they'll need to remember the places they've chosen when they do the writing task in D.

## 2 Role play

Combine the small groups into larger groups. Please allow enough time for both small groups to explain their excursion to the other.

## D Writing

The descriptions on SB page 105 can be a model for the paragraphs.

## Finally …

1 Remind everyone what the aims of this Lesson were. Have they been achieved?

2 To save time in Lesson 50, ask everyone to read the text *How to be a responsible tourist* on SB page 106 before the next Lesson.

# 50 The future of tourism

## Aim

Begin by explaining to the class that this Lesson focuses on discussion. The aim of Lesson 50 is to improve their ability to:

- talk about the ecological and social implications of tourism.

## Vocabulary

| | | |
|---|---|---|
| *behaving badly* | *job security* | *relative prosperity* |
| *benefits* | *profits* | *unemployed* |

in the text:

| | | |
|---|---|---|
| *endangered species* | *marked paths* | *shells* |
| *footprints* | *mounted butterflies* | *souvenirs* |
| *imported goods* | *multinational hotels* | *turtle* |

## First of all …

Ask the class how tourism in their region has changed over the years:

- What new facilities for tourists have been developed?
- Has the 'profile' of visitors changed (relative prosperity, nationalities, etc.)?
- Just suppose you were a foreign tourist, would you come to this region for a holiday? Why/Why not?

**A1** Play the recording right through and ask everyone to fill in the blanks in the Advantages during the first listening. Then play it again while they fill in the blanks in the Disadvantages.

### *Suggested answers*

| **Advantages** | **Disadvantages** |
|---|---|
| 1  employment | 1  security |
| 2  economy | 2  local |
| 3  currency | 3  country region |
| 4  farmers   fishermen | 4  abroad (or other regions) |
| 5  everybody else | 5  crime |

### Transcript  2 minutes  46 seconds

PRESENTER:  Hello. We have Tony King of Worldwide Holidays.
TONY:  Hello.
PRESENTER:  And Sarah Parker of Tourism Concern.
SARAH:  Hello.
PRESENTER:  So, is tourism a good thing or a bad thing for a country, or for a region? Tony?
TONY:  Oh, well, I think it's an excellent thing. I mean that firstly, let's take employment: um…any new hotel going up in…in an area is going to provide a…a huge amount of employment. I mean, not only for the…er…building trades, um…once the hotel is actually up, there are all the people who are going to…er…take all the jobs in the hotels: the chambermaids, the waiters, cleaners, swimming pool attendants, you know, all that kind of thing. That…that certainly can 'lift' a whole region.

PRESENTER:  Mm, Sarah?
SARAH:  Well, it doesn't always offer a lot of security. You see, in many places, the tourist season could only last between four and six months of the year. So, the rest of the year all the people that are working are unemployed.
PRESENTER:  What about the economy of the country?
TONY:  Well, yes, I think tourism really is of great benefit. The great thing is that the economy of the country is improved by the foreign currency coming in. It's the people coming in, spending their money, um…they…they go to the local shops, they buy things if there are, you know, arts and crafts things. That benefits all the local people. Um…th…th…they need guides, etc., etc.
SARAH:  Yes, um…I don't think that the benefits of tourism are…are really felt at a local level. For example, it's often staff from abroad, or perhaps from other regions, who…who do the better-paid and more senior management and accounting jobs. Often the…the profits from the larger hotels just go out of the country completely.
TONY:  Ah, yes, but you've got to look at the…the other people, I mean there are…there are the farmers, the…the fishermen, people growing crops and things, all…all that kind of thing…er…is sold to…to the hotels.
SARAH:  Yes, but lots of hotels don't buy local products. You know, they import…they import food and drink from abroad to suit…suit their customers' tastes, or …
TONY:  But there is this money that comes in. That money can be used, the profits from…from these things, can be used through taxes and things. It benefits, you know, everybody else if you build more roads, you know, etc., etc.
SARAH:  Tourism can generate social and political tensions though, you know. I mean, outside the…the comfortable environment of the hotel, often you see a lot of poverty, and…um…that can be very widespread. The relative prosperity of tourists may…may actually encourage crime.
TONY:  But in the end it is the local people who will benefit from this money coming in, from the hotels …

**PHOTOCOPIABLE** © Cambridge University Press 2005

**2** Arrange everyone into small groups. After they've discussed the questions, reassemble the class to pool ideas.

**B1** This can be done in pairs.

## Answers

- Don't waste water …
- Do stick to marked paths … don't damage …

- Don't pick ...
- Don't have ...
- Do buy local ...
- Do try to stay ...
- Do follow ... do ask people's permission ... don't leave too many footprints!
- Do take care ...
- Do turn off ...
- Don't buy souvenirs ...

**2** Arrange everyone into pairs. Not everyone may agree about staying in locally-owned hotels, especially if they work in a multinational!

**C1** Arrange everyone into pairs. Afterwards reassemble the class so that everyone can compare their ideas.

## 2 Writing

Brainstorm ideas in class before setting this as homework. But if this is your very last Lesson in the course, ask everyone to do this in note form in class, working in pairs. Then compare notes with another pair before doing the writing.

## Finally ...

**1** Ask everyone what they've learned during this course. (Their feedback will be useful for the next time you use this book with another class.) Perhaps ask for a written report.

**2** Ask everyone these questions:
- What job do you hope to do when you go out into the real world of travel and tourism?
- If you are working, what would you like to do next — work in a different job, get promotion, work abroad, etc?

## Attractions and activities: Vocabulary puzzle

Photocopy the Vocabulary puzzle on page 107 for everyone to do in pairs in class, or for homework.

### Answers

```
                    13
1              t  h  e  m  e      p  a  r  k
2     e  n  t  e  r  t  a  i  n  m  e  n  t  s
3           h  e  a  v  y      r  a  i  n
4              e  x  o  t  i  c
5              a  c  t  i  v  i  t  y
6           n  i  g  h  t  l  i  f  e
7           c  o  a  s  t
8           f  o  r  e  c  a  s  t
9     t  h  u  n  d  e  r  s  t  o  r  m
10       h  u  m  i  d
11       s  h  a  d  e
12       d  u  t  y      f  r  e  e
```

## If there's time ...

Photocopy this handout and ask the class to discuss which of the advice in the document is applicable to their country, and which is not.

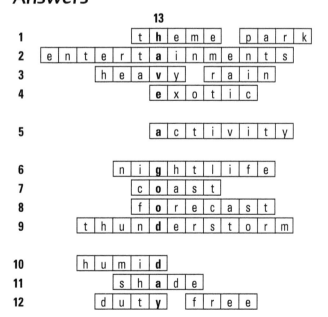

### THE HIMALAYAN TOURIST CODE

*By following these simple guidelines you can help to preserve the unique environment and ancient cultures of the Himalayas.*

#### PROTECT THE NATURAL ENVIRONMENT

▲ **Limit deforestation — make no open fires** and discourage others from doing so on your behalf. Where water is heated by scarce firewood, use as little as possible. When possible, choose accommodation that uses kerosene or fuel efficient wood stoves.

▲ **Remove litter, burn or bury paper** and carry out all non-degradable litter. Graffiti are permanent examples of environment pollution.

▲ **Keep local water clean and avoid using pollutants** such as detergents in streams or springs. If no toilet facilities are available, make sure you are at least 30 metres away from water sources and bury or cover wastes.

▲ **Plants should be left to flourish in their natural environment** — taking cuttings, seeds and roots is illegal in many parts of the Himalayas.

▲ **Help your guides and porters to follow conservation measures.**

▲ **When taking photographs, respect privacy** — ask permission and use restraint.

▲ **Respect Holy places** — preserve what you have come to see; never touch or remove religious objects. Shoes should be removed when visiting temples.

▲ **Giving to children encourages begging.** A donation to a project, health centre or school is a more constructive way to help.

▲ **You will be accepted and welcomed** if you follow local customs. Use only your right hand for eating and greeting. Do not share cutlery or cups, etc. It is polite to use both hands when giving or receiving gifts.

▲ **Respect for local etiquette earns you respect** — loose, lightweight clothes are preferable to revealing shorts, skimpy tops and tight-fitting action wear. Hand holding or kissing in public are disliked by local people.

▲ **Observe standard food and bed charges** but do not condone overcharging. Remember when you're shopping that the bargains you buy may only be possible because of low income to others.

▲ **Visitors who value local traditions encourage local pride and maintain local cultures;** please help local people gain a realistic view of life in Western Countries.

*The Himalayas may change you — please do not change them. As a guest, respect local traditions, protect local cultures, maintain local pride. Be patient, friendly and sensitive Remember — you are a guest*

**Tourism Concern**
Froebel College, Roehampton Lane, London SW15 5PU
Tel: 0181-878-9053

# Vocabulary puzzles

## Different kinds of people

Add the missing words to this puzzle.

1   A hotel receptionist works at the ....... .
2   It's important to make a good first ....... .
3   Are you working on the early or late ....... today?
4   The local ....... looks after clients on an inclusive tour.
5   In American English a *hall porter* is a ....... .
6   'What number do I ....... to get an outside line?'
7   'Dealing with the general ....... can be a nightmare!'
8   If there's a problem, ask the ....... ....... to speak to the guest.
9   Prices are lower during the low ....... .
10  A flight attendant has to wear a ....... .
11  ....... is served from 7.30pm. Last orders are at 10pm.
12  'Your ....... number is TG 404, and you have to check in at 2pm.'
13  We try to encourage ....... customers who stay with us regularly.
14  'For a room with a sea view there's a ....... of $15 to pay, madam.'
15  An inclusive tour can be called a ....... holiday.
16  How many members of ....... are there in the hotel?
17  The American English word for tap is ....... .
18  I'm afraid your departure has been ....... .
19  When talking to guests, try to sound ....... ....... ....... .

**19**

1   f r o n t   d e s k

## International travel

Add the missing words to this puzzle.

1   A Boeing 747 is a ....... ....... .
2   People going on vacation often fly on a ....... flight.
3   You have to ....... planes if you have a connecting flight.
4   Which ....... number does my flight leave from?
5   An ....... ticket is cheaper than a standard round trip.
6   Before boarding the plane, passengers wait in the departure ....... .
7   A ....... flight is more expensive than a charter flight.
8   If your money is stolen, you can claim on your travel ....... .
9   An ....... lists a traveller's flights and route.
10  Food and drink is served by a flight ....... .
11  You have to ....... your seat belt before the plane takes off.
12  It's important to read the safety ....... so that you know what to do in an emergency.
13  It's best to ....... in at least an hour before your flight.
14  Most flights between Europe and the USA are ....... - ....... .
15  'Our flight is now ....... , so we had better hurry up.'
16  You may have to reconfirm your ....... flight.
17  It's a ....... flight, so you won't have to change planes.
18  Never leave your ....... ....... at an airport.

**18**

1   j u m b o   j e t

# Phone calls

Add the missing words to this puzzle.

**1** Don't ....... someone when they're talking to you.
**2** 'You can make a call from your room or there's a ....... over there, sir.'
**3** 'Good morning, Royal Hotel. This is Maria ....... .'
**4** I make ....... during a call so as not to forget the important information.
**5** I phoned her yesterday but there was no ....... .
**6** A ....... phone is called a *cellphone* in American English.
**7** It's sometimes hard to sound both friendly and ....... on the phone.
**8** The ....... ....... is CB2 2RU.
**9** My phone number is 555 2123 and the ....... number is 333.
**10** 'I'll send you a ....... to confirm the booking.'
**11** 'I'm sorry, could you say that ......., please?'
**12** You would remember if you had ....... it down.
**13** 'She's not here at the moment. Can I ....... ....... ....... ?'

**13**

# Food and drink

Add the missing words to this puzzle.

**1** A table always looks nice if there's a vase of ....... on it.
**2** A woman who works behind the bar is a ....... .
**3** The ....... ....... is better value than an à la carte meal.
**4** 'Could you tell me what today's ....... are, please?'
**5** Cooks use ....... and spices to add flavour to a dish.
**6** Don't eat too much ....... or your breath will smell.
**7** Chinese cooks use a wok in which they ....... - ....... the ingredients.
**8** Another word for *hot* is ....... .
**9** 'You can get a ....... snack in the coffee shop, sir.'
**10** An Indian ....... can be made with meat, fish or vegetables.
**11** 'I'll bring you the ....... right away, sir.'
**12** You can get fresh fish and shellfish at a ....... restaurant.
**13** The American term for *starters* is ....... .
**14** Wine can be served in a bottle or a ....... .
**15** 'I'm afraid we don't have ....... beer, only bottled, sir.'
**16** Some people prefer ....... bread to white.
**17** Moslems don't eat ....... .
**18** 'Would you like your eggs fried or ......., madam?'
**19** ....... fries are also known as *chips*.
**20** A ....... doesn't eat meat.
**21** 'Would you like ice cream or fruit for ......., sir?'
**22** 'I'd like a glass of ....... ....... ....... juice, please.'

**22**

**Vocabulary puzzles**

# Correspondence

Add the missing words to this puzzle.

**1** May I ....... that you book early because we are likely to be very busy during August.

**2** I ....... our brochure and price list.

**3** Two bedrooms with a connecting door are ....... rooms.

4 I'm sorry that you were charged for an extra night. This amount will be ....... from your bill.

**5** 'How many people will there be in your ....... , sir?'

**6** A kingsize bed is a very large ....... bed.

**7** There's a full description of the hotel in the ....... .

**8** The Ritz is a five- ....... hotel.

**9** A large hotel usually has better ....... than a small one.

**10** A room with a ....... and sea view is more expensive.

**11** A suite is more ....... than a standard room.

**12** Thank you for your booking. I'll ....... ....... ....... ....... to confirm this.

# Accommodation

Add the missing words to this puzzle.

**1** In American English a wardrobe is a ....... .

**2** You use a ....... to dry yourself.

**3** His first name is Leo and his ....... is Jones.

**4** 'Would you like a room with a double bed or ....... ....... ?'

**5** 'Could you please fill out the ....... form, madam?'

**6** If you need a drink there's a ....... - ....... in your room.

**7** This ....... explains the facilities that are on offer.

**8** If you'd like us to do any dry-cleaning or ....... , please put it in the bag and call the room maid.

**9** 'I can't find the ....... ....... for the television.'

**10** 'My room's too hot. How can I turn down the ....... ?'

**11** ....... ....... is known as *American Plan* in American English.

**12** 'You can find an extra ....... in the cupboard in your room.'

**13** Benidorm is a well-known seaside ....... in Spain.

**14** The ....... is the manager in charge of guest bedrooms.

**15** A ....... is the person who cleans the rooms.

**16** 'I have to get up early tomorrow. Can I have a ....... - ....... ....... , please?'

**17** 'For breakfast please help yourself from the ....... , sir.'

**18** 'There's a hair-dryer in the ....... , madam'

**19** At an all- ....... hotel even the drinks are free.

**20** 'If you need a sunbed, please ask the pool ....... , sir.'

**21** ....... ....... is included in the price of the room.

# Money

Add the missing words to this puzzle.

**1** Departing passengers have to pay ....... ....... before going through passport control.

**2** 'You paid a deposit of $100, so the ....... is $123.40, sir.'

**3** You can pay in dollars or in the local ....... .

**4** In American English the ....... is called the check.

**5** The Japanese currency is the ....... .

**6** In some restaurants each diner has to pay a ....... ....... .

**7** Guests who have pre-paid their meals give a ....... to the waitress, rather than signing the bill.

**8** 'Tax and ....... are included in your bill, sir.'

**9** Some customers ....... ....... the bill to the nearest dollar.

**10** The porter should be given a ....... for carrying your bags.

**11** 'Could you explain this ....... on my bill, please?'

**12** 'As you're a regular guest, there's a ....... of 20% on your bill, sir.'

**13** 'The total was $49 and you gave me $50. Here's your ....... : $1.'

**14** 'Can you give me a ....... for this, please? I need it for my expenses.'

**15** Is that price in Australian, Canadian or US ....... ?

**16** 'Are you going to ....... ....... ....... ....... or in cash, sir?'

16

1
2
3
4
5
6
7
8
9
10
11
12
13
14
15

---

# Travelling around

Add the missing words to this puzzle.

**1** In American English the metro is called the ....... .

**2** A domestic flight can also be called an ....... flight.

**3** 'I'd like to rent a car with unlimited ....... .'

**4** Buses, cars and trucks are all ....... .

**5** If the ....... is very heavy, you may be delayed on your way to the airport by taxi.

**6** 'If you want to buy any ....... of your trip, I can recommend a good place to find them.'

**7** 'Can you tell me how much the taxi ....... to the station is likely to be?'

**8** 'The ....... ....... in town is 50 kph.'

**9** 'If you want to hire a car, you'll need an international driving ....... .'

**10** 'You can find out what's on at the cinema if you look at the local ....... .'

**11** 'Can you recommend a shop where I can buy ....... to take home to my family?'

**12** A passenger in a car has to wear a ....... ....... .

**13** 'There's a ....... at the top of the hill. You can take the cable car.'

**14** In American English the boot of a car is the ....... .

**15** A ....... sells medicines and drugs.

**16** Going on a ....... ....... is a good way to get to know a city or area.

16

1
2
3
4
5
6
7
8
9
10
11
12
13
14
15

**Vocabulary puzzles**

# Problems

Add the missing words to this puzzle.

**19**

1   Any valuables can be left in the ....... ....... box.

**1**   s a f e

2   A ....... is needed to lock or unlock the room.

**2**

3   For security, every guest is given a ....... which has to be shown at reception.

**3**

**4**

4   'I'd like to ....... for what has happened. I'll make sure it doesn't happen again.'

**5**

5   'Make sure the ....... is closed when you leave the room.'

**6**

6   'If you see anybody who looks ....... , please inform security.'

**7**

7   'There was a ....... with our computer but it's fixed now.'

**8**

8   'I'm afraid you can't have a warm shower because the ....... ....... system is not working.'

**9**

9   'I think I've been ....... — the total should be $10 less.'

**10**

10   'Is there a ....... phone number where we can reach you?'

**11**

11   Children aren't allowed in the deep end of the ....... ....... .

**12**

12   Even if you're angry, you must be ....... to guests.

**13**

13   Using drugs is ....... in this country.

**14**

14   'I'd like to speak to the duty ....... , please.'

**15**

15   You can ....... someone's identity by looking at their passport.

**16**

16   If you don't ....... someone, ask them to repeat what they said.

**17**

17   No ....... are allowed in your room after 11pm.

**18**

18   If a ....... offers you a lift in a car, it's wise to refuse politely.

19   Everyone has to be ready to ....... ....... ....... from guests or clients.

# Attractions and activities

Add the missing words to this puzzle.

**13**

1   Futuroscope is a ....... ....... .

**1**

2   There are plenty of ....... : clubs, cinemas, shows, etc.

**2**

3   It may be best to stay indoors because there's going to be ....... ....... this morning.

**3**

**4**

4   I love going to unusual places and trying ....... food.

5   There's always plenty to do on an ....... holiday.

**5**

6   It's very quiet in the evening; there's not much ....... .

**6**

7   There are some quieter beaches a little way up the ....... .

**7**

8   According to the weather ....... it's going to be cooler today.

**8**

9   The sky's getting very dark, I think there's going to be a ....... soon.

**9**

10   The weather seems hot because it isn't dry, it's ....... .

**10**

11   The tropical sun is very strong — you should stay in the ....... at midday.

**11**

12   Whisky is cheaper in the ....... ....... shop at the airport.

**12**

13   '....... ....... ....... ....... , sir!'
    — 'Thank you very much, I hope I will!'